Japanese for Busy People I

MW01256482

Japanese for Busy People I

Revised 4th Edition

Romanized Version

Association for
Japanese-Language Teaching

AJALT

This icon () means that there is free audio available. To download these contents, search for "Japanese for Busy People" at kodansha.us.

The Association for Japanese-Language Teaching (AJALT) was recognized as a nonprofit organization by the Ministry of Education in 1977. It was established to meet the practical needs of people who are not necessarily specialists on Japan but who wish to communicate effectively in Japanese. In 1992 AJALT was awarded the Japan Foundation Special Prize. In 2010 it became a public interest incorporated association. AJALT maintains a website at www.ajalt.org.

Published by Kodansha USA Publishing, LLC, 451 Park Avenue South, New York, NY 10016

Distributed in the United Kingdom and continental Europe by Kodansha Europe Ltd.

Copyright ©2022 by the Association for Japanese-Language Teaching. All rights reserved.

First published in Japan in 1984 by Kodansha International
Fourth edition 2022 published by Kodansha USA, an imprint of Kodansha USA Publishing

Printed in Italy
25 24 23 22   5 4 3 2 1

ISBN: 978-1-56836-619-7

Editorial supervision by Kodansha Editorial, Ltd.
Editing and DTP by Guild, Inc.
Illustrations by Shinsaku Sumi and Kaori Ikeda
Cover design by Masumi Akiyama

Audio narration by Yoko Ibe, Fumiaki Kimura, Shogo Nakamura, Asahi Sasagawa, Yuji Suzuki, Ai Tanaka, and Hiroaki Tanaka
Audio recording and editing by the English Language Education Council, Inc.

Photo credits: © kou/PIXTA, 19, 171. © cowardlion/Shutterstock.com, 49, 189. © iStock.com/Xavier Arnau, 1. © さるとびサスケ /PIXTA, 73. © レイコ /PIXTA, 95. © iStock.com/Yongyuan Dai, 141. © a-clip, 217.

Library of Congress Control Number: 2021950845

www.kodansha.us

KODANSHA

CONTENTS

PREFACE TO THE REVISED 4TH EDITION xi

INTRODUCTION xii

CHARACTERISTICS OF JAPANESE GRAMMAR xvii

FREQUENTLY USED EXPRESSIONS xviii

Audio, Script and Answers Download xx

UNIT **1** **AT THE OFFICE** **1**

LESSON **1** ## Meeting: Nice to Meet You **2**

- noun 1 **wa** noun 2 **desu.**
- noun 1 **wa** noun 2 **desu ka.**
- company **no** person
- Omission of the topic

- Sumisu-san wa Amerika-jin desu.
- Sumisu-san wa Amerika-jin desu ka.
- Kochira wa Nozomi Depāto no Tanaka-san desu.
- (Watashi wa) Sumisu desu.

CAN-DO
- Introduce yourself and others, at your workplace or at a party
- Talk about nationalities
- Give your name at the reception desk of a place you visit and give the name of the person you want to meet

WORD POWER
- Countries and nationalities
- Work affiliation

LESSON **2** ## Possession: Whose Pen Is This? **9**

- **Kore wa** noun **desu.**
- **Kore wa** noun **ja arimasen.**
- person **no** noun

- Kore wa tokei desu.
- Kore wa tokei ja arimasen.
- Kore wa Sumisu-san no tokei desu.

CAN-DO
- Talk about a nearby object and its owner
- Ask for telephone numbers
- Ask for words to be repeated when you do not understand

WORD POWER
- Numbers
- Business vocabulary
- Personal belongings

UNIT **2** **SHOPPING** **19**

LESSON **3** ## Asking the Time: What Time Is It? **20**

- **(Ima)** time **desu.**
- noun **wa** time 1 **kara** time 2 **made desu.**
- time 1 **no** time 2

- Ima 3-ji desu.
- Shigoto wa 9-ji kara 5-ji made desu.
- Kaigi wa ashita no 4-ji kara desu.

CAN-DO
- Talk about opening times and closing times
- Talk about the present time and time in cities overseas

WORD POWER
- Services and activities
- Numbers
- Times
- Time expressions

LESSON **4** ## Shopping (1): How Much Is This? **28**

- **kore/sore/are**
- noun **mo**
- noun **o kudasai.**/noun **o onegaishimasu.**
- noun 1 **to** noun 2

- Sore wa sumaho desu. Are wa taburetto desu.
- Kore wa 3,000-en desu. Are mo 3,000-en desu.
- Kore o kudasai.
- Karē to sarada o onegaishimasu.

CAN-DO
- Point to something and ask what it is
- Ask the prices of items in a store and make a purchase
- Place an order at a restaurant

WORD POWER
- Home appliances
- Food and drink
- Numbers

LESSON 5 **Shopping (2): Two Bottles of That Wine, Please** 38

- noun **wa** place **desu.**
- **kono/sono/ano** noun
- adjective + noun
- place **no** noun
- noun **o** number **kudasai.**

- Resutoran wa 5-kai desu.
- Kono T-shatsu wa 2,000-en desu.
- Ano aoi T-shatsu wa 3,000-en desu.
- Kore wa Furansu no wain desu.
- Sono wain o 2-hon kudasai.

CAN-DO
- Ask for the location of a facility or a shop
- In a shop, give the size and color of an item and ask its price
- Ask what country of origin of an item is, and buy the item
- Tell the shopkeeper that you want to buy more than one of an item

WORD POWER
- Items for sale
- Numbers and counters
- Floors

● **QUIZ 1** 48

UNIT **3** GETTING AROUND 49

LESSON 6 **Going Places (1): Where Are You Going?** 50

- Verbs
- person **wa** place/event **ni ikimasu.**
- Relative time expressions
- person **to**
- person **wa** place **kara kimashita.**

- Sumisu-san wa ashita ginkō ni ikimasu.
- Sumisu-san wa senshū Ōsaka ni ikimashita.
- Sumisu-san wa kinō tomodachi to resutoran ni ikimashita.
- Sumisu-san wa kyonen Amerika kara kimashita.

CAN-DO
- Talk about where, when, and with whom you will go/went somewhere
- Talk about from where and when you came
- By telephone, ask when someone will visit and with whom
- At the bus stop, ask if the bus goes to one's destination

WORD POWER
- Destinations
- Verbs
- Time expressions
- People

LESSON 7 **Going Places (2): I'm Going by Shinkansen** 61

- Specific time expressions
- transportation **de**
- noun 1 **wa** noun 2 **desu ka,** noun 3 **desu ka.**

- Ema-san wa 4-gatsu ni Nihon ni kimashita.
- Sumisu-san wa shinkansen de Ōsaka ni ikimasu.
- Kaigi wa yokka desu ka, yōka desu ka.

CAN-DO
- Talk about the date and day of the week of an event or meeting
- Talk about means of transportation
- Ask whether an event is on one day or another
- Speak words of greeting when entering someone's room

WORD POWER
- Verb
- Dates
- Means of transportation

UNIT **4** EATING OUT 73

LESSON 8 **Doing Things (1): I'm Going to Eat Tempura** 74

- person **wa** noun **o** verb.
- place/event **de**
- **nani mo** in a negative sentence

- Sumisu-san wa ashita tenisu o shimasu.
- Sumisu-san wa kinō resutoran de ban-gohan o tabemashita.
- Ema-san wa pātī de nani mo tabemasendeshita.

CAN-DO
- Talk about everyday activities—what, when, and where
- Make a reservation at a restaurant by telephone

WORD POWER
- Food and drink
- Verbs
- Numbers of people

| LESSON **9** | **Doing Things (2): Do You Often Come Here?** | **84** |

- person 1 **wa** person 2 **ni** verb.
- person 1 **wa** person 2/place **ni** noun **o** verb.
- Habitual action
- **amari/zenzen** in a negative sentence

- Sumisu-san wa ashita Tanaka-san ni aimasu.
- Sumisu-san wa Suzuki-san ni resutoran no basho o oshiemashita.
- Sumisu-san wa mainichi kōhī o nomimasu.
- Ema-san wa amari terebi o mimasen.

CAN-DO
- Talk about who you will meet
- Talk about to whom or to where to telephone
- State how frequently one does something
- At a restaurant, ask what is recommended

WORD POWER
- Verbs
- Family
- Time expressions
- Adverbs

● **QUIZ 2**   **94**

| UNIT **5** | **VISITING A JAPANESE HOME** | **95** |

| LESSON **10** | **Describing Things: It's Delicious** | **96** |

- Adjectives (1)

- Kono hon wa omoshiroi desu.
- Tōkyō no chikatetsu wa benri desu.
- Sumisu-san wa atarashii pasokon o kaimashita.
- Sumisu-san wa kinō yūmeina resutoran ni ikimashita.

CAN-DO
- Talk about the characteristics of things and places
- Entertain a guest and receive hospitality
- Talk about the weather

WORD POWER
- **i**-adjectives
- **na**-adjectives

| LESSON **11** | **Describing Impressions: It Was Beautiful** | **105** |

- Adjectives (2)
- clause 1 **ga**, clause 2.

- Kinō wa samukatta desu.
- Kinō no o-matsuri wa nigiyaka deshita.
- Sumisu-san wa depāto ni ikimashita ga, nani mo kaimasendeshita.

CAN-DO
- Express one's thoughts about experiences
- Express gratitude
- State something that differs from expectation

WORD POWER
- **i**-adjectives
- **na**-adjectives
- Verbs
- Events

| UNIT **6** | **WEEKEND TRIPS** | **113** |

| LESSON **12** | **Asking about Places: What Is at Nikko?** | **114** |

- place **ni** noun **ga arimasu/imasu**.
- Position words
- noun 1 **ya** noun 2

- 1-kai ni uketsuke ga arimasu.
- Uketsuke ni onna no hito ga imasu.
- Tēburu no ue ni hana ga arimasu.
- Nikkō ni o-tera ya jinja ga arimasu.

CAN-DO
- Talk about tourist destinations and one's hometown
- Say what or who is at a certain place
- Ask the meaning of a word you do not know

WORD POWER
- Parts of a building
- Things in a hotel room
- Features of a tourist site
- Positions

LESSON 13 · Asking for a Place: Where Is It? · 123

- place **ni** noun **ga** number **arimasu/ imasu**.
- noun **wa** place **ni arimasu/imasu**.
- place 1 **wa** place 2 **kara chikai/tōi desu**.

- Kaigi-shitsu ni isu ga muttsu arimasu.
- Kaigi-shitsu ni o-kyaku-san ga 4-nin imasu.
- Takushī-noriba wa eki no mae ni arimasu.
- Sumisu-san wa 2-kai ni imasu.
- Sumisu-san no uchi wa eki kara chikai desu.

CAN-DO
- Talk about the number of things or people in a certain place
- Talk about the whereabouts of things and people
- Ask if a certain place is near or far from some other place

WORD POWER
- Things near a train station
- Office supplies
- Demonstrative pronouns
- **i**-adjectives

LESSON 14 · Giving and Receiving: I Received It from My Friend · 131

- person 1 **wa** person 2 **ni** noun **o agemasu**.
- person 1 **wa** person 2 **ni** noun **o moraimasu**.
- person **wa** noun **ga arimasu**.

- Sumisu-san wa Nakamura-san ni hana o agemashita.
- Nakamura-san wa Sumisu-san ni hana o moraimashita.
- Sumisu-san wa ashita kaigi ga arimasu.

CAN-DO
- Talk about giving and receiving gifts
- Complement someone about clothing
- Talk about what one has

WORD POWER
- Verbs
- Gifts
- Words that can be used with **arimasu** ("have")

QUIZ 3 · 140

UNIT 7 MAKING LEISURE PLANS · 141

LESSON 15 · Talking about Preferences: I Like Japanese Anime · 142

- person **wa** noun **ga suki desu**.
  person **wa** noun **ga jōzu desu**.
- Verb dictionary form
- person **wa** verb [dictionary form] **no ga suki desu**.

- Chan-san wa wain ga suki desu.
- Chan-san wa Nihon-go ga jōzu desu.
- Sumisu-san wa sakkā o miru no ga suki desu.

CAN-DO
- Talk about someone's likes and skills
- Talk about what you like to do

WORD POWER
- **na**-adjectives
- Sports
- Dictionary form
- Verbs

LESSON 16 · Making an Invitation: Shall We Go Together? · 151

- place **de** event **ga arimasu**.
- verb [**masu**-form stem] **masen ka**.
- verb [**masu**-form stem] **mashō**.
- clause 1 **kara**, clause 2.

- Do-yōbi ni Asakusa de o-matsuri ga arimasu.
- Shūmatsu ni issho ni eiga o mimasen ka.
- Issho ni ikimashō.
- Ii tenki desu kara, kōen de hiru-gohan o tabemasen ka.

CAN-DO
- Tell where a certain event is taking place
- Invite someone to an event
- Receive or decline an invitation
- State a reason for declining an invitation

WORD POWER
- Events
- Parts of a train station
- Physical condition
- Variations on **masu**-form

LESSON 17 Stating a Wish: I Want to Buy a Souvenir 161

- (Watashi wa) verb [**masu**-form stem] **tai desu/takunai desu.**
- person **wa** noun **no mae ni** verb.
- person **wa** verb 1 [dictionary form] **mae ni** verb 2.

- (Watashi wa) oishii o-sushi o tabetai desu.
- Sumisu-san wa kaigi no mae ni shiryō o okurimasu.
- Sumisu-san wa mainichi neru mae ni sutoretchi o shimasu.

CAN-DO
- Talk about what you want to do
- State what someone will do/did before a certain event
- Talk about what one will do/did before doing something else

WORD POWER
- Hobbies
- Verbs

● CASUAL STYLE 1 169

UNIT 8   BUSINESS TRIPS 171

LESSON 18 Explaining Plans: I Will Go to Osaka and See Her 172

- Verb **te**-form
- person **wa** verb 1 [**te**-form], verb 2.
- person **wa** noun **no ato,** verb.

- Ema-san wa ashita Ōsaka-shisha ni itte, Chan-san ni aimasu.
- Sumisu-san wa kaigi no ato, repōto o kakimashita.

CAN-DO
- Talk about weekend plans, travel plans, and business trips
- Talk about schedules in detail
- Talk about a sequence of actions
- Ask and answer what someone will do/did after a certain event

WORD POWER
- te-form

LESSON 19 Making a Request: Please Give Her My Regards 180

- verb [**te**-form] **kudasai.**
- means **de**
- place/space **o**

- Chotto matte kudasai.
- Ema-san wa Chan-san ni mēru de shiryō o okurimashita.
- Tsugi no shingō o migi ni magatte kudasai.

CAN-DO
- Ask someone to do something for you
- Request delivery of something by a certain means at a certain time
- Give directions to a taxi driver

WORD POWER
- Verbs
- Positions and directions
- Means of delivery

● QUIZ 4 188

UNIT 9   AT THE MUSEUM 189

LESSON 20 Going Places (3): How Do You Go There? 190

- person **wa** place **de** transportation **ni norimasu.**
- person **wa** place **de** transportation **o orimasu.**
- place 1 **kara** place 2 **made** (transportation **de**) period **kakarimasu.**
- person **wa** place **ni** period **imasu.**

- Sumisu-san wa Tōkyō Eki de shinkansen ni norimasu.
- Sumisu-san wa Hiroshima Eki de shinkansen o orimasu.
- Tōkyō kara Hiroshima made shinkansen de 4-jikan kakarimasu.
- Sumisu-san wa Hiroshima ni 1-shūkan imasu.

CAN-DO
- Ask and answer about means of transportation, route, and time required to reach a destination
- Ask and answer departure and arrival times
- Ask and answer the period of one's stay

WORD POWER
- Verbs
- Periods

LESSON 21 Asking Permission: May I Have It? 199

- verb [te-form] mo ii desu ka.
- place/thing ni
- (Watashi wa) body part ga itai desu.

- Kono e no shashin o totte mo ii desu ka.
- Koko ni suwatte mo ii desu ka.
- (Watashi wa) atama ga itai desu.

CAN-DO
- Ask permission to do something
- Grant and refuse permission
- Talk about one's physical condition and explain a symptom

WORD POWER
- Verbs
- Parts of the body
- Symptoms

LESSON 22 Forbidding Actions: Please Don't Take Photos 209

- Verb nai-form
- verb [nai-form] de kudasai.
- place ni mo noun ga arimasu.

- Koko wa deguchi desu kara, kuruma o tomenaide kudasai.
- Wasabi o irenaide kudasai.
- Eki no mae ni konbini ga arimasu.
  Eki no naka ni mo (konbini ga) arimasu.

CAN-DO
- Give a reason and forbid someone from doing something
- When someone apologizes for something, tell them not to worry
- Say that something is in another place as well

WORD POWER
- Verbs
- nai-form
- Restrictions
- Adjective

UNIT 10 AT WORK AND AFTER WORK 217

LESSON 23 Explaining Actions: What Are You Doing Now? 218

- person wa verb [te-form] imasu. (1)
- Mō verb [masu-form stem] mashita ka.
- wa for contrast

- Sumisu-san wa ima hiru-gohan o tabete imasu.
- Sumisu-san wa Nihon-go o naratte imasu.
- Mō repōto o yomimashita ka.
- Gurīn-san wa tenpura wa suki desu ga, o-sushi wa suki ja arimasen.

CAN-DO
- Talk about what someone is doing now
- State whether an action is completed
- Talk about a regular activity

WORD POWER
- Verbs
- Lessons

LESSON 24 Work and Interests: I Work for an Apparel Maker 228

- person wa verb [te-form] imasu. (2)
- person wa noun ga wakarimasu.
- person wa noun o shitte imasu.
- noun wa verb [dictionary form] koto desu.

- Sumisu-san wa Tōkyō ni sunde imasu.
- Sumisu-san wa Nihon-go ga wakarimasu.
- Sumisu-san wa Chan-san o shitte imasu.
- Sumisu-san no shumi wa hon o yomu koto desu.

CAN-DO
- Talk about where one lives and works
- Talk about whether someone knows something
- Talk about what languages one understands
- Talk about someone's hobby

WORD POWER
- Verbs
- Family

QUIZ 5 237

CASUAL STYLE 2 238

APPENDIXES   List of Grammar Points 240   Target Dialogues (with kana) 251
GLOSSARY   Japanese-English Glossary 255   English-Japanese Glossary 261

PREFACE TO THE REVISED 4TH EDITION

Japanese for Busy People is composed of three levels: Book I (romanized version and kana version), Book II, and Book III. The first edition of *Japanese for Busy People I* was compiled on the basis of teaching materials developed over more than ten years by AJALT teachers involved in teaching Japanese language at various levels and published in 1984. It was designed for efficient mastery of Japanese by busy people and was used in many countries.

In 1994, when the textbooks were first revised, Book II was divided into two parts, Book II and Book III, and only minimal revisions were made to Book I. For the third edition published in 2006, a variety of changes were made, including grouping the lessons into units, adding the new features such as Culture Notes, Word Power, and Active Communication, and expanding the Exercises. These changes were made to clarify the situations for practical use of Japanese based on the latest results of research in Japanese-language education and to help learners feel confident in their communication skills.

This fourth edition carries on the editorial policy of the third edition, updating the vocabulary and dialogues and adding further explanation in Grammar and Notes in order to help learners studying independently. New pages introducing casual-style speech are also added.

We hope that *Japanese for Busy People* will help learners seeking to master Japanese amid busy lives get off to a pleasant start.

In the compilation of this revised edition, we would like to express our gratitude to Mio Urata of Kodansha Editorial and Makiko Ohashi of Guild, Inc. for their cooperation.

Acknowledgments for *Japanese for Busy People I* (1st edition, 1984)
Compilation of this textbook has been a cooperative endeavor, and we deeply appreciate the collective efforts and individual contributions of Sachiko Adachi, Nori Ando, Haruko Matsui, Shigeko Miyazaki, Sachiko Okaniwa, Terumi Sawada, and Yuriko Yobuko.
For English translations and editorial assistance, we wish to thank Dorothy Britton.

Acknowledgments for *Japanese for Busy People I, Revised Edition* (1994)
We would like to express our gratitude to the following people: Haruko Matsui, Junko Shinada, Keiko Ito, Mikiko Ochiai, and Satoko Mizoguchi.

Acknowledgments for the *Kana Version of Japanese for Busy People I, Revised Edition* (1995)
We would like to express our gratitude to the following people: Haruko Matsui, Junko Shinada, Mikiko Ochiai, and Satoko Mizoguchi.

Acknowledgments for *Japanese for Busy People I, Revised 3rd Edition* (2006)
We would like to express our gratitude to the following people: Yoko Hattori, Sakae Tanabe, Izumi Sawa, Motoko Iwamoto, Shigeyo Tsutsui, and Takako Kobayashi.

Acknowledgments for *Japanese for Busy People I, Revised 4th Edition*
Ten AJALT teachers have contributed to the writing of this textbook. They are Reiko Sawane, Hisako Aramaki, Eiko Ishida, Soko Onishi, Yuka Tanino, Yuko Hashimoto, Yumiko Matsuda, Yasuko Yako, Tomoko Waga, and Shinobu Aoki. They were assisted by Yuko Harada, Misuzu Imuta, and Yuko Takami. Preparation for this textbook was assisted by a grant from the Shoyu Club.

INTRODUCTION

Aims

This first volume of *Japanese for Busy People, Revised 4th Edition* has been developed to meet the needs of busy beginning learners seeking an effective method of acquiring a natural command of spoken Japanese in a limited amount of time. The book is suitable for both those studying with a teacher and those studying on their own. In order to minimize the burden on busy learners, the vocabulary and grammar items presented have been narrowed down to about a third of those introduced in a typical first-year course. However, the textbook is set up so that learners can use the material they have learned right away in conversations with speakers of Japanese. In other words, *Japanese for Busy People I* is a textbook for learning "survival Japanese."

Despite this, *Japanese for Busy People I* does not present simple, childish Japanese. That is, we do not focus on mere grammatical correctness. Instead, we place our emphasis on actual conversational patterns. Thus, by studying with this book, learners will acquire the most essential language patterns for everyday life, and be able to express their intentions in uncomplicated adult-level Japanese. They will also start to build a basis for favorable relations with the people around them by talking about themselves and their surroundings and circumstances, and asking about those of others.

This book is intended for beginners, but it can also provide a firm foundation for more advanced study. Learners can acquire a general idea of the nature of the Japanese language as they study the Target Dialogues, Speaking Practice, and Notes. For this reason, *Japanese for Busy People I* is also suitable as a review text for those who already know a certain amount of Japanese but want to confirm that they are using the language correctly.

Major Features of *Japanese for Busy People I, Revised 4th Edition*

Japanese for Busy People I, Revised 4th Edition, incorporates a number of features designed to make beginning study of Japanese enjoyable and effective.

FREQUENTLY USED EXPRESSIONS

The book begins with a list of expressions frequently used in daily life. Illustrations are provided to give a better idea of the situations where these expressions can be used. By repeated listening to the audio versions of these expressions, learners can accustom themselves to the sound of the Japanese language.

UNIT STRUCTURE

The book is divided into 10 units, each unit consisting of two or three lessons linked by a common theme. Studying these units with their interrelated social and cultural information, language information, and communications strategies is important to gaining a natural and appropriate mastery of Japanese.

CULTURE NOTES

Each unit begins with Culture Notes that describe Japanese customs and events as well as other aspects of life in Japan. Learners who can better understand people's lives and customs are sure to gain a greater desire to learn the language and deepen their understanding of it. We hope the social and cultural information presented in these notes will heighten learners' awareness of cultural diversity and give them specific mental images of the themes introduced in the units.

LESSONS

Each lesson is composed of the parts described below. Newly introduced vocabulary is given with English translations in the shaded sections at the bottom of the pages.

Target Dialogue

The first feature of each lesson is the Target Dialogue, which provides a specific example of the kind of dialogue the learner will be able to engage in after studying the lesson. The dialogues contain practical expressions and grammatical points necessary for daily conversation. Notes to explain particularly difficult expressions are provided.

Key Sentences
These are simple sentences incorporating the key points of study in each lesson. The Grammar section immediately below gives concise grammatical explanations of the sentences given in the Key Sentences that are easily accessible for self-study. Points under Key Sentences and Grammar that "are not used in normal speech but added for better understanding" are enclosed in parentheses. The explanations given here are provided as much as possible without requiring more advanced knowledge or information than is available in the grammatical notes provided in the current lesson.

Word Power
Basic vocabulary to be mastered before moving on to the Exercises is introduced here. The vocabulary is presented in clusters of related words so as to help the learner remember them efficiently. Most of the words given in this section are introduced in the illustrations and charts.

Exercises
In order to allow the learner to move smoothly from the basic expressions to more advanced applications, the exercises are presented in stages (I, II, III, etc.). The Exercises are composed of five types:
(1) Exercises for repeating vocabulary and conjugating verbs and adjectives.
(2) Standard sentence patterns for grasping Japanese sentence structures and learning their meanings.
(3) Substitution drills and dialogue-style drills linked to conversation practice.
(4) Conversation exercises geared to practical occasions and situations in which Japanese is used.
(5) Listening practice with questions to be answered after listening to the audio.
The goals of the exercise ("can-dos") to be mastered are set in italics so as to focus attention not just on doing the exercises but on the goal to be achieved through the exercises.

Speaking Practice
These relatively short conversations present useful expressions and various patterns of exchange. As with the Target Dialogue, cautions regarding use of the specific phrases and expressions are provided in the Notes below.

Active Communication
The last section of each lesson presents one or two tasks that can be used in actual situations or for communication activities in the classroom.

CASUAL STYLE
To respond to increased interest among students of Japanese in attaining comprehension of the informal language used in animation films, television dramas, or among the people around them, pages are set aside in two places to present the casual style.

OTHER FEATURES
Audio recordings may be downloaded for Frequently Used Expressions, Target Dialogue, Word Power, Listening Exercises, Speaking Practice, as well as the Sample Dialogues for the Casual Style pages. A Quiz is provided after every two units so as to help learners check their understanding and progress. The answers for Exercises and Quizzes are available on download for the convenience of those studying independently. The answers are based on the content learned in this textbook.

Using *Japanese for Busy People I*

Progress through this textbook should be flexible in accordance with the circumstances of the learners, but in general *Japanese for Busy People I* can be completed in about 60 hours. Each lesson will take about two to two-and-a-half hours to complete.

Whether using the textbook with a teacher's guidance or when studying from it independently, we recommend proceeding as follows:

Frequently Used Expressions	First, listen to the audio recording while looking at the illustrations. Next, the expressions should be practiced by either repeating after the recording or shadowing until they can be spoken fluently.
▼	
Contents	The items to be learned and goals of the lesson ("can-dos") are briefly outlined. Scan the contents to grasp the targets of the lesson.
▼	
Culture Notes	This section is aimed at expanding learners' awareness by providing social and cultural background to the topics treated in each unit.
▼	
Lesson	Each unit is made up of two or three lessons. Please proceed through each lesson following the instructions on the following page.
▼	
Quiz	A quiz is provided after every two units. First fill in the answers without looking anything up, and then check yourself using the answer sheet. To remedy mistakes or confirm understanding of the expressions, review the lesson for study of that item.
▼	
Casual Style	Pages introducing casual style are included after Unit 7 and Unit 10. Study of Casual Style (1) can be done after completing Unit 7 or both Casual Style (1) and (2) can be done after completing Unit 10. Intonation is very important in use of casual style, so please listen carefully to the audio.

Japanese for Busy People I : The Workbook for the Revised 4th Edition

The *Workbook* coordinated with *Japanese for Busy People I, Revised 4th edition* is available for sale. The effectiveness of studying with this textbook can be greatly enhanced by use of the *Workbook*.

How to Proceed through Each Lesson

Target Dialogue	This section presents the kind of dialogue one can engage in after completing the lesson. Listen to the audio and read the dialogue text alongside the English translation. At this point it is not necessary to spend too much time studying the dialogue. The lesson returns to this dialogue after the Exercises (see below). At this stage, you may skip over the Target Dialogue and keep going.
↓	
Key Sentences and Grammar	This section provides an explanation for the grammar points of this lesson. After grasping the grammar, listen to the audio and repeat the key sentences over several times so as to memorize them.
↓	
Word Power	The words used in the Exercises are collected here. Listen to the audio and practice saying them to commit the sound to memory.
↓	
Exercises	This section begins with repetition of vocabulary and practice with conjugation, practice creating sentences and exchanges, and proceeds toward re-creation of a full-fledged conversation. The listening practice at the end allows one to check listening and comprehension of conversations and sentences.
↓	
Speaking Practice	The conversations in this section include useful expressions to be learned in the lesson. Practice speaking thoroughly while listening to the audio. Once you can enunciate the words naturally, they will become useful for all kinds of situations.
↓	
Target Dialogue	The Target Dialogue is the summation of what is learned in the lesson. After completing the Exercises and Speaking Practice, listen to the Target Dialogue audio and read the script again. By now the conversation that seemed to be difficult when first read should now be more easily grasped. After reading the Notes in order to understand the details, listen to the audio and repeat consecutively or by shadowing.
↓	
Active Communication	The tasks here can be put into practice by the learner in person when circumstances allow. In the absence of a conversation partner, try imagining what one will say in each case.

Introducing the Characters

The following fictitious characters bring this textbook to life. Their names come up frequently in this book, so here we introduce their names, faces, and how they are related. Some of the characters are called by their first names and this is because in this fictional setting they prefer to be called that way.

Sumisu

Mike Smith is American. He is a member of the Product Development Department of the ABC Foods Tokyo branch.

Ema

Emma Robert is French. She is a member of the Product Development Department of the ABC Foods Tokyo branch.

Suzuki

Daisuke Suzuki is Japanese. He is a member of the Product Development Department of the ABC Foods Tokyo branch.

Nakamura

Mayumi Nakamura is Japanese. She is a member of the Product Development Department of the ABC Foods Tokyo branch.

Katō

Akira Kato is Japanese. He is section chief of the Product Development Department of the ABC Foods Tokyo branch.

Sasaki

Keiko Sasaki is Japanese. She is head of the Product Development Department of the ABC Foods Tokyo branch.

Gurīn

Frank Green is American. He is president of the Tokyo branch of ABC Foods.

Chan

Mei Chan is from Hong Kong. She works at the Osaka branch of ABC Foods.

Tanaka

Shingo Tanaka is Japanese. He works at Nozomi Department Store, which is a client of ABC Foods.

Raja

Naresh Raja is Indian. He is a student at the University of Tokyo.

Pōru

Paul Hudson is American. He is Mike Smith's cousin.

Risa

Lisa Smith is American. She is Mike Smith's younger sister.

CHARACTERISTICS OF JAPANESE GRAMMAR

The grammar presented in this textbook is not interpreted in accordance with grammatical constructions of Western languages but following the natural analysis of the Japanese language. Specialized terms are used selectively in order to assure a smooth transition from the basic level to more advanced learning.

The following are the basic characteristics of Japanese grammar. This list highlights in particular the differences between Japanese and English grammar.

1. Japanese nouns do not have gender or number. Some nouns express number by attachment of a suffix.

2. The verb (or copula **desu**) comes at the end of a clause or sentence.
   e.g. **Watashi wa Nihon-jin <u>desu</u>.**   "I am Japanese."
   Watashi wa Kyōto ni <u>ikimasu</u>.   "I go (or will go) to Kyoto."

3. In general, the gender, number, or person (first, second, or third) of the subject does not affect other parts of the sentence, but some sentences cannot be used depending on the person.

4. There are only two tenses of verbs: present and past. Whether "present form" refers to a customary action or refers to the future, and whether "past form" is equivalent to the past, present perfect, or past perfect must usually be judged according to the context.

5. Japanese adjectives are different from English adjectives in that they are inflected for present, past, positive, and negative forms.

6. The grammatical function of a noun is shown by the particle following it. The role of particles is similar to that of prepositions in English. As they always come after the word, they are sometimes called postpositions.
   e.g. **Tōkyō <u>de</u>**, "in Tokyo"
   nichi-yōbi <u>ni</u>, "on Sunday"

7. Politeness is expressed in various ways in Japanese, but the sentences used in this textbook adopt a style of courtesy that can be used when speaking to anyone.

NOTE: The following abbreviations are used in this book.

e.g.	example
aff.	affirmative
neg.	negative
i-adj.	**i**-adjective (see L10, GRAMMAR 1, p. 97)
na-adj.	**na**-adjective (see L10, GRAMMAR 1, p. 97)
R2	Regular 2 verb (see L15, GRAMMAR 2, p. 143)

*Regular 2 verbs are marked R2 in the Vocabulary sections for Lesson 15 and onward and the Glossary, but are not listed in the Vocabulary sections for Lesson 1 to 14.

FREQUENTLY USED EXPRESSIONS

① **Ohayō gozaimasu.**
Good morning.

② **Konnichiwa.**
Hello./Good afternoon. (A rather informal greeting used from about 10:00 A.M. until sundown.)

③ **Konbanwa.**
Good evening.

④ **Ja, mata.**
See you.

⑤ **Sayōnara.**
Good-bye.

⑥ **Shitsureishimasu.**
(Said when entering another person's room.)

⑦ **Shitsureishimasu.**
Good-bye. (Said on formal occasions.)

⑧ **A: O-saki ni shitsureishimasu.**
   Good-bye. (Said when leaving the office before other people.)
B: Otsukaresama (deshita).
   Good-bye. (Said when your colleague leaves the office before you.)

⑨ **A: Dōzo.**
   Please.
B: Arigatō gozaimasu.
   Thank you.
C: Iie.
   Not at all.

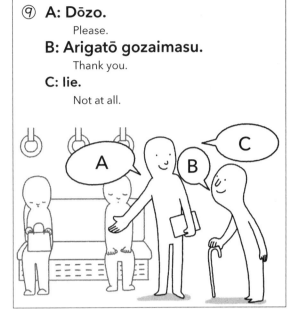

⑩ **Itadakimasu.**
   (Said before eating a meal.)

⑪ **Gochisōsama (deshita).**
   (Said after eating a meal.)

⑫ **Sumimasen.**
   Excuse me.

⑬ **Sumimasen.**
   I'm sorry.

⑭ **Chotto matte kudasai.**
   Wait just a moment, please.

⑮ **Mō ichi-do onegaishimasu.**
   Once more, please.

Audio, Script and Answers Download

The audio, script, and answers for this book can be downloaded to your smartphone, tablet, or PC, free of charge.

To download these contents, search for "Japanese for Busy People" at kodansha.us.

The audio files are in MP3 format and include Frequently Used Expressions, Target Dialogue, Key Sentences, Word Power, a part of the Exercises, Speaking Practice, and the Sample Dialogues for the Casual Style pages.

AT THE OFFICE

In Japan, people bow to each other on many occasions. They bow when meeting people, formally expressing gratitude, and apologizing for something. The typical way of bowing is to stand with the feet drawn together and bend the body at a 15 to 45 degree angle. Men tend to hold their hands at their sides while women hold their arms in front, elbows slightly bent, and hands folded. The eyes remain open during the bow, and the bowing person's line of sight moves with his or her torso rather than staying fixed on the other person. Generally, the deeper and slower the bow, the politer it is. Bowing properly is essential to making a good first impression.

Meeting: Nice to Meet You

TARGET DIALOGUE

🔊 016

Smith meets Tanaka for the first time. Tanaka is visiting ABC Foods.

Sumisu: **Sumimasen. Nozomi Depāto no Tanaka-san desu ka.**

Tanaka: **Hai, sō desu.**

Sumisu: **Hajimemashite. ABC Fūzu no Sumisu desu.**
Yoroshiku onegaishimasu.

(Hands over business card.)

Tanaka: **Hajimemashite. Tanaka desu.**

(Hands over business card.)

Kochirakoso, yoroshiku onegaishimasu.

Smith: Excuse me, are you Tanaka-san of the Nozomi Department Store?
Tanaka: Yes, I am.
Smith: Nice to meet you. I am Smith of ABC Foods. I look forward to working with you.
Tanaka: Nice to meet you, too. I am Tanaka.
          I look forward to working with you as well.

VOCABULARY

Sumimasen.	Excuse me.	**hai**	yes
Nozomi Depāto	Nozomi Department Store (fictitious company name)	**sō desu**	that's right
		Hajimemashite.	Nice to meet you.
depāto	department store	**ABC Fūzu**	ABC Foods (fictitious company name)
no	(particle; see GRAMMAR 3, p. 4)		
-san	Mr., Mrs., Ms., Miss	**Yoroshiku onegaishimasu.**	I look forward to working with you.
... desu	be		
ka	(particle; see GRAMMAR 2, p. 3)	**kochirakoso**	same here

NOTES

1. **Tanaka-san**

   San is a title of respect added to a person's name, so it cannot be used after one's own name. **San** is used regardless of gender and can be used with both the last name and the given name. In business situations, "last name + **san**" is the most common, but "first name + **san**" is also used.

2. **Hai, sō desu.**

   When replying to "noun **desu ka**," **sō** can be used instead of repeating the noun. When replying in the negative, say **Iie, chigaimasu.**

3. **Yoroshiku onegaishimasu.**

   A phrase used when being introduced, **Yoroshiku onegaishimasu** is usually combined with **Hajimemashite**. It is also used when taking one's leave after having asked a favor. **Yoroshiku** means "well" and is used as a request for the other person's favorable consideration in the future.

4. **Exchanging business cards**

   In business situations, people usually exchange business cards when meeting for the first time.

KEY SENTENCES

 017

1. **Sumisu-san wa Amerika-jin desu.**
2. **Sumisu-san wa Amerika-jin desu ka.**
3. **Kochira wa Nozomi Depāto no Tanaka-san desu.**
4. **(Watashi wa) Sumisu desu.**

1. Smith-san is an American.
2. Is Smith-san an American?
3. This is Tanaka-san of the Nozomi Department Store.
4. [I am] Smith.

GRAMMAR

1. noun 1 wa noun 2 desu.   (KEY SENTENCES 1, hereafter abbreviated as KS1)

The particle **wa** is the topic marker. It is used in the same sense as "as for" in English but is used much more frequently. The particle **wa** follows noun 1, singling it out as the "topic" of the sentence. Noun 2 is then identified, and the phrase is concluded with **desu**. The topic is the person or thing that the sentence is about. The topic is often the same as the subject but not necessarily.

2. noun 1 wa noun 2 desu ka.   (KS2)

It is easy to make questions in Japanese. Simply place the particle **ka** at the end of the sentence. No change in word order is required even when the question contains interrogatives like "who," "what," "when," etc. Intonation normally rises on **ka**, i.e., … **desu ka.** ↗
Hai is virtually the same as "yes," and **iie** is virtually the same as "no."

e.g. **Sumisu-san wa Amerika-jin desu ka.**	Is Smith-san American?
Hai, Amerika-jin desu.	Yes, (he is) American.
Iie, Igirisu-jin desu.	No, (he is) British.

VOCABULARY

wa	(particle; see GRAMMAR 1, above)	**kochira**	this one (polite for "this person")
Amerika-jin	American (person)	**watashi**	I

3. company **no** person

(KS3)

The particle **no** expresses belonging or affiliation. Here it shows that a person belongs to, in a sense that he works for, a company. Japanese customarily give their company name when being introduced in a business situation.

4. Omission of the topic

(KS4)

When the topic is clear to the other person, it is generally omitted. For example, **Tanaka-san desu ka** means "Are you Tanaka-san?" and since it is clear who the topic is, it is omitted. The same is true of the answer to the question; the topic is often omitted. (see GRAMMAR 2, p. 3)

WORD POWER

Ⅰ Countries and nationalities

 018

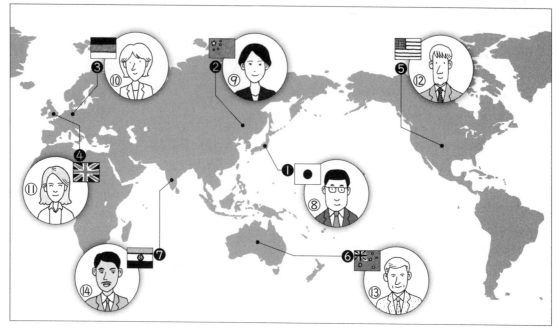

❶Nihon	❹Igirisu	❼Indo	⑩Doitsu-jin	⑬Ōsutoraria-jin
❷Chūgoku	❺Amerika	⑧Nihon-jin	⑪Igirisu-jin	⑭Indo-jin
❸Doitsu	❻Ōsutoraria	⑨Chūgoku-jin	⑫Amerika-jin	

Ⅱ Work affiliation

019

①depāto   ②ginkō   ③daigaku   ④taishikan

VOCABULARY

Nihon	Japan	**Amerika**	United States	**ginkō**	bank
Chūgoku	China	**Ōsutoraria**	Australia	**daigaku**	university, college
Doitsu	Germany	**Indo**	India	**taishikan**	embassy
Igirisu	United Kingdom	**-jin**	-ese, -ian (person from)		

EXERCISES

I *State someone's nationality.* Make up sentences following the pattern of the example. Substitute the underlined parts with the alternatives given.

| Sumisu-san | Hofuman-san | Buraun-san | Chan-san | Tanaka-san |

e.g. **Sumisu-san wa Amerika-jin desu.**

1. .... (Hofuman-san, Doitsu-jin)

2. .... (Buraun-san, Igirisu-jin)

3. .... (Chan-san, Chūgoku-jin)

4. .... (Tanaka-san, Nihon-jin)

II Make up dialogues following the patterns of the examples. Substitute the underlined parts with the alternatives given.

A. *Ask and answer what someone's nationality is.*

e.g. **A: Sumisu-san wa Amerika-jin desu ka.**

B: Hai, Amerika-jin desu.

1. A: .... (Hofuman-san, Doitsu-jin)

   B: .... (Doitsu-jin)

2. A: .... (Buraun-san, Igirisu-jin)

   B: .... (Igirisu-jin)

3. A: .... (Chan-san, Chūgoku-jin)

   B: .... (Chūgoku-jin)

4. A: .... (Tanaka-san, Nihon-jin)

   B: .... (Nihon-jin)

VOCABULARY

Hofuman	Hoffman (surname)
Buraun	Brown (surname)

B. *Ask and answer what someone's nationality is.*

e.g. **A:** Sumisu-san wa Igirisu-jin desu ka.

   B: Iie, Amerika-jin desu.

1. A: .... (Hofuman-san)

   B: .... (Doitsu-jin)

2. A: .... (Chan-san)

   B: .... (Chūgoku-jin)

III *Confirm the identity of someone you are meeting for the first time.* Make up dialogues following the pattern of the example and based on the information provided.

| ABC Fūzu Sumisu-san | Berurin Mōtāzu Hofuman-san | Rondon Ginkō Buraun-san | Tōkyō Daigaku Raja-san | Ōsutoraria Taishikan Harisu-san |

e.g. **Anata:** Sumimasen. ABC Fūzu no Sumisu-san desu ka.

   Sumisu: Hai, sō desu.

1. Anata: ....

   Hofuman: ....

2. Anata: ....

   Buraun: ....

3. Anata: ....

   Raja: ....

4. Anata: ....

   Harisu: ....

VOCABULARY

iie	no	Tōkyō Daigaku	University of Tokyo
Berurin Mōtāzu	Berlin Motors (fictitious company name)	Tōkyō	Tokyo
Berurin	Berlin	Harisu	Harris (surname)
Rondon Ginkō	Bank of London (fictitious bank name)	anata	you
Rondon	London		

IV *Introduce yourself.* Make up dialogues following the pattern of the example. Substitute the underlined parts with the alternatives given.

    e.g. Sumisu: Hajimemashite. ABC Fūzu no Sumisu desu.

                  Yoroshiku onegaishimasu.

       Hofuman: Hajimemashite. <u>Berurin Mōtāzu</u> no <u>Hofuman</u> desu.

                  Yoroshiku onegaishimasu.

   1. Buraun: ....

                                          (Rondon Ginkō, Buraun)

   2. Raja: ....

                                          (Tōkyō Daigaku, Raja)

   3. Harisu: ....

                                      (Ōsutoraria Taishikan, Harisu)

V *Introduce people.* Referring to the illustration, introduce A and B to each other.

e.g. A   you   B

A: Berurin Mōtāzu
   Hofuman-san

B: ABC Fūzu
   Sumisu-san

1. A   you   B

A: Rondon Ginkō
   Buraun-san

B: Tōkyō Daigaku
   Raja-san

2. A   you   B

A: Nozomi Depāto
   Tanaka-san

B: Ōsutoraria Taishikan
   Harisu-san

   e.g. Anata: Kochira wa <u>Berurin Mōtāzu</u> no <u>Hofuman-san</u> desu.

               Kochira wa <u>ABC Fūzu</u> no <u>Sumisu-san</u> desu.

   1. Anata: ....

               ....

   2. Anata: ....

               ....

VI Listen to the audio and fill in the blanks based on the information you hear. 🔊 020-022

   1. Sumisu-san wa .... desu.

   2. Raja-san wa .... desu.

   3. Chan-san wa .... desu.

SPEAKING PRACTICE

1. Tanaka and Smith, who have just met for the first time, are talking. 🔊 023

   Tanaka: Sumisu-san, o-kuni wa dochira desu ka.
   Sumisu: Amerika desu.

   Tanaka: Smith-san, what country are you from?
   Smith: I'm from the United States.

2. Sasaki introduces Brown to Tanaka. 🔊 024

   Sasaki: Tanaka-san, kochira wa Rondon Ginkō no Buraun-san desu.
   Buraun: Hajimemashite. Buraun desu.
   Yoroshiku onegaishimasu.
   Tanaka: Hajimemashite. Nozomi Depāto no Tanaka desu.
   Yoroshiku onegaishimasu.

   Sasaki: Tanaka-san, this is Brown-san of the Bank of London.
   Brown: Nice to meet you. I am Brown. I look forward to working with you.
   Tanaka: Nice to meet you. I am Tanaka of the Nozomi Department Store. I look forward to
             working with you.

3. Smith is visiting the Nozomi Department Store. 🔊 025

   Sumisu: ABC Fūzu no Sumisu desu. Tanaka-san o onegaishimasu.
   Uketsuke: Hai.

   Smith: I am Smith of ABC Foods. I would like to see Tanaka-san.
   Receptionist: Yes [, just a moment].

NOTES

1. **O-kuni wa dochira desu ka.**

   The prefix **o** is added to the word **kuni** to specify the country or birthplace of the person you are talking to. The basic word for "where" is **doko**, but **dochira** is more polite.

2. **Tanaka-san o onegaishimasu.**

   Use "person **o onegaishimasu**" when asking a receptionist to summon somebody you want to see. **Onegaishimasu** is a very convenient phrase often used in making polite requests.

Active Communication

1. Introduce yourself to a classmate. Then introduce two classmates to each other.

2. Try introducing yourself when you meet a Japanese person.

VOCABULARY

o-kuni	your country	**... o onegaishimasu**	please (get me...) (see NOTES 2,
o-	(honorific prefix)		above)
kuni	country	**uketsuke**	reception desk, receptionist
dochira	where (polite word for **doko**)		

Possession: Whose Pen Is This?

TARGET DIALOGUE
🔊 026

A meeting has just ended. Nakamura finds a pen on the floor.

Nakamura: Kore wa dare no pen desu ka.

Suzuki: Sā, wakarimasen.

(Turning toward Smith.)

Sumisu-san no desu ka.

Sumisu: Iie, watashi no ja arimasen.

Nakamura runs after Tanaka, who left the meeting room earlier.

Nakamura: Tanaka-san, kore wa Tanaka-san no pen desu ka.

Tanaka: Hai, watashi no desu. Arigatō gozaimasu.

Nakamura: Whose pen is this?
Suzuki: I don't know. Is it yours, Smith-san?
Smith: No, it isn't mine.

Nakamura: Tanaka-san, is this your pen?
Tanaka: Yes, it is. Thank you.

VOCABULARY

kore	this one	**pen**	pen	**Sumisu-san no**	Smith-san's
dare no	whose	**Sā, wakarimasen.**	(See NOTES 1, p. 10)	**watashi no**	my, mine
dare	who			**... ja arimasen**	is/are not
no	(particle; see GRAMMAR 3, p. 10)	**wakarimasen**	I don't know	**Arigatō gozaimasu.**	Thank you.

9

NOTES

1. Sā, wakarimasen.

The **sā** here expresses the speaker's hesitation about immediately answering, "I don't know."

2. Sumisu-san no desu ka.

In Japanese, the word **anata** is the equivalent of "you," but here Suzuki doesn't say **Anata no desu ka**. In Japanese conversation, the word **anata** is little used other than for members of one's family and other close associates. **Anata** is never used with people of higher status. Instead of **anata** they are addressed by their "surname/first name + **san**" or by their job title.

3. Arigatō gozaimasu.

This is the frequently used way of expressing thanks. Saying **Dōmo arigatō gozaimasu** gives greater weight or formality to an expression of thanks. The casual form is either **Arigatō** or **Dōmo arigatō**.

KEY SENTENCES

 027

1. **Kore wa tokei desu.**
2. **Kore wa tokei ja arimasen.**
3. **Kore wa Sumisu-san no tokei desu.**

1. This is a watch.
2. This is not a watch.
3. This is Smith-san's watch.

GRAMMAR

1. Kore wa noun **desu.** (KS1)

Kore is a pronoun that indicates something near to the speaker (see L4, GRAMMAR 1, p. 29).

2. Kore wa noun **ja arimasen.** (KS2)

... ja arimasen or **... dewa arimasen** is the negative form of **... desu**. **Ja** is more informal than **dewa**, but commonly used; otherwise they are the same. The chart below summarizes the forms of **... desu**.

Present form		Past form	
aff.	*neg.*	*aff.*	*neg.*
... desu	... ja arimasen ... dewa arimasen	... deshita	... ja arimasendeshita ... dewa arimasendeshita
is	is not	was	was not

3. person no noun (KS3)

The particle **no** connects two nouns, and the noun-**no** combination modifies the word that comes after it. Particle **no** has various functions and here it expresses possession (see L1, GRAMMAR 3, p. 4). In cases when the noun is obvious from the situation, the noun may be omitted.

e.g. **Kore wa watashi no pen desu.**   This is my pen.

Kore wa watashi no desu.   This is mine.

VOCABULARY

| tokei | watch, clock |

WORD POWER

Ⅰ Numbers

 028

0	1	2	3	4	5	6	7	8	9
zero/rei	ichi	ni	san	yon/shi	go	roku	nana/shichi	hachi	kyū/ku

Ⅱ Business vocabulary

029

① ②のぞみデパート ③田中真吾 ④東京都港区虎ノ門 3–25–2 ⑤(03)3459-9620* (090)8765-4321 ⑥ s.tanaka@nozomidpt.com	Nozomi Department Store Shingo Tanaka 3–25–2 Toranomon, Minato-ku, Tokyo (03)3459-9620 (090)8765-4321 E-MAIL: s.tanaka@nozomidpt.com

①meishi　　　　③namae　　⑤denwa-bangō

②kaisha no namae　④jūsho　　⑥mēru-adoresu

*The area code for Tokyo is 03. When saying a phone number aloud, put **no** between the area code (e.g., 03) and the exchange, and between the exchange and the last four numbers. The phone number here is pronounced **zero-san no san-yon-go-kyū no kyū-roku-ni-zero**.

NOTE: The 0 used in telephone numbers is usually pronounced **zero**.

Ⅲ Personal belongings

030

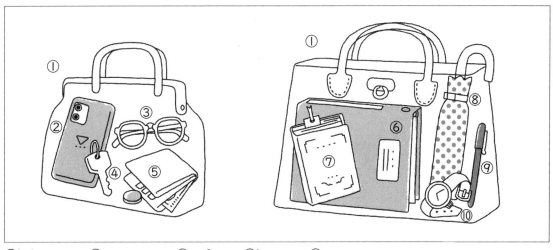

①kaban　　③megane　　⑤saifu　　⑦hon　　⑨pen

②sumaho　④kagi　　　⑥fairu　　⑧kasa　　⑩tokei

VOCABULARY

meishi	business card	denwa-bangō	telephone number	megane	glasses
kaisha no namae		denwa	telephone	kagi	key
	company name	bangō	number	saifu	wallet
kaisha	company	mēru-adoresu	mail address	fairu	file
namae	name	kaban	bag	hon	book
jūsho	address	sumaho	smart phone	kasa	umbrella

EXERCISES

I Make up sentences following the patterns of the examples. Substitute the underlined part with the alternatives given.

    A. *State what an object is.*

        e.g. Kore wa <u>hon</u> desu.

        1. .... (kagi)

        2. .... (tokei)

    B. *State what an object is not.*

        e.g. Kore wa <u>hon</u> ja arimasen.

        1. .... (kagi)

        2. .... (tokei)

II Make up dialogues following the patterns of the examples and based on the information provided.

    A. *Ask and answer whether or not an object is what it appears to be.*

        e.g. A: Kore wa <u>hon</u> desu ka.

        B: Hai, <u>hon</u> desu.

        1. A: ....

           B: ....

        2. A: ....

           B: ....

        3. A: ....

           B: ....

B. *Answer whether or not an object is what it appears to be.*

e.g. A: Kore wa kasa desu ka.

B: Iie, <u>kasa</u> ja arimasen.

1. A: Kore wa saifu desu ka.

B: ....

2. A: Kore wa tokei desu ka.

B: ....

3. A: Kore wa hon desu ka.

B: ....

Ⅲ *Ask and answer what an object is.* Make up dialogues following the pattern of the example and based on the information provided.

e.g. A: Kore wa nan desu ka.

B: <u>Hon</u> desu.

1. A: ....

B: ....

2. A: ....

B: ....

3. A: ....

B: ....

VOCABULARY

| **nan** | what |

IV *State who the owner of an object is.* Make up sentences following the pattern of the example and based on the information provided.

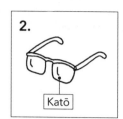

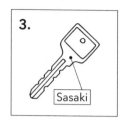

e.g. **Kore wa <u>Sumisu-san</u> no <u>hon</u> desu.**

1. ....

2. ....

3. ....

V Make up dialogues following the patterns of the examples and based on the information provided.

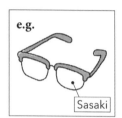

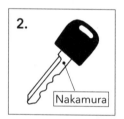

A. *Ask and answer whether or not an object belongs to someone.*

e.g. **A: Kore wa <u>Sasaki-san</u> no <u>megane</u> desu ka.**

   B: Hai, <u>Sasaki-san no</u> desu.

1. A: ....

   B: ....

2. A: ....

   B: ....

3. A: ....

   B: ....

B. *Answer whether or not an object belongs to someone.*

    e.g. **A: Kore wa Nakamura-san no megane desu ka.**

        B: Iie, <u>Nakamura-san no</u> ja arimasen.

   1. A: Kore wa Sasaki-san no sumaho desu ka.

       B: ....

   2. A: Kore wa Ema-san no kagi desu ka.

       B: ....

   3. A: Kore wa Sumisu-san no saifu desu ka.

       B: ....

C. *Ask and answer who an object's owner is.*

    e.g. **A: Kore wa dare no <u>megane</u> desu ka.**

        B: <u>Sasaki-san no</u> desu.

   1. A: ....

       B: ....

   2. A: ....

       B: ....

   3. A: ....

       B: ....

Ⅵ Make up sentences or dialogues following the patterns of the examples based on the information in the table.

Name	Telephone number	Name	Telephone number
e.g. Sumisu	080-1234-5678	4. ginkō	03-5690-3111
1. Sasaki	080-5642-2963	5. Nozomi Depāto	03-3459-9620
2. Tanaka	090-8765-4321	6. taishikan	03-3225-1116
3. Suzuki	030-6435-2187		

A. *State someone's phone number.*

e.g. **Sumisu-san no denwa-bangō wa zero-hachi-zero no ichi-ni-san-yon no go-roku-nana-hachi desu.**

1. ....

....

2. ....

....

3. ....

....

B. *Ask for and provide someone's phone number.*

e.g. **A: Sumisu-san no denwa-bangō o oshiete kudasai.**

B: Zero-hachi-zero no ichi-ni-san-yon no go-roku-nana-hachi desu.

4. A: ....

B: ....

5. A: ....

B: ....

6. A: ....

B: ....

VOCABULARY

| ... o oshiete kudasai please tell me

VII *Talk about who an object's owner is.* Make up dialogues following the pattern of the example and based on the information provided.

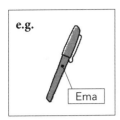

e.g. **Sumisu:** **Kore wa Nakamura-san no <u>pen</u> desu ka.**

Nakamura: (*looking at the pen*) **Iie, watashi no ja arimasen.**

Sumisu: **Dare no desu ka.**

Nakamura: <u>**Ema-san no**</u> **desu.**

1. Sumisu: ....

Nakamura: ....

Sumisu: ....

Nakamura: ....

2. Sumisu: ....

Nakamura: ....

Sumisu: ....

Nakamura: ....

3. Sumisu: ....

Nakamura: ....

Sumisu: ....

Nakamura: ....

VIII Listen to the audio and fill in the blanks based on the information you hear. 🔊 031, 032

1. Sumisu-san no denwa-bangō wa ....

.... desu.

2. Kaban wa .... no desu.

SPEAKING PRACTICE

1. Smith finds something in the break room.   🔊 033

Sumisu: **Kore wa nan desu ka.**
Nakamura: Nihon no o-kashi desu. Dōzo.
Sumisu: Arigatō gozaimasu.

Smith: What are these?
Nakamura: They are Japanese sweets. Please help yourself.
Smith: Thank you!

2. Smith and Nakamura are working at the office.   🔊 034

Sumisu: Nozomi Depāto no denwa-bangō o oshiete kudasai.
Nakamura: 03-3459-9620 desu.
Sumisu: Sumimasen. Mō ichi-do onegaishimasu.

Smith: Please tell me the telephone number of the Nozomi Department Store.
Nakamura: It is 03-3459-9620.
Smith: Excuse me. Could you say that again?

NOTES

1. **Dōzo.**

Dōzo is used when handing something to someone. It is also used when asking a visitor to enter a room or office.

Active Communication   If you're in Japan, ask an employee of a restaurant or store what the establishment's phone number is.

VOCABULARY

Nihon no o-kashi	Japanese sweets	Mō ichi-do onegaishimasu.		onegaishimasu	
o-kashi	sweets		One more time, please.		please (lit. "I request you")
o-	(polite prefix)	mō ichi-do	one more time		
kashi	sweets	mō	more		
Dōzo.	Please (have one).	ichi-do	one time		

18

SHOPPING

Japan is a paradise for shoppers. There are many kinds of stores, from grand department stores and luxury brand goods shops to small shops in local town street malls, 100-yen shops, and more, so there are many ways to enjoy shopping. Large-scale shopping centers that have numerous shops, restaurants, and movie theaters are always crowded with families and young people. Shopkeepers are courteous and kind. People who enter a store, are almost always greeted with the word, "Irasshaimase!"

Asking the Time: What Time Is It?

TARGET DIALOGUE

🔊 035

Smith is calling the "Sushiyoshi" sushi shop.

Mise no hito: Sushiyoshi desu.

Sumisu: Sumimasen. Ranchi-taimu wa nan-ji kara desu ka.

Mise no hito: 11-ji han kara desu.

Sumisu: Nan-ji made desu ka.

Mise no hito: 2-ji han made desu.

Sumisu: Rasuto-ōdā wa nan-ji desu ka.

Mise no hito: 2-ji desu.

Sumisu: Arigatō gozaimasu.

■ **Ranchi-taimu wa 11-ji han kara 2-ji han made desu.**

Restaurant employee: This is Sushiyoshi.
Smith: Excuse me. What time does lunchtime start?
Restaurant employee: From 11:30.
Smith: What time does lunchtime end?
Restaurant employee: It goes until 2:30.
Smith: What time is the last order?
Restaurant employee: 2:00.
Smith: Thank you.

■ Lunchtime is from 11:30 to 2:30.

VOCABULARY

mise no hito	restaurant employee	**nan-ji**	what time	**made**	until (particle; see GRAMMAR 2, p. 21)
mise	restaurant, shop	**kara**	from (particle; see GRAMMAR 2, p. 21)		
hito	person, employee			**2-ji han**	2:30, two-thirty, half past two
Sushiyoshi	Sushiyoshi (fictitious restaurant name)	**11-ji han**	11:30, eleven-thirty, half past eleven		
				rasuto-ōdā	last order
ranchi-taimu	lunchtime	**... han**	...thirty, half past (hour)	**2-ji**	2:00, two o'clock

20

KEY SENTENCES

 036

1. Ima 3-ji desu.
2. Shigoto wa 9-ji kara 5-ji made desu.
3. Kaigi wa ashita no 4-ji kara desu.

1. It is 3:00 now.
2. Work is from 9:00 to 5:00.
3. The meeting is tomorrow, from 4:00.

GRAMMAR

1. (Ima) time desu. (KS1)

When stating the present time, no subject is given. Sometimes **ima** may be added adverbially. When speaking of the present time in a specified place, the geographical name will be made the topic and accompanied by **wa**.

2. noun wa time 1 kara time 2 made desu. (KS2)

The particle **kara** attached to a time indicates a starting time and the particle **made** indicates ending time. These particles are used when stating business hours.

3. time 1 no time 2 (KS3)

When more than one expression of time is used, the series begins with the larger unit, followed by the smaller unit(s) linked together with the particle **no**. Sometimes **no** is omitted. When asking "When is the event?" the expression "event **wa itsu desu ka**" is used.

WORD POWER

① Services and activities

 037

①súpā

②resutoran

③jimu

④shigoto

⑤kaigi

⑥hiru-yasumi

⑦pātī

VOCABULARY

ima	now	kaigi	meeting	jimu	gym
3-ji	3:00, three o'clock	ashita	tomorrow	hiru-yasumi	lunch break
shigoto	work	4-ji (yo-ji)	4:00, four o'clock	hiru	noon
9-ji (ku-ji)	9:00, nine o'clock	súpā	supermarket	yasumi	break, time off
5-ji	5:00, five o'clock	resutoran	restaurant	pātī	party

Ⅱ Numbers

 038

10	jū	20	nijū	30	sanjū
11	jūichi	21	nijūichi	40	yonjū
12	jūni	22	nijūni	50	gojū
13	jūsan	23	nijūsan	60	rokujū
14	jūyon/jūshi	24	nijūyon/nijūshi	70	nanajū
15	jūgo	25	nijūgo	80	hachijū
16	jūroku	26	nijūroku	90	kyūjū
17	jūnana/jūshichi	27	nijūnana/nijūshichi		
18	jūhachi	28	nijūhachi		
19	jūkyū/jūku	29	nijūkyū/nijūku	100	hyaku

Ⅲ Times

 039

1:00	ichi-ji	3:05	san-ji go-fun	3:10	san-ji juppun
2:00	ni-ji	3:15	san-ji jūgo-fun	3:20	san-ji nijuppun
3:00	san-ji	3:25	san-ji nijūgo-fun	3:30	san-ji sanjuppun/han
4:00	yo-ji	3:35	san-ji sanjūgo-fun	3:40	san-ji yonjuppun
5:00	go-ji	3:45	san-ji yonjūgo-fun	3:50	san-ji gojuppun
6:00	roku-ji	3:55	san-ji gojūgo-fun		
7:00	shichi-ji				
8:00	hachi-ji				
9:00	ku-ji			4:00 A.M.	gozen yo-ji
10:00	jū-ji			9:00 P.M.	gogo ku-ji
11:00	jūichi-ji				
12:00	jūni-ji				

NOTE: Hours and minutes are written in hiragana here, but throughout the rest of the book they are written with numerals, e.g., **1-ji** for "1:00," **10-ji 20-pun** for "10:20," etc.

Ⅳ Time expressions

040

①kyō   ②ashita

VOCABULARY

-ji	...o'clock	kyō	today
-fun/pun	...minute(s)		
gozen	A.M., in the morning		
gogo	P.M., in the afternoon		

EXERCISES

I *State the time.* Practice telling the times indicated below.

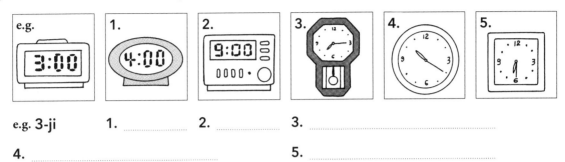

e.g. **3-ji** 1. .... 2. .... 3. ....

4. .... 5. ....

II *Ask and give the time.* Make up dialogues following the pattern of the example. Substitute the underlined part with the times indicated in EXERCISES I.

e.g. **A: Ima nan-ji desu ka.**

B: 3-ji desu.

1. A: ....

   B: ....

2. A: ....

   B: ....

3. A: ....

   B: ....

4. A: ....

   B: ....

5. A: ....

   B: ....

Ⅲ Make up sentences following the patterns of the examples. Substitute the underlined part(s) with the alternatives given.

A. *State the opening time.*

e.g. **Sūpā wa 9-ji kara desu.**

1. .... (8:00)

2. .... (10:00)

B. *State the closing time.*

e.g. **Depāto wa 8-ji made desu.**

1. .... (7:00)

2. .... (9:00)

C. *State the opening and closing times.*

e.g. **Shigoto wa 9-ji kara 5-ji made desu.**

1. .... (9:30, 5:30)

2. .... (10:00, 6:00)

Ⅳ Make up dialogues following the patterns of the examples. Substitute the underlined parts with the alternatives given.

A. *Ask and answer what the opening time is.*

e.g. **A: Depāto wa nan-ji kara desu ka.**
    B: 10-ji kara desu.

1. A: .... (resutoran)

   B: .... (11:30)

2. A: .... (ginkō)

   B: .... (9:00)

B. *Ask and answer what the closing time is.*

e.g. **A: Resutoran wa nan-ji made desu ka.**

B: Gogo 11-ji made desu.

1. A: .... (kaigi)

   B: .... (4:30)

2. A: .... (jimu)

   B: .... (gogo 9:00)

C. *Ask and answer what the opening and closing times are.*

e.g. **A: Kaigi wa nan-ji kara nan-ji made desu ka.**

B: 1-ji kara 3-ji made desu.

1. A: .... (hiru-yasumi)

   B: .... (12:30, 1:30)

2. A: .... (happī awā)

   B: .... (4:00, 7:00)

V *Ask and answer when events are held.* Make up dialogues following the pattern of the example. Substitute the underlined parts with the alternatives given.

e.g. **A: Kaigi wa itsu desu ka.**

B: Ashita no 9-ji kara desu.

1. A: .... (purezen)

   B: .... (kyō no 3-ji)

2. A: .... (pātī)

   B: .... (ashita no 5-ji)

3. A: .... (konsāto)

   B: .... (kyō no 6-ji)

VOCABULARY

happī awā	happy hour
itsu	when
purezen	presentation
konsāto	concert

VI *Talk about the opening time.* Make up dialogues following the pattern of the example. Substitute the underlined parts with the alternatives given.

Smith is staying at a hotel. He asks about the hotel services.

e.g. **Sumisu:** **Sumimasen. <u>Asa-gohan</u> wa nan-ji kara desu ka.**

Furonto: **<u>7-ji</u> kara desu.**

Sumisu: **Arigatō gozaimasu.**

1. Sumisu: .... (ban-gohan)

Furonto: .... (6:00)

Sumisu: ....

2. Sumisu: .... (pūru)

Furonto: .... (8:00 A.M.)

Sumisu: ....

3. Sumisu: .... (jimu)

Furonto: .... (9:00 A.M.)

Sumisu: ....

VII Listen to the audio and fill in the blanks based on the information you hear. 🔊 041, 042

1. Jimu wa .... kara .... made desu.

2. Asa-gohan wa .... kara .... made desu.

VOCABULARY

asa-gohan	breakfast	ban-gohan	evening meal, dinner,
asa	morning		supper
gohan	meal, cooked rice	ban	evening
furonto	reception desk	pūru	swimming pool

SPEAKING PRACTICE

1. Sasaki wants to call the London branch of her company. 🔊 043

Sasaki:	**Nakamura-san, ima nan-ji desu ka.**
Nakamura:	**4-ji han desu.**
Sasaki:	**Rondon wa ima nan-ji desu ka.**
Nakamura:	**Gozen 8-ji han desu.**
Sasaki:	**Sō desu ka. Dōmo arigatō.**

Sasaki:	Nakamura-san, what time is it now?
Nakamura:	It's 4:30.
Sasaki:	What time is it in London now?
Nakamura:	It's 8:30 in the morning.
Sasaki:	I see. Thank you.

NOTES

1. Sō desu ka.

This expression, meaning "I see." or "Is that so?" is used as a comment on what someone else has said. It is spoken with falling intonation.

Active Communication

1. Ask someone for the time.

2. If you're in Japan, try asking for the business hours of a restaurant or other facilities you are interested in.

VOCABULARY

Sō desu ka.	I see. (see NOTES 1, above)
Dōmo arigatō.	Thank you.

Shopping (1): How Much Is This?

Smith is shopping.

Mise no hito:	**Irasshaimase.**
Sumisu:	(*Pointing.*) **Sore o misete kudasai.**
Mise no hito:	**Hai, dōzo.**
Sumisu:	**Arigatō. Kore wa ikura desu ka.**
Mise no hito:	**3,000-en desu.**
Sumisu:	(*Pointing.*) **Are wa ikura desu ka.**
Mise no hito:	**Are mo 3,000-en desu.**
Sumisu:	**Ja, kore o kudasai.**
Mise no hito:	**Hai, arigatō gozaimasu.**

Salesperson:	May I help you?
Smith:	Please show me that item.
Salesperson:	Here you go.
Smith:	Thank you. How much is this?
Salesperson:	It is 3,000 yen.
Smith:	How much is that one over there?
Salesperson:	That one over there is also 3,000 yen.
Smith:	All right. I'll take this one.
Salesperson:	Fine. Thank you.

Irasshaimase.	May I help you?, Welcome.		**-en**	...yen
sore	that one		**are**	that one over there
misete kudasai	please show me		**mo**	also, too, either (particle; see GRAMMAR 2, p. 29)
ikura	how much		**ja**	well then
3,000-en (sanzen-en)	3,000 yen		**kudasai**	please give me

NOTES

1. **Irasshaimase.**

   This phrase is used in shops etc. to welcome customers. Literally it means "Please come in."

2. **Sore o misete kudasai.**

   When you want to take a closer look at an item in a store, use "thing **o misete kudasai**" ("please show me…").

3. **Ja, kore o kudasai.**

   Ja and **dewa** correspond to "well" or "well then," interjections that express conclusion or resignation.

KEY SENTENCES

 045

1. **Sore wa sumaho desu. Are wa taburetto desu.**
2. **Kore wa 3,000-en desu. Are mo 3,000-en desu.**
3. **Kore o kudasai.**
4. **Karē to sarada o onegaishimasu.**

1. That is a smart phone. That one over there is a tablet.
2. This one is 3,000 yen. That one over there is also 3,000 yen.
3. I would like this one, please.
4. I would like curry and salad, please.

GRAMMAR

1. **kore/sore/are**   (KS1, 2, 3)

Whereas English has only "this" and "that," Japanese has three separate demonstrative pronouns: **kore**, **sore**, and **are**. **Kore** (see ① right) indicates something near the speaker, **sore** (see ② right) something near the listener, and **are** (see ③ right) something distant from either person.

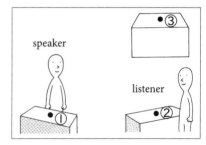

2. **noun mo**   (KS2)

The particle **mo** means "too," "also," "either," etc. It is used in both affirmative and negative sentences.

> e.g. **Kore wa watashi no kasa ja arimasen. Sore mo watashi no ja arimasen.**
>
> This is not my umbrella. That is not mine either.

Mo is always used with a noun.

3. **noun o kudasai./noun o onegaishimasu.**   (KS3, 4)

"noun **o kudasai**" means "please give me," and can be used when shopping or placing an order in a restaurant. "noun **o onegaishimasu**" can be used not only for making purchases or placing a restaurant order but for asking someone to do something or for requesting a service.

VOCABULARY

taburetto	tablet
karē	curry
to	and (particle; see GRAMMAR 4, p. 30)
sarada	salad

4. noun 1 **to** noun 2 (KS4)

The particle **to** ("and") is used to connect two or more nouns. It is used only to connect nouns. It cannot be used to connect verbs, adjectives or clauses.

WORD POWER

Ⅰ Home appliances 046

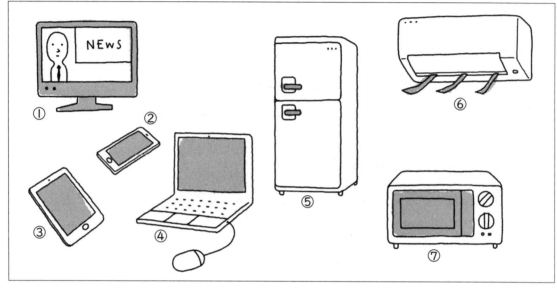

①terebi	③taburetto	⑤reizōko	⑦denshi-renji
②sumaho	④pasokon	⑥eakon	

Ⅱ Food and drink 047

①kōhī ②kōcha ③jūsu ④sandoitchi ⑤karē ⑥sarada

VOCABULARY

terebi	television	**denshi-renji**	microwave oven	**sandoitchi**	sandwich
pasokon	(personal) computer	**kōhī**	coffee		
reizōko	refrigerator	**kōcha**	(black) tea		
eakon	air conditioner	**jūsu**	juice		

Ⅲ Numbers

 048

100	hyaku	1,000	sen	10,000	ichiman
200	nihyaku	2,000	nisen	20,000	niman
300	sanbyaku	3,000	sanzen	30,000	sanman
400	yonhyaku	4,000	yonsen	40,000	yonman
500	gohyaku	5,000	gosen	50,000	goman
600	roppyaku	6,000	rokusen	60,000	rokuman
700	nanahyaku	7,000	nanasen	70,000	nanaman
800	happyaku	8,000	hassen	80,000	hachiman
900	kyūhyaku	9,000	kyūsen	90,000	kyūman

Intermediate numbers are made by combining the numbers composing them.

e.g. 135 **hyaku-sanjūgo**   1,829 **sen-happyaku-nijūkyū**

NOTE: Large numbers are written in hiragana here, but throughout the rest of the book, numerals are used to write them, e.g., **3,000-en** for "3,000 yen."

PLUS ONE

The system of counting large numbers is different in Japanese and English. The chart below shows how to count from a thousand to a trillion.

1,000	sen
10,000	ichi-man
100,000	jū-man
1,000,000	hyaku-man
10,000,000	sen-man
100,000,000	ichi-oku
1,000,000,000	jū-oku
10,000,000,000	hyaku-oku
100,000,000,000	sen-oku
1,000,000,000,000	itchō

chō oku man

2,222,222,222,222

nichō-nisen-nihyaku-nijūni-oku-nisen-nihyaku-nijūni-man-
nisen-nihyaku-nijūni

Decimals (The word for "decimal point" is **ten**.)

0.7	rei-ten-nana
0.29	rei-ten-ni-kyū
0.538	rei-ten-go-san-hachi

Fractions (**Bun** means "part.")

1/2	ni-bun no ichi	2/3	san-bun no ni
1/4	yon-bun no ichi		

EXERCISES

I *State an item's price.* Look at the illustrations and state the price of each item.

e.g.	1.	2.	3.	4.
¥90	¥100	¥120	¥300	¥400

5.	6.	7.	8.	9.
¥860	¥1,200	¥3,000	¥6,800	¥79,000

e.g. **kyūjū-en**

1. .... 4. .... 7. ....

2. .... 5. .... 8. ....

3. .... 6. .... 9. ....

II *Ask and answer an item's price.* Make up dialogues following the pattern of the example and based on the information provided.

e.g.

1.

2.

3.

e.g. **A: Kore wa ikura desu ka.**

B: 500-en desu.

1. A: ....

   B: ....

2. A: ....

   B: ....

3. A: ....

   B: ....

III *Ask and give an item's price.* Make appropriate questions for each of the answers given and based on the information provided.

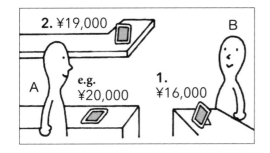 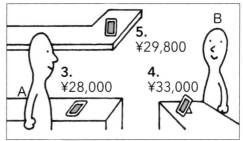

e.g. **A: <u>Kore wa ikura desu ka.</u>**

   B: 20,000-en desu.

1. A: ....

   B: 16,000-en desu.

2. A: ....

   B: 19,000-en desu.

3. A: ....

   B: 28,000-en desu.

4. A: ....

   B: 33,000-en desu.

5. A: ....

   B: 29,800-en desu.

IV *Give two things and state what they have in common.* Make up sentences following the pattern of the example. Substitute the underlined parts with the alternatives given.

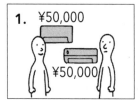   

e.g. Kore wa 90,000-en desu. Sore mo 90,000-en desu.

1. .... (kore, 50,000-en, sore)

2. .... (kore, tokei, sore)

3. ....
.... (Tanaka-san, Nihon-jin, Sasaki-san)

4. ....
.... (Tōkyō, gozen 10-ji, Souru)

V *Ask the price of more than one item.* Make up dialogues following the patterns of the examples. Substitute the underlined parts with the alternatives given.

A. e.g. Sumisu: **Kore wa ikura desu ka.**

    Mise no hito: **8,000-en desu.**

    Sumisu: **Are mo 8,000-en desu ka.**

    Mise no hito: **Hai, are mo 8,000-en desu.**

1.   Sumisu: ....

    Mise no hito: .... (7,000-en)

    Sumisu: .... (7,000-en)

    Mise no hito: .... (7,000-en)

2.   Sumisu: ....

    Mise no hito: .... (9,000-en)

    Sumisu: .... (9,000-en)

    Mise no hito: .... (9,000-en)

Souru	Seoul

B. e.g. **Sumisu:**   **Kore wa ikura desu ka.**

       Mise no hito: <u>5,000-en</u> **desu.**

       Sumisu: **Are mo** <u>5,000-en</u> **desu ka.**

       Mise no hito: Iie, are wa <u>5,000-en</u> **ja arimasen.**

                      4,000-en desu.

1. Sumisu: ....

     Mise no hito: .... (3,000-en)

     Sumisu: .... (3,000-en)

     Mise no hito: .... (3,000-en)

     ....

2. Sumisu: ....

     Mise no hito: .... (4,500-en)

     Sumisu: .... (4,500-en)

     Mise no hito: .... (4,500-en)

     ....

VI *Place your order at a restaurant.* Make up sentences following the pattern of the example and based on the information provided.

e.g.   1.   2. orenji-jūsu   3. chokorēto-kēki

e.g. **Sandoitchi to kōhī o onegaishimasu.**

1. ....

2. ....

3. ....

VOCABULARY

orenji-jūsu	orange juice
chokorēto-kēki	chocolate cake

VII *Talk about some item, ask its price, and say what you want to buy.* Make up dialogues following the pattern of the example. Substitute the underlined parts with the alternatives given.

    e.g. **Sumisu:**   Sumimasen. Are wa <u>pasokon</u> desu ka.

        Mise no hito: Iie, <u>taburetto</u> desu.

        Sumisu: Sore wa <u>pasokon</u> desu ka.

        Mise no hito: Hai, sō desu.

        Sumisu: Ikura desu ka.

        Mise no hito: <u>50,000-en</u> desu.

        Sumisu: Ja, sore o kudasai.

1. Sumisu: .... (bōrupen)

     Mise no hito: .... (shāpen)

     Sumisu: .... (bōrupen)

     Mise no hito: ....

     Sumisu: ....

     Mise no hito: .... (170-en)

     Sumisu: ....

2. Sumisu: .... (denshi-renji)

     Mise no hito: .... (tōsutā)

     Sumisu: .... (denshi-renji)

     Mise no hito: ....

     Sumisu: ....

     Mise no hito: .... (13,000-en)

     Sumisu: ....

VIII Listen to the audio and fill in the blanks based on the information you hear. 🔊 049-051

    1. Denshi-renji wa .... desu.

    2. Taburetto wa .... desu.

    3. Reizōko wa .... desu.

VOCABULARY

bōrupen	ballpoint pen
shāpen	mechanical pencil
	(colloquial shortening of **shāpu-penshiru**)
tōsutā	toaster

SPEAKING PRACTICE

1. Smith is placing his order at a coffee shop. 🔊 052

Sumisu: Sumimasen. Sandoitchi to kōhī o onegaishimasu.
Mise no hito: Hai.

Smith: Excuse me. I would like a sandwich and coffee, please.
Server: Thank you.

2. Smith is shopping in a store. 🔊 053

Sumisu: Kore o kudasai.
Mise no hito: 8,300-en desu.
Sumisu: Kādo de onegaishimasu.
Mise no hito: Hai.

Smith: I would like this, please.
Shopkeeper: That will be 8,300 yen.
Smith: I would like to pay by credit card.
Shopkeeper: Yes [, that will be fine].

NOTES

1. **Kādo de onegaishimasu.**
When stating a means or method of payment, the particle **de** is used.

Active Communication
If you're in Japan, try asking the prices of items at vendors where prices are not listed or are written in *kanji*.

VOCABULARY

kādo	credit card
de	by means of (particle; see NOTES 1, above)

Shopping (2): Two Bottles of That Wine, Please

TARGET DIALOGUE 🔊 054

Smith is at the information desk in a shopping mall.

Sumisu:	Sumimasen. Wain-shoppu wa doko desu ka.
Infomēshon no hito:	Chika 1-kai desu.
Sumisu:	Dōmo arigatō.

(In the liquor store.)

Sumisu:	Sumimasen. Sono wain wa doko no desu ka.
Mise no hito:	Furansu no desu.
Sumisu:	Ikura desu ka.
Mise no hito:	2,600-en desu.
Sumisu:	Ja, sore o 2-hon kudasai.
	Fukuro mo 2-mai kudasai.

Smith:	Excuse me. Where is the wine shop?
Information desk staff:	It is in the first-floor basement.
Smith:	Thank you.

Smith:	Excuse me. Where is that wine from?
Salesperson:	It is from France.
Smith:	How much is it?
Salesperson:	It is 2,600 yen.
Smith:	I see. Then I would like to have two bottles. Please let me have two bags as well.

VOCABULARY

wain-shoppu	wine shop		**sono**	that
doko	where		**wain**	wine
infomēshon	information desk		**Furansu**	France
chika 1-kai (ikkai)	first-floor basement		**2-hon**	two (long objects)
chika	basement		**fukuro**	bag
1-kai	first floor		**2-mai**	two (flat objects)

NOTES

1. **Sore o 2-hon kudasai.**

   -hon (bon/pon) is a unit for counting long, slender objects like pencils and bottles. Japanese has two numerical systems: the **hitotsu, futatsu, mittsu** system and the abstract **ichi, ni, san** system. Counting things can be done in two ways: (1) using the **hitotsu, futatsu, mittsu** system independently (see WORD POWER II, p. 40), or (2) using the **ichi, ni, san** system combined with a counter such as **-hon (bon/pon)** or **-mai**, the latter for thin, flat objects like shirts and pieces of paper.

   The **hitotsu, futatsu, mittsu** system, however, only goes as far as **tō** (10), after which the **ichi, ni, san** system is used: **jū-ichi, jū-ni, jū-san**, etc.

KEY SENTENCES

 055

1. **Resutoran wa 5-kai desu.**
2. **Kono T-shatsu wa 2,000-en desu.**
3. **Ano aoi T-shatsu wa 3,000-en desu.**
4. **Kore wa Furansu no wain desu.**
5. **Sono wain o 2-hon kudasai.**

1. The restaurant is on the 5th floor.
2. This T-shirt is 2,000 yen.
3. That blue T-shirt over there is 3,000 yen.
4. This is a wine from France. / This is a French wine.
5. I would like two bottles of that wine, please.

GRAMMAR

1. noun **wa** place **desu.**   (KS1)

This is the expression used when stating the location or place of a thing or person. When asking the location of the thing or person, say "noun **wa doko desu ka.**"

2. **kono/sono/ano** noun   (KS2, 3, 5)

Kono, **sono**, and **ano** have similar meanings to **kore**, **sore**, **are**, but they modify nouns.

3. adjective + noun   (KS3)

When the adjective modifies a noun, it is placed before the noun.

4. place **no** noun   (KS4)

The place which comes before the noun indicates the place of production or manufacture of the thing or product that follows.

5. noun **o** number **kudasai.**   (KS5)

When purchasing or ordering multiple items, the number comes after "noun **o.**" There is no particle after the number.

VOCABULARY

5-kai	fifth floor	**ano**	that (over there)
kono	this	**aoi**	blue
T-shatsu	T-shirt		

WORD POWER

I Items for sale

 056

red blue black white

①T-shatsu	④kuroi	⑦wain	⑩ringo
②akai	⑤shiroi	⑧(o-) sara	⑪ōkii
③aoi	⑥bīru	⑨koppu	⑫chiisai

II Numbers and counters

🔊 057

	👕 etc.	🍾☂ etc.	🍎🍔 etc.
1	ichi-mai (1-mai)	ippon (1-pon)	hitotsu
2	ni-mai (2-mai)	ni-hon (2-hon)	futatsu
3	san-mai (3-mai)	san-bon (3-bon)	mittsu
4	yon-mai (4-mai)	yon-hon (4-hon)	yottsu
5	go-mai (5-mai)	go-hon (5-hon)	itsutsu
6	roku-mai (6-mai)	roppon (6-pon)	muttsu
7	nana-mai (7-mai)	nana-hon (7-hon)	nanatsu
8	hachi-mai (8-mai)	happon (8-pon)	yattsu
9	kyū-mai (9-mai)	kyū-hon (9-hon)	kokonotsu
10	jū-mai (10-mai)	juppon (10-pon)	tō

III Floors

🔊 058

①ikkai (1-kai)	④yon-kai (4-kai)	⑦chika ikkai (1-kai)
②ni-kai (2-kai)	⑤go-kai (5-kai)	
③san-gai (3-gai)	⑥rokkai (6-kai)	

VOCABULARY

akai	red	ringo	apple	-hon/bon/pon	(counter for long,
kuroi	black	ōkii	big, large		slender objects)
shiroi	white	chiisai	small	ni-kai (2-kai)	second floor
bīru	beer	-mai	(counter for	san-gai (3-gai)	third floor
(o-) sara	dish, plate		flat objects)	yon-kai (4-kai)	fourth floor
koppu	glass			rokkai (6-kai)	sixth floor

-kai/gai	...floor

EXERCISES

I *Ask for the location of a shop or where certain goods are sold.* Make up dialogues following the pattern of the example. Substitute the underlined parts with the alternatives given.

> e.g. **A: Wain-shoppu** wa doko desu ka.
>
> **B: 1-kai** desu.

1. A: .... (resutoran)

    B: .... (6-kai)

2. A: .... (sōjiki)

    B: .... (3-gai)

3. A: .... (pasokon)

    B: .... (chika 1-kai)

II *Single out a specific item and state its price.* Make up sentences following the pattern of the example and based on the information provided.

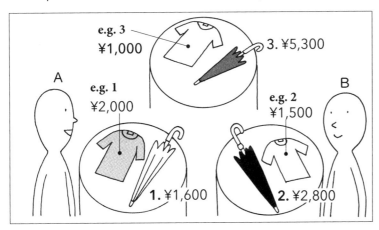

e.g. 3 ¥1,000
3. ¥5,300
A
e.g. 1 ¥2,000
e.g. 2 ¥1,500
B
1. ¥1,600
2. ¥2,800

e.g. 1   A: Kono T-shatsu wa 2,000-en desu.

e.g. 2   A: Sono T-shatsu wa 1,500-en desu.

e.g. 3   A: Ano T-shatsu wa 1,000-en desu.

1. A: ....

2. A: ....

3. A: ....

VOCABULARY

| sōjiki | vacuum cleaner |

III *Ask and give a specific item's price.* Make up dialogues following the pattern of the example and based on the information provided.

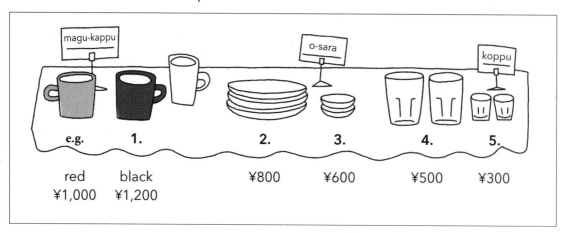

e.g. **A: Akai magu-kappu wa ikura desu ka.**

B: 1,000-en desu.

1. A: ....

   B: ....

2. A: ....

   B: ....

3. A: ....

   B: ....

4. A: ....

   B: ....

5. A: ....

   B: ....

IV Make up dialogues following the patterns of the examples and based on the information provided.

A. *Ask and answer whether an item is from a given country.*

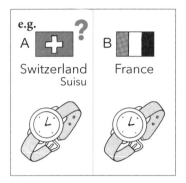 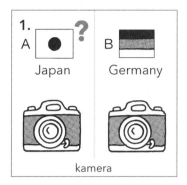 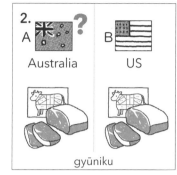

e.g. **A: Kore wa Suisu no tokei desu ka.**

B: Iie, Suisu no ja arimasen. Furansu no desu.

1. A: ....

   B: ....

2. A: ....

   B: ....

B. *Ask and answer what an item's country of origin is.*

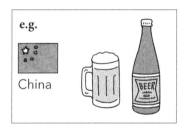  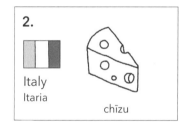

e.g. **A: Kore wa doko no bīru desu ka.**

B: Chūgoku no desu.

1. A: ....

   B: ....

2. A: ....

   B: ....

VOCABULARY

Suisu	Switzerland		**Itaria**	Italy
kamera	camera		**chīzu**	cheese
gyūniku	beef			
kutsu	shoes			

V *Ask the price of more than one item.* Make up dialogues following the pattern of the example and based on the information provided. Change the pronoun to fit each item.

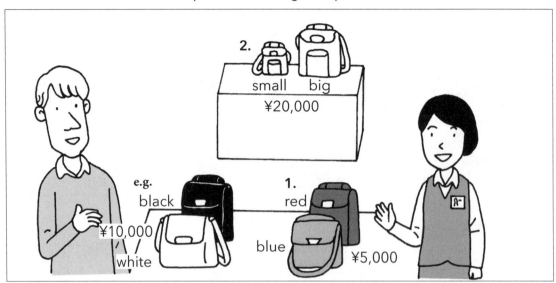

e.g. **Sumisu:**   <u>Kono shiroi kaban</u> wa ikura desu ka.

Mise no hito: <u>10,000-en</u> desu.

Sumisu: <u>Kono kuroi kaban</u> mo <u>10,000-en</u> desu ka.

Mise no hito: Hai, <u>sore</u> mo <u>10,000-en</u> desu.

1. Sumisu: ....

   Mise no hito: ....

   Sumisu: ....

   Mise no hito: ....

2. Sumisu: ....

   Mise no hito: ....

   Sumisu: ....

   Mise no hito: ....

VI *State what you want to buy and the quantity.* Make up sentences following the pattern of the example and based on the information provided.

e.g. **Sumisu:** Sono mikan o mittsu kudasai.

1. Sumisu: ....

2. Sumisu: ....

3. Sumisu: ....

4. Sumisu: ....

VII *Ask the price of an item and where it was made. State how many you want.* Make up dialogues following the pattern of the example. Substitute the underlined parts with the alternatives given.

e.g. **Sumisu:** Sumimasen. Sono <u>wain</u> wa ikura desu ka.

Mise no hito: <u>1,200</u>-en desu.

Sumisu: Sore wa doko no <u>wain</u> desu ka.

Mise no hito: <u>Furansu</u> no desu.

Sumisu: Ja, sore o <u>2-hon</u> kudasai.

1. Sumisu: .... (kōhī-kappu)

   Mise no hito: ....

   Sumisu: .... (kōhī-kappu)

   Mise no hito: .... (Igirisu)

   Sumisu: .... (muttsu)

mikan	mikan orange	**kōhī-kappu**	coffee cup
aka-wain	red wine (In the case of wine, red wine is not **akai wain**, but **aka-wain**. Likewise, white wine is **shiro-wain**.)		

2. Sumisu: .... (taoru)

   Mise no hito: ....

   Sumisu: .... (taoru)

   Mise no hito: .... (Itaria)

   Sumisu: .... (4-mai)

VIII Listen to the audio and choose the correct answers. 🔊 059

   1. Where is the beer from?

   ⓐ Nihon   ⓑ Amerika   ⓒ Doitsu

   2. How much does the beer cost?

   ⓐ 300-en   ⓑ 200-en   ⓒ 100-en

   3. How many bottles did the man buy?

   ⓐ 1-pon   ⓑ 5-hon   ⓒ 10-pon

SPEAKING PRACTICE

1. Smith is shopping in a clothing store. 🔊 060

   Sumisu: **Sumimasen. Ano T-shatsu wa ikura desu ka.**
   Mise no hito: **Dore desu ka.**
   Sumisu: **Ano aoi T-shatsu desu.**
   Mise no hito: **2,000-en desu.**

   Smith: Excuse me. How much is that T-shirt over there?
   Shopkeeper: Which one is it?
   Smith: That blue T-shirt.
   Shopkeeper: That one is 2,000 yen.

taoru	towel
dore	which one (of three or more things; see NOTES 1, p. 47)

2. Chan is shopping in a cake shop.　　　　　　　　　　　　　　　　061

> **Mise no hito: Irasshaimase.**
> **Chan:　　　　 Chīzu-kēki o mittsu to appuru-pai o futatsu kudasai.**
> **Mise no hito: Hai. 2,500-en desu.**

> Shopkeeper: Hello, how are you today.
> Chan:　　　　I would like three of the cheese cakes and two of the apple pies.
> Shopkeeper: All right. That will be 2,500 yen.

3. Chan is asking something to a shopkeeper in a shopping mall.　　　　062

> **Chan:　　　　 Otearai wa doko desu ka.**
> **Mise no hito: Achira desu.**
> **Chan:　　　　 Dōmo.**

> Chan:　　　　Can you tell me where the restroom is?
> Shopkeeper: It is over there.
> Chan:　　　　Thanks.

NOTES

1. Dore desu ka.

Dore is used when asking about an item among three or more. **Dochira** is used when asking about one of two items.

2. Achira desu.

Achira is the demonstrative pronoun used for a place distant from both the speaker and the listener. **Achira** is the polite form of the pronoun **asoko**.

3. Dōmo.

This is a colloquial shortening of **Dōmo arigatō**.

Active Communication

1. Ask people around you where an item they own is from (i.e., what its country of origin is).

2. If you're in Japan, go shopping and buy more than one of an item. Be sure to use the pattern "number of items **kudasai**."

VOCABULARY

chīzu-kēki	cheese cake		**Dōmo.**	Thanks.
appuru-pai	apple pie			
otearai	restroom			
achira	over there			

I Complete the dialogues by choosing words from the box below. Do not use the same word more than once.

nan	dare	itsu	doko	nan-ji	ikura

1. Sumisu: Kore wa (   ) no pen desu ka.

   Suzuki: Watashi no desu.

2. Sasaki: Rondon wa ima (   ) desu ka.

   Nakamura: Gozen 9-ji desu.

3. Sumisu: Kaigi wa (   ) desu ka.

   Nakamura: Ashita no 4-ji kara desu.

4. Sumisu: Are wa (   ) desu ka.

   Suzuki: Tokei desu.

5. Sumisu: Sore wa (   ) no wain desu ka.

   Mise no hito: Nihon no desu.

   Sumisu: (   ) desu ka.

   Mise no hito: 1,200-en desu.

II What do you say in the following situations?

1. You order curry and salad at a restaurant.

   ....

2. You want to know where the restrooms are.

   ....

3. In a shop, you want to see something located near the salesperson.

   ....

4. You ask a restaurant employee when the lunchtime begins and ends.

   ....

22番線　今度の電車
やまびこ　203号　6:40　仙台　自由席1〜5号車
停車駅　宇・新白河・郡山・福島・仙台
やまびこ・つばさ 123号　7:12　船山形 紀伊　つばさ16.17自由席号車
停車駅　つばさ
たにがわ　77号　7:28　ガーラ湯沢　自由席1〜4号車

Next Departure

6:09

Next Departure
やまびこ　201号
停車駅　原・新白河・
たにがわ　401
停車駅　崎・上毛高原
あさま　601
（情報）（5時30分現在

UNIT

3

GETTING AROUND

Japan boasts one of the most convenient transportation systems in the world. All major cities from Kagoshima in southern Japan to Tokyo in the east and Hakodate in the north are connected by bullet train. Other train systems connect towns and outlying suburbs of cities. In large metropolitan areas such as Tokyo, Nagoya, and Osaka, there are also extensive subway systems. All modes of public transportation depart and arrive on exact schedules. Some trains show news and advertising in video formats.

Going Places (1): Where Are You Going?

TARGET DIALOGUE

🔊 063

Smith calls Chan at the Osaka branch office at her mobile phone.

Chan: Hai, Chan desu.

Sumisu: Tōkyō-shisha no Sumisu desu. Ohayō gozaimasu.

Chan: Ohayō gozaimasu.

Sumisu: Ashita sochira ni ikimasu. Kaigi wa 1-ji kara desu ne.

Chan: Hai, 1-ji kara desu. Hitori de kimasu ka.

Sumisu: Iie, Katō-san to ikimasu.

Chan: Sō desu ka. Dewa, ashita.

Sumisu: Shitsureishimasu.

Chan: Shitsureishimasu.

■ Sumisu-san wa ashita Katō-san to Ōsaka-shisha ni ikimasu.

Chan: Hello, this is Chan.
Smith: This is Smith, of the Tokyo branch. Good morning.
Chan: Good morning.
Smith: I will visit you tomorrow.
        The meeting is from 1:00 P.M., right?
Chan: Yes, it is from 1:00. Will you be coming alone?
Smith: No, I'm going with Kato-san.
Chan: I see. Well, we will see you tomorrow, then.
Smith: Good bye.
Chan: Good bye.

■ Smith-san will go to the Osaka branch office
with Kato-san tomorrow.

VOCABULARY

Tōkyō-shisha	Tokyo branch
shisha	branch (office of a company)
Ohayō gozaimasu.	Good morning.
sochira	there [where you are]
ni	to (particle; see GRAMMAR 2, p. 52)
ikimasu	go
ne	right?, isn't it? (particle; see NOTES 2, p. 51)
hitori de	alone
kimasu	come
to	with, together with (particle; see GRAMMAR 4, p. 52)
dewa	well then
Shitsureishimasu.	Good bye.
Ōsaka-shisha	Osaka branch
Ōsaka	Osaka (city in western Japan)

NOTES

1. **Hai, Chan desu.**

   When answering the phone people often say **hai** before giving their name.

2. **Kaigi wa 1-ji kara desu ne.**

   The particle **ne** comes at the end of a sentence or phrase and, like "isn't it?" in English, seeks confirmation from the other person. It is spoken with a rising intonation. **Ne** is used when expressing admiration and praise, seeking agreement or empathy, and agreeing with what one's listener says, but in that case is pronounced with a falling intonation, sometimes drawing out the vowel: **nē**.

3. **Hitori de kimasu ka.**

   Iie, Katō-san to ikimasu.

   The Japanese verbs **ikimasu** and **kimasu** are always used from the point of view of the speaker. **Ikimasu** expresses the idea of moving from where the speaker is now to some other place. **Kimasu**, on the other hand, expresses the idea of moving toward the place where the speaker is now. Therefore, unlike in English, a speaker talking about going to the place where the listener is located, as in the above exchange, uses **ikimasu** rather than **kimasu**.

4. **Shitsureishimasu.**

   This expression is used as a form of "good-bye" when hanging up the phone or leaving a house or room. It is also used when entering a house or room, passing in front of someone, leaving in the middle of a gathering, and so on, to mean "excuse me."

KEY SENTENCES

 064

1. **Sumisu-san wa ashita ginkō ni ikimasu.**
2. **Sumisu-san wa senshū Ōsaka ni ikimashita.**
3. **Sumisu-san wa kinō tomodachi to resutoran ni ikimashita.**
4. **Sumisu-san wa kyonen Amerika kara kimashita.**

1. Smith-san is going to the bank tomorrow.
2. Smith-san went to Osaka last week.
3. Smith-san went to a restaurant with a friend yesterday.
4. Smith-san came from the United States last year.

GRAMMAR

1. Verbs   (KS1, 2, 3, 4)

Japanese sentences end with a verb (or some other element followed by **desu**, which behaves like a verb). The endings of verbs show the tense and whether the verb is affirmative or negative. Tenses of Japanese verbs can be divided roughly into two large categories:

(1) The present form   (KS1)

The present form, or **masu**-form—so called because verbs in this tense end in **masu**—also expresses a future action.

VOCABULARY

senshū	last week	**kyonen**	last year
ikimashita	went	**kara**	from (particle; see
kinō	yesterday		GRAMMAR 5, p. 52)
tomodachi	friend	**kimashita**	came

(2) The past form (KS2, 3, 4)

When expressing the past tense, **masu** changes to **mashita**.

The chart below summarizes the tenses of Japanese verbs and shows the endings—affirmative and negative—that correspond to each.

Present form		Past form	
aff.	*neg.*	*aff.*	*neg.*
-masu	-masen	-mashita	-masendeshita

To ask a question like "will you go?" that contains a verb, simply add **ka** to the verb. Answers to such questions can be brief, as in the examples below.

> e.g. **Sumisu-san wa ashita Kyōto ni ikimasu ka.**   Smith-san, will you go to Kyoto tomorrow?
> **Hai, ikimasu.**   Yes, (I) will go.
> **Iie, ikimasen.**   No, (I) will not go.

2. person **wa** place/event **ni ikimasu.** (KS1, 2, 3)

The role of the preposition "to" in English is played by the particle **ni** in Japanese. **Ni** is placed after a noun that denotes a place or an event. It indicates the direction of movement with motion verbs such as **ikimasu** ("go"), **kimasu** ("come"), **kaerimasu** ("return").

In this pattern, the particle "**e**" (written "**he**" in hiragana) can also be used in place of "**ni.**"

> e.g. **Sumisu-san wa pātī ni/e ikimasu.**
> Smith-san is going to the party.

3. Relative time expressions (KS1, 2, 3, 4)

Relative time expressions like **ashita** ("tomorrow"), **raishū** ("next week"), **kongetsu** ("this month"), and **kyonen** ("last year") generally do not take particles.

4. person **to** (KS3)

Use the particle **to** ("with") to indicate the person accompanied.

5. person **wa** place **kara kimashita.** (KS4)

When explaining that someone moved from one place to another, attach the particle **kara** to the place of departure. **Doko kara kimashita ka** means "Where did you come from?" and when Japanese ask non-Japanese this question, it usually means they want to know their country of origin.

WORD POWER

I Destinations

 065

| ①kūkō | ②eki | ③shisha | ④kōen | ⑤tomodachi no uchi |

II Verbs

 066

①ikimasu ②kimasu

III Time expressions

067

	Last	This	Next
day	kinō	kyō	ashita
week	senshū	konshū	raishū
month	sengetsu	kongetsu	raigetsu
year	kyonen	kotoshi	rainen

IV People

068

①tomodachi ②dōryō ③jōshi ④kazoku ⑤gakusei

VOCABULARY

kūkō	airport	raishū	next week	rainen	next year
eki	station	sengetsu	last month	dōryō	colleague, coworker
kōen	park	kongetsu	this month	jōshi	boss, superior
uchi	house, home	raigetsu	next month	kazoku	family
konshū	this week	kotoshi	this year	gakusei	student

EXERCISES

I *Practice conjugating verbs.* Repeat the verbs below and memorize their forms—present and past, affirmative and negative.

	Present form		Past form	
	aff.	*neg.*	*aff.*	*neg.*
go	**ikimasu**	**ikimasen**	**ikimashita**	**ikimasendeshita**
come	**kimasu**	**kimasen**	**kimashita**	**kimasendeshita**

II Make up sentences following the patterns of the examples. Substitute the underlined part with the alternatives given.

A. *State where someone will go.*

e.g. Sumisu-san wa <u>ginkō</u> ni ikimasu.

1. .... (kūkō)

2. .... (Kankoku)

3. .... (konsāto)

B. *State when someone will go to a particular place.*

e.g. Sumisu-san wa <u>ashita</u> Kyōto ni ikimasu.

1. .... (raishū)

2. .... (raigetsu)

3. .... (asatte)

C. *State when someone went to a particular place.*

e.g. Sumisu-san wa <u>kinō</u> Honkon ni ikimashita.

1. .... (senshū)

2. .... (sengetsu)

3. .... (ototoi)

VOCABULARY

Kankoku	South Korea, ROK	**ototoi**	day before yesterday
Kyōto	Kyoto		
asatte	day after tomorrow		
Honkon	Hong Kong		

III Make up dialogues following the patterns of the examples. Substitute the underlined part with the alternatives given.

A. *Ask and answer whether someone will go to a particular place.*

e.g. **A: Sumisu-san wa ashita** <u>Kyōto</u> **ni ikimasu ka.**

B: Hai, ikimasu.

1. A: ....

(Tōkyō Eki)

B: ....

2. A: ....

(Ginza no depāto)

B: ....

B. *Ask and answer whether someone will go to a particular place.*

e.g **A: Sumisu-san wa ashita** <u>ginkō</u> **ni ikimasu ka.**

B: Iie, ikimasen.

1. A: ....

(Ōsaka-shisha)

B: ....

2. A: .... (kūkō)

B: ....

C. *Ask and answer whether someone went to a particular place.*

e.g. **A: Sumisu-san wa kinō** <u>Ōsaka-shisha</u> **ni ikimashita ka.**

B: Hai, ikimashita.

1. A: .... (pātī)

B: ....

2. A: ....

(tomodachi no uchi)

B: ....

VOCABULARY

Tōkyō Eki	Tokyo Station
Ginza	Ginza (district in Tokyo)

D. *Ask and answer whether someone went to a particular place.*

e.g. **A: Sumisu-san wa kinō <u>taishikan</u> ni ikimashita ka.**

B: Iie, ikimasendeshita.

1. A: .... (jimu)

B: ....

2. A: .... (ginkō)

B: ....

Ⅳ Make up dialogues following the patterns of the examples. Substitute the underlined part with the alternatives given.

A. *Ask and answer where someone will go.*

e.g. **A: Sumisu-san wa ashita doko ni ikimasu ka.**

B: <u>Nozomi Depāto</u> ni ikimasu.

1. A: ....

B: .... (Hokkaidō)

2. A: ....

B: .... (tomodachi no uchi)

B. *Ask and answer when someone will go to a particular place.*

e.g. **A: Katō-san wa itsu Ōsaka-shisha ni ikimasu ka.**

B: <u>Raishū</u> ikimasu.

1. A: ....

B: .... (ashita)

2. A: ....

B: .... (raigetsu)

| **Hokkaidō** | Hokkaido (island in northern Japan) |

V *State whom someone will go somewhere with.* Make up sentences following the pattern of the example. Substitute the underlined word with the alternatives given.

    e.g. **Chan-san wa <u>tomodachi</u> to resutoran ni ikimasu.**

    1. .... (Nakamura-san)

    2. .... (Ema-san)

    3. .... (dōryō)

VI *Ask and answer whom someone will go somewhere with.* Make up dialogues following the pattern of the example. Substitute the underlined part with the alternatives given.

    e.g. **A: Sumisu-san wa ashita dare to Nozomi Depāto ni ikimasu ka.**

        B: <u>Katō-san</u> to ikimasu.

    1. A: ....

       B: .... (Ema-san)

    2. A: ....

       B: .... (jōshi)

VII Make up sentences following the patterns of the examples. Substitute the underlined parts with the alternatives given.

    A. *State who came to a particular place.*

    e.g. **<u>Sumisu-san</u> wa <u>kyonen</u> Nihon ni kimashita.**

    1. .... (Buraun-san, sengetsu)

    2. .... (Aren-san, ototoi)

    3. ....
        (Harisu-san, senshū)

    B. *State where someone came from.*

    e.g. **<u>Sumisu-san</u> wa kyonen <u>Amerika</u> kara kimashita.**

    1. .... (Chan-san, Honkon)

    2. .... (Ema-san, Furansu)

    3. .... (Hofuman-san, Doitsu)

VOCABULARY

| **Aren** | Allen (surname) |

VIII *State when, where, and with whom someone will travel/traveled to a destination.* Make up sentences following the pattern of the example and based on the information provided.

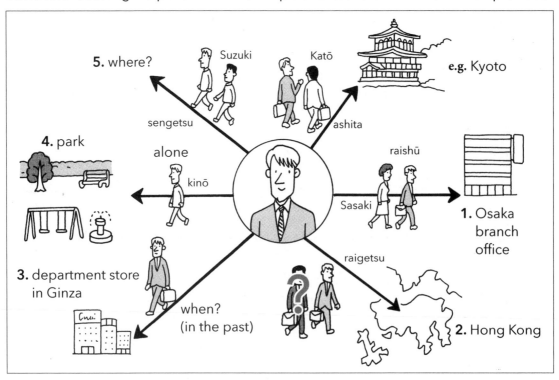

5. where? Suzuki   Katō   **e.g.** Kyoto

sengetsu   ashita

4. park   alone   raishū

kinō

1. Osaka branch office

Sasaki

raigetsu

3. department store in Ginza

when?
(in the past)

2. Hong Kong

e.g. **Sumisu-san wa ashita Katō-san to Kyōto ni ikimasu.**

1. ....

2. ....

3. ....

4. ....

5. ....

IX *Talk about when and with whom you are going somewhere.* Make up dialogues following the pattern of the example. Substitute the underlined parts with the alternatives given.

Smith is talking on the phone with a person from the Yokohama branch office.

e.g. **Yokohama-shisha no hito: Sumisu-san wa itsu Yokohama-shisha ni kimasu ka.**

Sumisu: Ashita ikimasu.

Yokohama-shisha no hito: Dare to kimasu ka.

Sumisu: Sasaki-san to ikimasu.

Yokohama-shisha no hito: Sō desu ka.

| **Yokohama**   Yokohama (city near Tokyo)

1. Yokohama-shisha no hito: ....

Sumisu: .... (raishū)

Yokohama-shisha no hito: ....

Sumisu: .... (Suzuki-san)

Yokohama-shisha no hito: ....

2. Yokohama-shisha no hito: ....

Sumisu: .... (asatte)

Yokohama-shisha no hito: ....

Sumisu: .... (Katō-san)

Yokohama-shisha no hito: ....

🅧 Listen to the audio and fill in the blanks based on the information you hear. 🔊069-071

1. Sumisu-san wa asatte .... to .... ni ikimasu.

2. Sumisu-san wa kinō .... to .... ni ikimashita.

3. Ema-san wa kyonen .... kara kimashita.

SPEAKING PRACTICE

1. From today, Raja is starting an internship at ABC Foods. 🔊 072

Sasaki: Kochira wa intān no Raja-san desu.
Raja: Hajimemashite. Raja desu. Indo kara kimashita.
Tōkyō Daigaku no gakusei desu.
Kyō kara yoroshiku onegaishimasu.
Kaisha no hito-tachi: Yoroshiku onegaishimasu.

Sasaki: This is Raja-san, our intern.
Raja: Nice to meet you. My name is Raja. I am from India.
I am a student at the University of Tokyo.
[From today] I look forward to working with you.
Company staff: Nice to meet you!

intān	intern
no	(particle; see NOTES 1, p. 60)
hito-tachi	people
-tachi	(plural for people)

2. At a bus stop, Smith asks the driver a question before boarding. 🔊 073

Sumisu:	**Sumimasen. Kono basu wa Shibuya ni ikimasu ka.**
Basu no untenshu:	**Iie, ikimasen.**
Sumisu:	**Dono basu ga ikimasu ka.**
Basu no untenshu:	**6-ban no basu ga ikimasu.**
Sumisu:	**Arigatō gozaimasu.**

Smith:	Excuse me. Does this bus go to Shibuya?
Bus driver:	No, it doesn't go to Shibuya.
Smith:	Which bus goes there?
Bus driver:	The No. 6 bus goes there.
Smith:	Thank you.

NOTES

1. **intān no Raja-san**

   This particle **no** here expresses apposition, not possession or affiliation, and it means Raja is an intern.

2. **dono basu**

   Dore is used alone to mean "which," but if "which" is to be followed by a noun, then **dono** is used.

   e.g. **dore**   which one

       dono basu   which bus

3. **Dono basu ga ikimasu ka.**

   6-ban no basu ga ikimasu.

   The particle **ga**, the subject marker, is used instead of the topic marker **wa** after interrogatives like **dore** and **dono**. **Ga** is repeated in replies to questions of the **dore ga** or **dono ... ga** pattern, as in the exchange here.

Active Communication

Ask people around you where they are going tomorrow, next week, next month, and so on.

VOCABULARY

basu	bus	**ga**	(particle; see NOTES 2, above)
Shibuya	Shibuya (district in Tokyo)	**-ban**	number... (suffix for number)
untenshu	driver		
dono	which (of three or more things)		

Going Places (2): I'm Going by Shinkansen

TARGET DIALOGUE 074

Smith is carrying a suitcase. Nakamura notices and calls out to him.

Nakamura: A, Sumisu-san, shutchō desu ka.

Sumisu: Ee, Katō-san to Ōsaka-shisha ni ikimasu.
Kin-yōbi ni Tōkyō ni kaerimasu.

Nakamura: Hikōki de ikimasu ka.

Sumisu: Iie, shinkansen de ikimasu.

Nakamura: Sō desu ka. Itterasshai.

■ Sumisu-san wa Katō-san to shinkansen de Ōsaka ni ikimasu.
Kin-yōbi ni Tōkyō ni kaerimasu.

Nakamura: Ah! Smith-san, are you going on a business trip?
Smith: Yes. I'm going to the Osaka branch office with Kato-san. I'll be back to Tokyo on Friday.
Nakamura: Are you going by airplane?
Smith: No. We're going by Shinkansen.
Nakamura: I see. Have a good trip.

■Smith-san will go to Osaka with Kato-san by Shinkansen.
They will return to Tokyo on Friday.

VOCABULARY

a	ah, oh (see NOTES 1, p. 62)	**hikōki**	airplane
shutchō	business trip	**de**	by means of (particle; see GRAMMAR 2, p. 62)
ee	yes (a softer way of saying **hai**)	**shinkansen**	superexpress train, Shinkansen
kin-yōbi	Friday	**Itterasshai.**	Have a good trip., Have a good day.
ni	at, in, on (particle; see GRAMMAR 1, p. 62)		
kaerimasu	return, come back		

1. **A, Sumisu-san, shutchō desu ka.**

    A is an utterance expressing having just noticed something. It is also used to get someone's attention.

2. **Shutchō desu ka.**

    Nakamura asks if Smith is going on a business trip because he is carrying a suitcase and is clearly on his way somewhere. She means, "Are you going on business?"

KEY SENTENCES

 075

1. **Ema-san wa 4-gatsu ni Nihon ni kimashita.**
2. **Sumisu-san wa shinkansen de Ōsaka ni ikimasu.**
3. **Kaigi wa yokka desu ka, yōka desu ka.**

1. Emma-san came to Japan in April.
2. Smith-san is going to Osaka by Shinkansen.
3. Is the meeting on the 4th or on the 8th?

GRAMMAR

1. Specific time expressions (KS1)

When stating the time of a certain action, unlike relative time expressions (see L6, GRAMMAR 3, p. 52), specific time expressions take the particle **ni**.

e.g. **5-ji ni**   at 5:00

do-yōbi ni   on Saturday

12-nichi ni   on the twelfth

2025-nen ni   in 2025

2. transportation **de** (KS2)

When indicating means of movement, the particle **de** is attached to the noun indicating the means of transportation.

e.g. **basu de**   by bus

takushī de   by taxi

But to say "by foot," use **aruite**, e.g., **aruite kimashita**, (I) walked here.

To ask the means by which someone will go somewhere, use **nan de**.

e.g. **Nan de ikimasu ka.**   How will you go?

Basu de ikimasu.   I'll go by bus.

Since **nan de** means "Why?" in colloquial speech, **nani de** can be used in place of **nan de** to avoid confusion.

3. noun 1 **wa** noun 2 **desu ka**, noun 3 **desu ka.** (KS3)

This is the expression for confirming which of two alternatives (noun 2 or noun 3) is correct. The intonation rises for **ka** in each case.

4-gatsu (shigatsu)	April	yōka	8th, eighth (of the month)
yokka	4th, fourth (of the month)		

WORD POWER

① Verb

 076

kaerimasu

② Dates

076... 077

Years		
1998-nen	**sen kyūhyaku kyūjū hachi-nen**	the year 1998
2022-nen	**nisen nijūni-nen**	the year 2022

Days of the week	
nichi-yōbi	Sunday
getsu-yōbi	Monday
ka-yōbi	Tuesday
sui-yōbi	Wednesday
moku-yōbi	Thursday
kin-yōbi	Friday
do-yōbi	Saturday

Months			
ichi-gatsu	January	**shichi-gatsu**	July
ni-gatsu	February	**hachi-gatsu**	August
san-gatsu	March	**ku-gatsu**	September
shi-gatsu	April	**jū-gatsu**	October
go-gatsu	May	**jūichi-gatsu**	November
roku-gatsu	June	**jūni-gatsu**	December

Days of the month					
tsuitachi	1st	**jūichi-nichi**	11th	**nijūichi-nichi**	21st
futsuka	2nd	**jūni-nichi**	12th	**nijūni-nichi**	22nd
mikka	3rd	**jūsan-nichi**	13th	**nijūsan-nichi**	23rd
yokka	4th	**jūyokka**	14th	**nijūyokka**	24th
itsuka	5th	**jūgo-nichi**	15th	**nijūgo-nichi**	25th
muika	6th	**jūroku-nichi**	16th	**nijūroku-nichi**	26th
nanoka	7th	**jūshichi-nichi**	17th	**nijūshichi-nichi**	27th
yōka	8th	**jūhachi-nichi**	18th	**nijūhachi-nichi**	28th
kokonoka	9th	**jūku-nichi**	19th	**nijūku-nichi**	29th
tōka	10th	**hatsuka**	20th	**sanjū-nichi**	30th
				sanjūichi-nichi	31st

NOTE: Months and dates are written in hiragana here, but elsewhere in the book numerals are used to write them, e.g., **1-gatsu** for "January," **11-nichi** for "the eleventh," etc.

VOCABULARY

-nen	the year…
-yōbi	day of the week
-gatsu	month
-nichi	day

III Means of transportation

 078

①densha

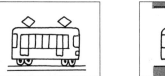
②chikatetsu

③kuruma

④takushī

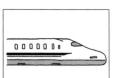
⑤shinkansen

⑥hikōki

⑦baiku

⑧jitensha

EXERCISES

I *State when an event will be held.* Make up sentences following the pattern of the example. Substitute the underlined part with the alternatives given.

e.g. **Kaigi wa sui-yōbi desu.**

1. .... (getsu-yōbi)

2. .... (4-gatsu hatsuka)

II Make up dialogues following the patterns of the examples. Substitute the underlined parts with the alternatives given.

A. *Ask and answer when an event will be held.*

e.g. **A: O-matsuri wa nan-gatsu desu ka.**

B: 9-gatsu desu.

1. A: .... (nan-nichi)

   B: .... (17-nichi)

2. A: .... (nan-yōbi)

   B: .... (nichi-yōbi)

densha	train	**baiku**	motorbike	**nan-nichi**	what day
chikatetsu	subway	**jitensha**	bicycle	**nan-yōbi**	what day of the week
kuruma	car	**(o-) matsuri**	festival		
takushī	taxi	**nan-gatsu**	what month		

B. *Ask and answer the questions about events.*

e.g. **A: Tanjōbi wa itsu desu ka.**

B: 8-gatsu 19-nichi desu.

1. A: .... (kaigi)

B: .... (7-gatsu tsuitachi)

2. A: .... (pātī)

B: .... (raishū no do-yōbi)

3. A: .... (purezen)

B: .... (konshū no kin-yōbi)

4. A: .... (konsāto)

B: .... (9-gatsu 19-nichi)

C. *Ask and answer when an event will be held.*

e.g. **A: Natsu-yasumi wa itsu kara itsu made desu ka.**

B: 9-gatsu futsuka kara nanoka made desu.

1. A: .... (shutchō)

B: ....

(getsu-yōbi, moku-yōbi)

2. A: .... (ryokō)

B: ....

(4-gatsu 29-nichi, 5-gatsu itsuka)

VOCABULARY

tanjōbi	birthday		**ryokō**	trip
natsu-yasumi	summer vacation			
natsu	summer			
yasumi	vacation			

Ⅲ Make up sentences or dialogues following the patterns of the examples and based on the information provided.

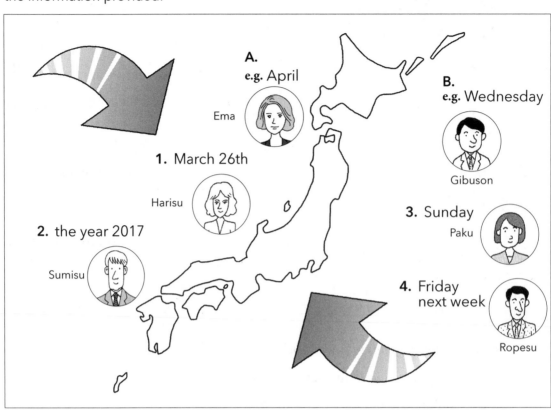

A.
e.g. April

Ema

B.
e.g. Wednesday

Gibuson

1. March 26th

Harisu

3. Sunday

Paku

2. the year 2017

Sumisu

4. Friday
next week

Ropesu

A. *State when someone came to a particular place.*

e.g. **Ema-san** wa **4-gatsu** ni Nihon ni kimashita.

1. ....

2. ....

B. *Ask and answer when someone will come to Japan.*

e.g. A: **Gibuson-san** wa itsu Nihon ni kimasu ka.

B: **Sui-yōbi** ni kimasu.

3. A: ....

B: ....

4. A: ....

B: ....

Gibuson	Gibson (surname)
Paku	Pak, Park (surname)
Ropesu	Lopez (surname)

IV *State how someone got home.* Make up sentenes following the pattern of the example. Substitute the underlined part with the alternatives given.

e.g. **Sumisu-san wa <u>chikatetsu de</u> uchi ni kaerimashita.**

1. .... (takushī de)

2. .... (densha de)

3. .... (aruite)

V *Ask and answer how someone will go to Osaka.* Make up dialogues following the pattern of the example. Substitute the underlined part with the alternatives given.

e.g. **A: Sumisu-san wa nan de Ōsaka ni ikimasu ka.**

B: <u>Kuruma</u> de ikimasu.

1. A: ....

   B: .... (shinkansen)

2. A: ....

   B: .... (hikōki)

VOCABULARY

aruite	on foot, walking
nan de	by what means

VI *State when and how someone traveled.* Make up sentences following the pattern of the example and based on the information provided.

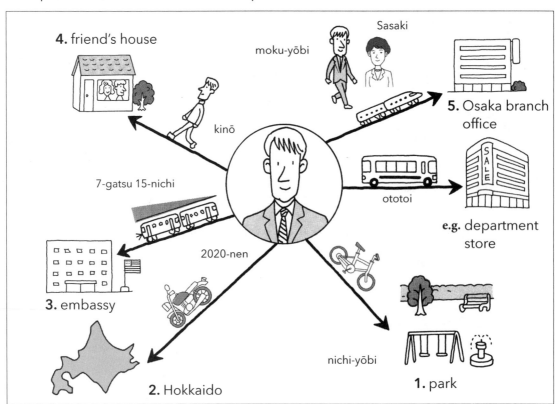

e.g. **Sumisu-san wa** <u>ototoi basu de depāto ni ikimashita.</u>

1. ....

2. ....

3. ....

4. ....

5. ....

VII *Describe a schedule.* Make up sentences following the pattern of the example and based on the information provided in the page from Smith's weekly planner.

e.g.	Mon.	12:00	Go to Tokyo Hotel (by taxi, with Suzuki-san)
	Tue.		
1.	Wed.		Go to Osaka branch office (by airplane, alone)
	Thu.		
2.	Fri.	1:00	Go to Nozomi Department Store
		4:00	Go to Yokohama branch office (with Sasaki-san)
		6:00	Go to the American Embassy
	Sat.		
3.	Sun.	9:00 a.m.	Go to the park (with friends)
		7:00 p.m.	Go to Suzuki-san's house (with colleagues)

e.g. **Sumisu-san wa getsu-yōbi no 12-ji ni Suzuki-san to takushī de Tōkyō Hoteru ni ikimasu.**

1. ....

    ....

2. ....

    ....

3. ....

    ....

VIII *Ask whether the event time is one or another day/hour.* Make up dialogues following the pattern of the example. Substitute the underlined parts with the alternatives given.

e.g. **A: Kaigi wa <u>yokka</u> desu ka, <u>yōka</u> desu ka.**

   B: <u>Yokka</u> desu.

1. A: ....(mikka, muika)

    B: ....(mikka)

2. A: ....(4:00, 5:00)

    B: ....(5:00)

Tōkyō Hoteru   Tokyo Hotel (fictitious hotel name)
   hoteru   hotel

IX *Talk about when and how to travel.* Make up dialogues following the pattern of the example and based on the information provided.

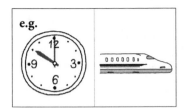
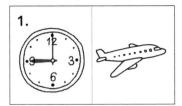

e.g.   1.   2.

Smith is talking over the phone with Chan of the Osaka branch office.

e.g. **Chan:** **Raishū no getsu-yōbi ni sochira ni ikimasu.**

Sumisu: Nan-ji ni kimasu ka.

Chan: <u>**10-ji**</u> **ni ikimasu.**

Sumisu: Nan de kimasu ka.

Chan: <u>**Shinkansen**</u> **de ikimasu.**

Sumisu: Sō desu ka.

1. Chan: ....

   Sumisu: ....

   Chan: ....

   Sumisu: ....

   Chan: ....

   Sumisu: ....

2. Chan: ....

   Sumisu: ....

   Chan: ....

   Sumisu: ....

   Chan: ....

   Sumisu: ....

X Listen to the audio and choose the correct answers.   079, 080

1. When and how will Emma go to Osaka?

1) ⓐ getsu-yōbi   ⓑ moku-yōbi   ⓒ sui-yōbi

2) ⓐ    ⓑ 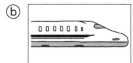   ⓒ

2. What time is the meeting?

ⓐ 1-ji   ⓑ 7-ji

SPEAKING PRACTICE

1. Kato and Smith arrive at the Osaka branch office and Chan shows them to the meeting room.   081

Chan: (*Opening the door.*) **Dōzo.**
Katō: **Shitsureishimasu.** (*Enters the room.*)
Sumisu: Shitsureishimasu. (*Enters the room.*)
Chan: Dōzo okake kudasai.
Sumisu: Arigatō gozaimasu.

Chan: Please go on in.
Kato: Thank you. (Excuse me.)
Smith: Thank you. (Excuse me.)
Chan: Please have a seat.
Smith: Thank you.

2. Nakamura and Raja are talking during their break.   082

Nakamura: Raja-san wa itsu Nihon ni kimashita ka.
Raja: Kyonen no 9-gatsu ni kimashita.
Nakamura: Sō desu ka. Natsu-yasumi ni Indo ni kaerimasu ka.
Raja: Iie, kaerimasen. Tomodachi to Hokkaidō ni ikimasu.

Nakamura: Raja-san, when did you come to Japan?
Raja: I came in September last year.
Nakamura: Ah, I see. Will you go back to India during the summer vacation?
Raja: No, I won't go back. I'm going to Hokkaido with a friend.

VOCABULARY

Shitsureishimasu.	Excuse me.
Okake kudasai.	Please have a seat.

3. Smith and Emma are working. 🔊 083

Sumisu: **Kaigi wa itsu desu ka.**
Ema: **Raigetsu no yōka desu.**
Sumisu: **E? Yokka desu ka, yōka desu ka.**
Ema: **Yōka desu.**
Sumisu: **Yōka desu ne.**

Smith: When is the meeting?
Emma: It's on the 8th of next month.
Smith: What? Is it the 4th or the 8th?
Emma: It's the 8th.
Smith: Right, the 8th.

NOTES

1. E? Yokka desu ka, yōka desu ka.

   E is an utterance expressing uncertainty about what one has heard. It may be used when one is surprised.

Active
Communication

1. Ask people around you when their birthdays are.

2. Ask people around you when their summer vacations are.

VOCABULARY

e   (see NOTES 1, above)

EATING OUT

The most famous type of Japanese food worldwide may be sushi, but numerous other dishes include tempura, shabu-shabu, yakitori, and soba. These dishes can be enjoyed in a wide range of establishments, from high-end restaurants to simple stalls people stop by on their way home from work. There are also places for eating and drinking late into the night, among which the izakaya are especially popular. Many restaurants around the cities, especially Tokyo, serve authentic world cuisines, so you can even get a sense of world travel by eating at the restaurants from different countries.

Doing Things (1): I'm Going to Eat Tempura

TARGET DIALOGUE

 084

Smith and Sasaki are talking during their break.

Sasaki: Shūmatsu ni nani o shimasu ka.

Sumisu: Do-yōbi ni Ginza de Suzuki-san to tenpura o tabemasu.

Sasaki: Sō desu ka. Ii desu ne.

Sumisu: Sasaki-san wa?

Sasaki: Nichi-yōbi ni tomodachi to kabuki o mimasu.

Sumisu: Ii desu ne.

- Sumisu-san wa do-yōbi ni Ginza de Suzuki-san to tenpura o tabemasu.
  Sasaki-san wa nichi-yōbi ni tomodachi to kabuki o mimasu.

Sasaki: What are you going to do over the weekend?
Smith: On Saturday, I'm going to eat tempura in Ginza with Suzuki-san.
Sasaki: Really. That sounds nice.
Smith: How about you, Sasaki-san?
Sasaki: On Sunday, I'm going to see kabuki
        with a friend.
Smith: Oh, that sounds great.

- Smith-san is going to eat tempura in Ginza
  with Suzuki-san on Saturday.
  Sasaki-san is going to see kabuki
  with a friend on Sunday.

VOCABULARY

shūmatsu	weekend	**de**	at, in, on (particle; see GRAMMAR 2, p. 75)	**Ii desu ne.**	That's good. (see NOTES 1, p. 75)
nani	what				
o	(particle; see GRAMMAR 1, p. 75)	**tenpura**	tempura	**kabuki**	kabuki (see NOTES 3, p. 75)
		tabemasu	eat	**mimasu**	see
shimasu	do				

74

NOTES

1. **Ii desu ne.**

   This is the phrase that is used to express admiration or praise of the words or actions of someone.

2. **Sasaki-san wa?**

   Spoken with a rising intonation, this means, "How about you, Sasaki-san, what are you going to do?"

3. **kabuki**

   Kabuki is a traditional performing art performed by male actors.

KEY SENTENCES

 085

1. **Sumisu-san wa ashita tenisu o shimasu.**
2. **Sumisu-san wa kinō resutoran de ban-gohan o tabemashita.**
3. **Ema-san wa pātī de nani mo tabemasendeshita.**

1. Smith-san will play tennis tomorrow.
2. Smith-san ate supper at a restaurant yesterday.
3. Emma-san did not eat anything at the party.

GRAMMAR

1. person wa noun o verb. (KS1, 2)

Placed after a noun, the particle **o**, the object marker, indicates that the noun is the object of the sentence. **O** is used with verbs like **mimasu** ("see"), **yomimasu** ("read"), **nomimasu** ("drink"), **kaimasu** ("buy") and a host of others.

2. place/event de (KS2, 3)

The particle **de** is used when indicating the place or event in which a certain action is taken. It has the meaning of "at," "in," "on" in English. Word order in general: person **wa** time **(ni)** place/event **de** noun **o** verb.

3. nani mo in a negative sentence (KS3)

Nani mo is always used in negative statements such as **Watashi wa nani mo tabemasendeshita.**, meaning "I didn't eat anything." Likewise, **Dare mo ikimasendeshita.** means "Nobody went."

VOCABULARY

tenisu o shimasu	play tennis	tabemasendeshita	did not eat
tabemashita	ate		
nani mo tabemasendeshita	didn't eat anything		
nani mo -masen	nothing (see GRAMMAR 3, above)		

WORD POWER

I Food and drink

 086

①asa-gohan	④rāmen	⑦tenpura	⑩o-cha
②hiru-gohan	⑤(o-) sushi	⑧sūpu	⑪mizu
③ban-gohan	⑥sutēki	⑨nihonshu	⑫aisu-kurīmu

II Verbs

086 087

①tabemasu	②nomimasu	③kaimasu	④yomimasu	⑤kikimasu

⑥mimasu	⑦tenisu o shimasu	⑧benkyō o shimasu	⑨kaimono o shimasu	⑩shigoto o shimasu

NOTE: For more on the "noun **o shimasu**" verb type, see APPENDIX D, p. 246.

VOCABULARY

hiru-gohan	lunch	o-cha	green tea	kikimasu	listen to
rāmen	ramen (Chinese noodle)	mizu	water	benkyō o shimasu	study
(o-) sushi	sushi	aisu-kurīmu	ice cream	kaimono o shimasu	shop
sutēki	steak	nomimasu	drink	shigoto o shimasu	work
sūpu	soup	kaimasu	buy		
nihonshu	sake (Japanese rice liquor)	yomimasu	read		

Ⅲ Numbers of people

088

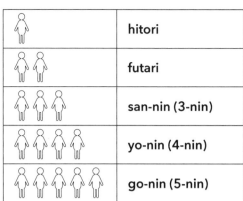

👤	hitori
👤👤	futari
👤👤👤	san-nin (3-nin)
👤👤👤👤	yo-nin (4-nin)
👤👤👤👤👤	go-nin (5-nin)
?	nan-nin

EXERCISES

I *Practice conjugating verbs.* Repeat the verbs below and memorize their forms—present and past, affirmative and negative.

	Present form		Past form	
	aff.	*neg.*	*aff.*	*neg.*
eat	tabemasu	tabemasen	tabemashita	tabemasendeshita
drink	nomimasu	nomimasen	nomimashita	nomimasendeshita
buy	kaimasu	kaimasen	kaimashita	kaimasendeshita
read	yomimasu	yomimasen	yomimashita	yomimasendeshita
listen to	kikimasu	kikimasen	kikimashita	kikimasendeshita
see	mimasu	mimasen	mimashita	mimasendeshita
do	shimasu	shimasen	shimashita	shimasendeshita

hitori	one person
futari	two people
-nin	...people
nan-nin	how many people

II Make up sentences following the patterns of the examples. Substitute the underlined part with the alternatives given.

A. *State what someone will see.*

e.g. **Suzuki-san wa <u>terebi</u> o mimasu.**

1. ....(eiga)

2. ....(kabuki)

B. *State what someone will listen to.*

e.g. **Suzuki-san wa <u>ongaku</u> o kikimasu.**

1. ....(rajio)

2. ....(nyūsu)

III Make up sentences or dialogues following the patterns of the examples and based on the information provided.

A. *State what someone will do.*

e.g. **Sumisu-san wa sutēki o tabemasu.**

1. ....

2. ....

3. ....

4. ....

VOCABULARY

eiga	movie
ongaku	music
rajio	radio
nyūsu	news

B. *Ask and answer what someone will do.*

e.g. **A: Sumisu-san wa nani o tabemasu ka.**

B: Sutēki o tabemasu.

1. A: ....

B: ....

2. A: ....

B: ....

3. A: ....

B: ....

4. A: ....

B: ....

IV Make up sentences following the patterns of the examples. Substitute the underlined part with the alternatives given.

A. *State where someone will drink something.*

e.g. **Suzuki-san wa <u>uchi</u> de bīru o nomimasu.**

1. .... (resutoran)

2. .... (hoteru no bā)

B. *State where someone will buy something.*

e.g. **Suzuki-san wa <u>konbini</u> de mizu o kaimasu.**

1. .... (sūpā)

2. .... (kūkō)

VOCABULARY

bā   bar
konbini   convenience store

Make up sentences or dialogues following the patterns of the examples and based on the information provided.

e.g. resutoran	1. toshokan	2. kaisha	3. konbini	4. kōen
			 sandwich	

A. *State where someone will do something.*

e.g. **Sumisu-san wa resutoran de ban-gohan o tabemasu.**

1. ....

2. ....

3. ....

4. ....

B. *Ask and answer where someone will do something.*

e.g. **A: Sumisu-san wa doko de ban-gohan o tabemasu ka.**

   B: Resutoran de tabemasu.

1. A: ....

   B: ....

2. A: ....

   B: ....

3. A: ....

   B: ....

4. A: ....

   B: ....

VI *Ask and answer what someone did at an event.* Make up dialogues following the pattern of the example. Substitute the underlined parts with the appropriate forms of the alternatives given.

> e.g. **A: O-matsuri de nani o <u>tabemashita</u> ka.**
>
> **B: Nani mo <u>tabemasendeshita</u>.**

1. A: .... (kaimasu)

   B: .... (kaimasu)

2. A: .... (nomimasu)

   B: .... (nomimasu)

VII *Answer how many are in your party at a restaurant.* Make up dialogues following the pattern of the example and based on the information provided.

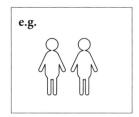 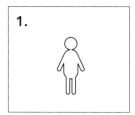 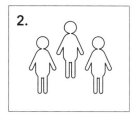 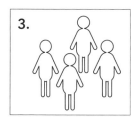

> e.g. **A: Nan-mei sama desu ka.**
>
> **B: Futari desu.**

1. A: Nan-mei sama desu ka.

   B: ....

2. A: Nan-mei sama desu ka.

   B: ....

3. A: Nan-mei sama desu ka.

   B: ....

| **Nan-mei sama desu ka.** | How many people? (polite expression of **Nan-nin desu ka**) |

Ⅷ *Talk about what you did, where, and with whom.* Make up dialogues following the pattern of the example. Substitute the underlined parts with the alternatives given.

e.g. **Katō:** **Shūmatsu ni nani o shimashita ka.**

Sumisu: <u>Tomodachi</u> to <u>gorufu</u> o shimashita.

Katō: **Doko de shimashita ka.**

Sumisu: <u>Hakone</u> de shimashita.

Katō: **Sō desu ka.**

1. Katō: ....

Sumisu: ....

(Gurīn-san, tenisu)

Katō: ....

Sumisu: ....

(hoteru no tenisu-kōto)

Katō: ....

2. Katō: ....

Sumisu: ....

(Suzuki-san, kaimono)

Katō: ....

Sumisu: ....

(Ginza no depāto)

Katō: ....

Ⅸ Listen to the audio and fill in the blanks based on the information you hear. 🔊 089

1. Ema-san wa Ginza de .... o kaimashita.

2. Ema-san wa .... de hiru-gohan o tabemashita.

VOCABULARY

gorufu o shimasu	play golf
Hakone	Hakone (popular travel destination southwest of Tokyo)
tenisu-kōto	tennis court

SPEAKING PRACTICE

1. Suzuki phones a tempura restaurant called "Tenmasa." 🔊 090

Mise no hito: Tenmasa de gozaimasu.
Suzuki: Yoyaku o onegaishimasu.
Mise no hito: Hai, arigatō gozaimasu.
Suzuki: Do-yōbi no 7-ji ni onegaishimasu.
Mise no hito: Nan-mei sama desu ka.
Suzuki: Futari desu.
Mise no hito: Hai, wakarimashita. Dewa, o-namae to o-denwa-bangō o onegaishimasu.

Restaurant employee: This is Tenmasa.
Suzuki: I'd like to make a reservation.
Restaurant employee: Thank you.
Suzuki: Please make the reservation for 7:00 P.M. on Saturday.
Restaurant employee: How many people in your party?
Suzuki: For two, please.
Restaurant employee: Yes, well then. Please give me your name and your telephone number.

2. On Monday morning, Nakamura is talking to Smith. 🔊 091

Nakamura: Kinō nani o shimashita ka.
Sumisu: Furī-māketto ni ikimashita.
Nakamura: Nani o kaimashita ka.
Sumisu: Nani mo kaimasendeshita.

Nakamura: What did you do yesterday?
Smith: I went to a flea market.
Nakamura: What did you buy?
Smith: I didn't buy anything.

Active Communication

1. Talk to people around you about your plans for the weekend.
2. Tell people around you about what you did the previous weekend.

Tenmasa	Tenmasa (fictitious restaurant name)	**wakarimasu**	understand, see, get it
... de gozaimasu	(polite form of **... desu**)	**o-namae**	your name
yoyaku	reservation	**o-denwa-bangō**	your phone number
wakarimashita	understood, I see, I understand	**furī-māketto**	flea market

Doing Things (2): Do You Often Come Here?

TARGET DIALOGUE

🔊 092

Smith and Suzuki have arrived at a tempura restaurant in Ginza.

Mise no hito:	**Irasshaimase.**
Suzuki:	**Suzuki desu.**
Mise no hito:	**Suzuki-sama desu ne. Dōzo kochira e.**
Sumisu:	**Ii mise desu ne.**
	Suzuki-san wa yoku kono mise ni kimasu ka.
Suzuki:	**Ee, tokidoki kimasu.**
	Senshū wa koko de Gurīn-san ni aimashita.
Sumisu:	**E, hontō desu ka.**

(*Branch president Green comes into the restaurant.*)

Sumisu and Suzuki: A, Gurīn-san!

■ **Sumisu-san to Suzuki-san wa Ginza no tenpura-ya de Gurīn-san ni aimashita.**

Restaurant employee:	Welcome.
Suzuki:	I am Suzuki.
Restaurant employee:	Thank you, Mr. Suzuki. This way, please.
Smith:	It's a nice restaurant. Do you often come here?
Suzuki:	Yes, I come here sometimes. Last week, I met Green-san here.
Smith:	Really?

Smith and Suzuki: Oh, Green-san!

■ Smith-san and Suzuki-san met Green-san at the tempura restaurant in Ginza.

Suzuki-sama	Mr. Suzuki	**koko**	here
-sama	Mr., Mrs., Ms., Miss (more polite than **-san**)	**ni**	(particle; see GRAMMAR 1, 2, p. 85)
Dōzo kochira e.	Please come in.	**aimasu**	meet
ii	nice, good	**Hontō desu ka.**	Really?
ne	(particle; see L6, NOTES 2, p. 51)	**tenpura-ya**	tempura restaurant
yoku	often	**-ya**	(suffix for shop or restaurant)
tokidoki	sometimes		

NOTES

1. **Senshū wa koko de Gurīn-san ni aimashita.**

The particle **wa** in **senshū wa** identifies **senshū** as the topic from among the times Suzuki has come to this restaurant.

KEY SENTENCES

 093

1. **Sumisu-san wa ashita Tanaka-san ni aimasu.**
2. **Sumisu-san wa Suzuki-san ni resutoran no basho o oshiemashita.**
3. **Sumisu-san wa mainichi kōhī o nomimasu.**
4. **Ema-san wa amari terebi o mimasen.**

1. Smith-san will meet Tanaka-san tomorrow.
2. Smith-san told Suzuki-san the location of the restaurant.
3. Smith-san drinks coffee every day.
4. Emma-san does not watch television very often.

GRAMMAR

1. person 1 wa person 2 ni verb.   (KS1)

The particle **ni** can also serve as an object marker, as in the example here, where **Tanaka-san** is the object of the verb **aimasu** ("meet"). Essentially, **ni** indicates the person or thing an action is directed at.

2. person 1 wa person 2/place ni noun o verb.   (KS2)

With verbs like **denwa-bangō o oshiemasu** ("tell someone's telephone number"), **mēru o okurimasu** ("send e-mail"), and **denwa o shimasu** ("telephone"), **ni** indicates the receiver of the action.

3. Habitual action   (KS3)

The present form of verbs also expresses habitual actions when they are used with adverbs of frequency or words used with every time, such as **mainichi** ("every day"), **maishū** ("every week"), and **maiasa** ("every morning").

4. amari/zenzen in a negative sentene   (KS4)

The adverb **amari** occurs in negative sentences, meaning "not often," "not very." **Zenzen** is also used in negative sentences, meaning "not at all."

VOCABULARY

basho	location
oshiemasu	tell, teach
mainichi	every day
amari ... -masen	not often, not very

WORD POWER

ⓘ Verbs

🔊 094

①denwa o shimasu　②okurimasu　③aimasu　④kikimasu　⑤oshiemasu

ⓘⓘ Family

🔊 095

①Tanaka-san no go-kazoku　　⑤kazoku　　　　　　⑨Sasaki-san no go-shujin
②Tanaka-san no otōsan　　　　⑥chichi　　　　　　⑩otto/shujin
③Tanaka-san no okāsan　　　　⑦haha
④Tanaka-san no okusan　　　　⑧tsuma/kanai

denwa o shimasu	telephone	**otōsan**	(another person's) father	**tsuma/kanai**	(my) wife
okurimasu	send	**okāsan**	(another person's) mother	**go-shujin**	(another person's)
kikimasu	ask	**okusan**	(another person's) wife		husband
go-kazoku	(another person's) family	**chichi**	(my) father	**otto/shujin**	(my) husband
go-	(honorific prefix)	**haha**	(my) mother		

III Time expressions

🔊 096

	Day	Morning	Evening	Week
Every	**mainichi**	**maiasa**	**maiban**	**maishū**

IV Adverbs

🔊 097

Frequency

100%	**itsumo**	always
	yoku	often
	tokidoki	sometimes
	amari … -masen	not often
0%	**zenzen … -masen**	not at all

EXERCISES

I *Practice conjugating verbs.* Repeat the verbs below and memorize their forms—present and past, affirmative and negative.

	Present form		Past form	
	aff.	*neg.*	*aff.*	*neg.*
telephone	denwa o shimasu	denwa o shimasen	denwa o shimashita	denwa o shimasendeshita
send	okurimasu	okurimasen	okurimashita	okurimasendeshita
meet	aimasu	aimasen	aimashita	aimasendeshita
ask	kikimasu	kikimasen	kikimashita	kikimasendeshita
tell, teach	oshiemasu	oshiemasen	oshiemashita	oshiemasendeshita

II Make up sentences following the patterns of the examples. Substitute the underlined part with the alternatives given.

A. *State whom someone will telephone.*

e.g. **Sumisu-san wa** <u>**Tanaka-san**</u> **ni denwa o shimasu.**

1. .... (okāsan)

2. .... (Sasaki-san)

3. .... (taishikan)

VOCABULARY

maiasa every morning
maiban every evening
maishū every week
itsumo always

zenzen … -masen not at all

B. *State to whom someone will send an e-mail.*

e.g. **Sumisu-san wa** Tanaka-san **ni mēru o okurimasu.**

1. .... (otōsan)

2. .... (Katō-san)

3. .... (Nozomi Depāto)

III *Ask and answer who will telephone, or e-mail whom.* Make up dialogues following the patterns of the examples and based on the information provided.

e.g. 1. Nakamura-san	**1)** Ōsaka-shisha no Chan-san	**2)** Nozomi Depāto no shachō	**e.g. 2.** ginkō	**3)** Ginza no hoteru	**4)** Nihon-go no gakkō

1. e.g. 1. A: Sumisu-san wa dare ni denwa o shimasu ka.

　　　　B: Nakamura-san **ni shimasu.**

　　１）A: ....

　　　　B: ....

　　２）A: ....

　　　　B: ....

e.g. 2. A: Sumisu-san wa doko ni denwa o shimasu ka.

　　　　B: Ginkō **ni shimasu.**

　　３）A: ....

　　　　B: ....

　　４）A: ....

　　　　B: ....

mēru	e-mail	**Nihon-go**	Japanese	**gakkō**	school
shachō	president (of a company)	**-go**	language		

2. e.g. 1. **A: Sumisu-san wa dare ni mēru o okurimasu ka.**

       B: <u>Nakamura-san</u> ni okurimasu.

  1) A: ....

      B: ....

  2) A: ....

      B: ....

e.g. 2. **A: Sumisu-san wa doko ni mēru o okurimasu ka.**

      B: <u>Ginkō</u> ni okurimasu.

  3) A: ....

      B: ....

  4) A: ....

      B: ....

IV Make up sentences following the patterns of the examples and based on the information provided.

A. *State who asked whom for what.*

  e.g. **Sumisu-san wa Nakamura-san ni <u>denwa-bangō</u> o kikimashita.**

  1. ....

  2. ....

B. *State who told whom what.*

  e.g. **Nakamura-san wa Sumisu-san ni <u>denwa-bangō</u> o oshiemashita.**

  1. ....

  2. ....

V *Describe a schedule.* Make up sentences following the pattern of the example and based on the information in the page from Smith's weekly planner.

	Day	Time	Place	Person
e.g.	Mon.	4:00	Tōkyō Eki	Suzuki-san
1.	Tue.	10:00	Nozomi Depāto	Tanaka-san
2.	Wed.	7:00	Resutoran Rōma	Rondon Ginkō no Buraun-san
3.	Thu.	11:00	Sapporo-shisha	shisha no hito

e.g. **Sumisu-san wa getsu-yōbi no 4-ji ni Tōkyō Eki de Suzuki-san ni aimasu.**

1. ....

2. ....

3. ....

VI *State what someone does regularly.* Make up sentences following the pattern of the example and based on the information provided.

e.g. every day

1. every morning
yōguruto

2. every evening
okusan
bīru

3. every week
okāsan

e.g. **Katō-san wa mainichi sanpo o shimasu.**

1. ....

2. ....

3. ....

VII *Ask and answer about how often something is done.* Make up dialogues following the pattern of the example and based on the information provided.

e.g. often

1. sometimes

2. not often

3. not at all
yasai-jūsu

VOCABULARY

Resutoran Rōma	Restaurant Rome (fictitious restaurant name)
Rōma	Rome
Sapporo-shisha	Sapporo branch
Sapporo	Sapporo (city on the island of Hokkaido)

yōguruto	yogurt
sanpo o shimasu	take a walk
yasai-jūsu	vegetable juice
yasai	vegetable

e.g. **A: Sumisu-san wa yoku <u>hon</u> o <u>yomimasu</u> ka.**

B: Hai, <u>yoku yomimasu</u>.

1. A: ....

B: Hai, ...

2. A: ....

B: Iie, ...

3. A: ....

B: Iie, ...

VIII *State what you want to order and the quantity.* Make up sentences following the pattern of the example and based on the information provided.

e.g. **Sumisu:** <u>Bīru o 2-hon onegaishimasu.</u>

1. Sumisu: ....

2. Sumisu: ....

3. Sumisu: ....

VOCABULARY

gurasu   glass, wine glass

IX *Talk about what you do and how often.* Make up dialogues following the pattern of the example. Substitute the underlined parts with the alternatives given.

e.g. **Suzuki: Kondo no shūmatsu ni nani o shimasu ka.**

Ema: **<u>Shibuya Toshokan</u> ni ikimasu.**

Suzuki: Ema-san wa yoku <u>Shibuya Toshokan</u> ni ikimasu ka.

Ema: **Hai, <u>yoku</u> ikimasu.**

1. Suzuki: ....

Ema: .... (Tenmasa)

Suzuki: .... (Tenmasa)

Ema: .... (tokidoki)

2. Suzuki: ....

Ema: .... (kōen)

Suzuki: .... (kōen)

Ema: .... (maishū)

X Listen to the audio and fill in the blanks based on the information you hear. 🔊 098

Smith and Nakamura are talking together.

1. Sumisu-san wa Nakamura-san ni Nozomi Depāto no denwa-bangō o

....

2. Nakamura-san wa Sumisu-san ni Nozomi Depāto no denwa-bangō o

....

3. Nozomi Depāto no denwa-bangō wa .... desu.

VOCABULARY

kondo   next, next time
Shibuya Toshokan   Shibuya Library (fictitious library name)

SPEAKING PRACTICE

1. Suzuki is in a restaurant with a friend and is about to order. 🔊 099

> **Suzuki:**   Kyō no o-susume wa nan desu ka.
> **Mise no hito:** Kochira desu.
> **Suzuki:**   Ja, sore o futatsu onegaishimasu.
> **Mise no hito:** Hai. O-nomimono wa?
> **Suzuki:**   Nama-bīru o futatsu onegaishimasu.
> **Mise no hito:** Hai.

Suzuki:	What do you recommend today?
Restaurant employee:	Here, how about this?
Suzuki:	Okay. Please let us have that for two.
Restaurant employee:	Fine. Would you like anything to drink?
Suzuki:	Yes, please let us have two draft beers.
Restaurant employee:	Yes, certainly.

2. Having finished their meal, they call the restaurant employee. 🔊 100

> **Suzuki:**   Sumimasen. O-kaikei o onegaishimasu.
> **Mise no hito:** Hai.
> **Suzuki:**   Betsubetsu ni onegaishimasu.
> **Mise no hito:** Hai.

Suzuki:	Excuse me. May we have the bill, please?
Restaurant employee:	Yes, certainly.
Suzuki:	We would like to pay separately.
Restaurant employee:	Yes [, that will be fine].

NOTES

1. **Betsubetsu ni onegaishimasu.**

   Expression used in a restaurant when each person wants to pay separately. **Betsubetsu de onegaishimasu** is also used.

Active Communication

If you're in Japan, go to a restaurant and ask what they recommend on the menu; place an order.

VOCABULARY

o-susume	recommendation		**(o-) kaikei**	bill, check
kochira	(polite word for **kore**)		**betsubetsu ni**	separately
(o-) nomimono	beverage			
nama-bīru	draft beer			

I Complete the dialogues by choosing words from the box below. Do not use the same word more than once. Some are not needed.

nan	nani	dare	itsu	doko	dono	dore

1. Suzuki: Ema-san wa (   ) Nihon ni kimashita ka.

   Ema: Kyonen no 10-gatsu ni kimashita.

   Suzuki: (   ) to kimashita ka.

   Ema: Hitori de kimashita.

2. Suzuki: Shūmatsu ni (   ) o shimashita ka.

   Raja: Tenisu o shimashita.

   Suzuki: (   ) de shimashita ka.

   Raja: Daigaku de shimashita.

3. Sumisu: (   ) basu ga Shibuya ni ikimasu ka.

   Untenshu: 6-ban no basu ga ikimasu.

4. Sumisu: Shūmatsu ni Hakone ni ikimasu.

   Suzuki: (   ) de ikimasu ka.

   Sumisu: Kuruma de ikimasu.

II What do you say in the following situations?

1. In a restaurant, you want to ask what the recommended dish of the day is.

   ....

2. You want to ask Smith-san if he often drinks beer.

   ....

3. You want to ask Emma-san when she will meet Chan-san.

   ....

4. You are now at the company. You ask your colleague, Suzuki-san, what time he came to the company today.

   ....

VISITING A JAPANESE HOME

Many people today live in Western-style houses or condominiums and the number who live in traditional-style dwellings has decreased, but even Western-style homes incorporate various Japanese features to suit local preferences and conditions. Shoes are not worn inside the home, so there is always space at the entrance for removing shoes. Many homes have rooms with tatami floors. The main form of seating in a tatami room is a square cushion called a zabuton. Even today, the Japanese-style room is considered a comforting and relaxing kind of space.

Describing Things: It's Delicious

Emma is visiting the Sasakis' home. She is enjoying their hospitality.

Sasaki: O-cha o dōzo.

Ema: Arigatō gozaimasu.

Sasaki: O-kashi wa ikaga desu ka.

Ema: Hai, itadakimasu. Kireina o-kashi desu ne.
Nihon no o-kashi desu ka.

Sasaki: Ee, sō desu. Kyōto no o-kashi desu.

Ema: Totemo oishii desu.

■ **Ema-san wa Sasaki-san no uchi de kireina Nihon no o-kashi o tabemashita.**

Sasaki: Please, have some tea.
Emma: Thank you.
Sasaki: How about a sweet?
Emma: Yes, please. Isn't this a beautiful sweet! Is it a Japanese sweet?
Sasaki: Yes, it is. It's a sweet from Kyoto.
Emma: Hmm. It's really delicious.

■ Emma-san ate a pretty Japanese sweet at Sasaki-san's house.

VOCABULARY

Ikaga desu ka.	How about...? (see NOTES 2, p. 97)
itadakimasu	(see NOTES 3, p. 97)
kirei (na)	pretty, beautiful, clean
totemo	very
oishii	delicious, tasty

NOTES

1. **O-cha o dōzo.**

   "Thing **o dōzo** ("please help yourself to…")" is used to offer something to someone.

2. **Ikaga desu ka.**

   "Thing **wa ikaga desu ka**" is often used when politely offering things like food or drink. It means "Would you like one?" or "How about some?"

3. **Hai, itadakimasu.**

   This phrase is spoken when taking something that is offered. It implies both acceptance and gratitude.

KEY SENTENCES

 102

1. **Kono hon wa omoshiroi desu.**
2. **Tōkyō no chikatetsu wa benri desu.**
3. **Sumisu-san wa atarashii pasokon o kaimashita.**
4. **Sumisu-san wa kinō yūmeina resutoran ni ikimashita.**

1. This book is interesting.
2. Tokyo subways are convenient.
3. Smith-san bought a new computer.
4. Smith-san went to a famous restaurant yesterday.

GRAMMAR

1. Adjectives (1)

(KS1, 2, 3, 4)

Japanese adjectives can either modify nouns by directly preceding them, or act as predicates. In this they resemble English adjectives. There are two kinds of adjectives: **i**-adjectives (KS1, KS3) and **na**-adjectives (KS2, KS4).

Modifying noun: adjective + noun		
i-adj.	ōkii kōen	big park
na-adj.	kireina hana	pretty flower

Unlike English, Japanese adjectives are conjugated. The present affirmative and negative forms are listed below.

	As predicate: adjective + **desu**	
	aff.	*neg.*
i-adj.	ōkii desu ii desu	ōkikunai desu yokunai desu*
na-adj.	kirei desu	kirei ja arimasen kirei dewa arimasen**

* exceptional inflection
** more formal

VOCABULARY

omoshiroi	interesting
benri (na)	convenient
atarashii	new, fresh
yūmei (na)	famous

WORD POWER

I i-adjectives

🔊 103

①ōkii

②chiisai

③takai

④yasui

⑤atarashii

⑥furui

⑦ii

⑧warui

⑨atsui

⑩samui

⑪atatakai

⑫suzushii

⑬omoshiroi

⑭oishii

II na-adjectives

🔊 104

①nigiyaka (na)

②shizuka (na)

③benri (na)

④yūmei (na)

⑤kirei (na)

VOCABULARY

takai	expensive	**atsui**	hot	**nigiyaka (na)**	lively
yasui	inexpensive	**samui**	cold	**shizuka (na)**	quiet
furui	old	**atatakai**	warm		
warui	bad	**suzushii**	cool

EXERCISES

I *Practice conjugating* **i**-*adjectives.* Repeat the adjectives below and memorize their forms.

	As predicate: present form		Modifying
	aff.	*neg.*	noun
big, large	**ōkii desu**	**ōkikunai desu**	**ōkii**
small	**chiisai desu**	**chiisakunai desu**	**chiisai**
expensive	**takai desu**	**takakunai desu**	**takai**
inexpensive	**yasui desu**	**yasukunai desu**	**yasui**
new, fresh	**atarashii desu**	**atarashikunai desu**	**atarashii**
old	**furui desu**	**furukunai desu**	**furui**
good, nice	**ii desu**	**yokunai desu**	**ii**
bad	**warui desu**	**warukunai desu**	**warui**
hot	**atsui desu**	**atsukunai desu**	**atsui**
cold	**samui desu**	**samukunai desu**	**samui**
warm	**atatakai desu**	**atatakakunai desu**	**atatakai**
cool	**suzushii desu**	**suzushikunai desu**	**suzushii**
interesting	**omoshiroi desu**	**omoshirokunai desu**	**omoshiroi**
delicious	**oishii desu**	**oishikunai desu**	**oishii**

II *State a characteristic of something.* Make up sentences following the pattern of the example. Substitute the underlined parts with the alternatives given.

e.g. **Kono hon wa omoshiroi desu.**

1. .... (kono kamera, yasui desu)

2. ....

(Katō-san no uchi, atarashii desu)

III Make up dialogues following the patterns of the examples. Substitute the underlined parts with the appropriate forms of the alternatives given.

A. *Ask and answer about the characteristics of things.*

> e.g. **A: Sono wain wa takai desu ka.**
>
> **B: Hai, takai desu.**

1. A: .... (kono pasokon, atarashii desu)

   B: .... (atarashii desu)

2. A: .... (sono o-bentō, oishii desu)

   B: .... (oishii desu)

B. *Ask and answer about the weather in a distant place.*

> e.g. **A: Tōkyō wa atsui desu ka.**
>
> **B: Iie, atsukunai desu.**

1. A: .... (Rondon, samui desu)

   B: .... (samui desu)

2. A: .... (Shidonī, suzushii desu)

   B: .... (suzushii desu)

IV *Practice conjugating* **na**-*adjectives.* Repeat the adjectives below and memorize their forms.

	As predicate: present form		Modifying
	aff.	*neg.*	noun
lively	**nigiyaka desu**	**nigiyaka ja arimasen**	**nigiyakana**
quiet	**shizuka desu**	**shizuka ja arimasen**	**shizukana**
convenient	**benri desu**	**benri ja arimasen**	**benrina**
famous	**yūmei desu**	**yūmei ja arimasen**	**yūmeina**
pretty, clean	**kirei desu**	**kirei ja arimasen**	**kireina**

V *Describe something.* Make up sentences following the pattern of the example. Substitute the underlined parts with the alternatives given.

> e.g. **Tōkyō no chikatetsu wa benri desu.**

1. .... (Fujisan, yūmei desu)

2. .... (kono hana, kirei desu)

VOCABULARY

(o-) bentō	box lunch, bento	**Fujisan**	Mt. Fuji
Shidonī	Sydney	**hana**	flower

VI Make up dialogues following the patterns of the examples. Substitute the underlined parts with the appropriate forms of the alternatives given.

A. *Ask and give one's opinion about a place.*

e.g. **A: Toshokan wa shizuka desu ka.**

B: Hai, shizuka desu.

1. A: .... (Roppongi, nigiyaka desu)

   B: .... (nigiyaka desu)

2. A: .... (Okinawa no umi, kirei desu)

   B: .... (kirei desu)

B. *Ask and give one's opinion about something.*

e.g. **A: Kono e wa yūmei desu ka.**

B: Iie, yūmei ja arimasen.

1. A: .... (sono apuri, benri desu)

   B: .... (benri desu)

2. A: .... (ano resutoran, shizuka desu)

   B: .... (shizuka desu)

VII *Describe something someone has purchased.* Make up sentences following the pattern of the example and based on the information provided.

e.g.	1. kēki	2. sētā	3.
old	small	expensive	delicious

e.g. **Sumisu-san wa furui tokei o kaimashita.**

1. ....

2. ....

3. ....

Roppongi	Roppongi (district in Tokyo)	**apuri**	application
Okinawa	Okinawa (islands in southern Japan)	**kēki**	cake
umi	ocean	**sētā**	sweater
e	painting, picture		

VIII *Describe the place where someone went.* Make up sentences following the pattern of the example and based on the information provided.

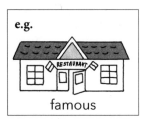

e.g.

famous

1.

quiet

2.

lively

e.g. **Sumisu-san wa kinō yūmeina resutoran ni ikimashita.**

1. ....

2. ....

IX *Talk about one's opinion of a place.* Make up dialogues following the pattern of the example. Substitute the underlined parts with the alternatives given.

e.g. **A: Shūmatsu ni Nikkō ni ikimasu.**

B: Nikkō wa donna tokoro desu ka.

A: Kireina tokoro desu yo.

1. A: .... (Asakusa)

   B: .... (Asakusa)

   A: .... (nigiyakana)

2. A: .... (Odaiba)

   B: .... (Odaiba)

   A: .... (omoshiroi)

VOCABULARY

Nikkō	Nikko (scenic area north of Tokyo)	**Odaiba**	Odaiba (district in Tokyo)
donna	what kind of		
tokoro	place		
Asakusa	Asakusa (district in Tokyo)		

X *State something in a place you are visiting.* Smith visits the home of a friend. Praise something in the friend's house as if you are Smith.

e.g. big

1. interesting   **2.** very old   **3.** pretty

e.g. **Sumisu: Ōkii uchi desu ne.**

1. Sumisu: ....

2. Sumisu: ....

3. Sumisu: ....

XI *Talk about the weather.* Make up dialogues following the pattern of the example. Substitute the underlined parts with the alternatives given.

e.g. **A: Kyō wa <u>samui</u> desu ne.**

B: Ee, hontō ni <u>samui</u> desu ne.

1. A: .... (atatakai)

    B: .... (atatakai)

2. A: .... (ii tenki)

    B: .... (ii tenki)

XII Listen to the audio and fill in the blank based on the information you hear. 105

    1. Hakone wa .... tokoro desu.

VOCABULARY

hontō ni	really
tenki	weather

SPEAKING PRACTICE

1. Emma visits the Sasakis' home. She rings the doorbell. 🔊 106

> **Sasaki: Hai, donata desu ka.**
> **Ema: Ema desu.**
> **Sasaki: A, chotto matte kudasai.**
> _(Opens the door.)_ **Dōzo.**
> **Ema: Ojamashimasu.**

Sasaki: Yes. Who is it?
Emma: It's Emma.
Sasaki: Ah, just a minute. Please come in!
Emma: Thank you.

2. Smith is looking at rice bowls in an antique shop. 🔊 107

> **Sumisu: Kore wa ikura desu ka.**
> **Mise no hito: 8,000-en desu.**
> **Sumisu: Chotto takai desu ne.**
> **Mise no hito: Kochira wa 6,500-en desu.**
> **Sumisu: Ja, sore o kudasai.**

Smith: How much is this?
Shopkeeper: It's 8,000 yen.
Smith: It's a bit expensive.
Shopkeeper: This one is 6,500 yen.
Smith: Okay. I'll take that one.

NOTES

1. **Ojamashimasu.**
   Customary expression used when entering private space as a guest.

Active Communication) Tell people around you about where you come from and tell them what kind of place it is.

VOCABULARY

donata	who (polite word for **dare**)
chotto	a little bit
matte kudasai	please wait
machimasu	wait

Ojamashimasu.	May I come in? (see NOTES 1, above)

Describing Impressions: It Was Beautiful

TARGET DIALOGUE
🔊 108

At the Sasakis' house, Emma is talking with the Sasakis.

Ema: Senshū Fujisan ni noborimashita.
Sasaki: Dō deshita ka.
Ema: Totemo kirei deshita.
Sasaki: Shashin o torimashita ka.
Ema: Ee, kore desu.

(*Shows photos on her smart phone.*)

Sasaki: Hontō ni kirei desu ne. Donokurai arukimashita ka.
Ema: 8-jikan gurai arukimashita.
Taihen deshita ga, tanoshikatta desu.

■ **Ema-san wa Sasaki-san to Sasaki-san no go-shujin ni shashin o misemashita.**

Emma: Last week, I climbed Mt. Fuji.
Sasaki: How was it?
Emma: It was really beautiful.
Sasaki: Did you take photos?
Emma: Yes. Here they are.
Sasaki: It really is beautiful.
How long did you walk?
Emma: I walked for about eight hours.
It was hard, but it was also enjoyable.

■ Emma-san showed her photos to the Sasakis.

VOCABULARY

noborimasu	climb	**arukimasu**	walk	**ga**	but (particle; see GRAMMAR 2, p. 106)
Dō deshita ka.	How was it?	**8-jikan**	8 hours		
dō	how (in question)	**-jikan**	(number of) hours	**tanoshikatta desu**	it was fun, it was enjoyable
kirei deshita	it was beautiful	**... gurai**	about (amount) (see NOTES 1, p. 106)		
shashin	photo			**tanoshii**	fun, pleasant, enjoyable
torimasu	take (a photo)	**taihen deshita**	it was hard		
donokurai	how long	**taihen (na)**	hard, tough	**misemasu**	show

NOTES

1. **Donokurai arukimashita ka.**
   8-jikan gurai arukimashita.

   Here, **donokurai** means "how long." **Kurai** may also be pronounced **gurai**. The **gurai** in Emma's response, **8-jikan gurai**, is used with certain periods of time, with prices, and with amounts and means "about" or "approximately." **Gurai** may also be pronounced **kurai**.

   e.g. **5-fun gurai**   about 5 minutes
   1,000-en gurai   about 1,000 yen
   500-nin gurai   about 500 people

KEY SENTENCES

🔊 109

1. **Kinō wa samukatta desu.**
2. **Kinō no o-matsuri wa nigiyaka deshita.**
3. **Sumisu-san wa depāto ni ikimashita ga, nani mo kaimasendeshita.**

1. Yesterday, it was cold.
2. Yesterday's festival was lively.
3. Smith-san went to the department store, but he did not buy anything.

GRAMMAR

1. Adjectives (2)   (KS1, 2)

Japanese adjectives are conjugated not only for affirmative and negative but according to tense.

	As predicate: adjective + desu			
	Present form		Past form	
	aff.	*neg.*	*aff.*	*neg.*
i-adj.	ōkii desu ii desu	ōkikunai desu yokunai desu*	ōkikatta desu yokatta desu*	ōkikunakatta desu yokunakatta desu*
na-adj.	kirei desu	kirei ja arimasen	kirei deshita	kirei ja arimasendeshita

* exceptional inflection

2. clause 1 ga, clause 2.   (KS3)

This **ga** is a conjunction that joins two clauses. It can be translated as "but."

VOCABULARY

samukatta desu   it was cold
nigiyaka deshita   it was lively

WORD POWER

Ⅰ i-adjectives

🔊 110

①tanoshii

②tsumaranai

③muzukashii

④isogashii

Ⅱ na-adjectives

🔊 111

①kantan (na)

②taihen (na)

③hima (na)

Ⅲ Verbs

🔊 112

①noborimasu

②arukimasu

③(shashin o) torimasu

④misemasu

Ⅳ Events

🔊 113

①(o-) matsuri

②konsāto

③kurasu

VOCABULARY			
tsumaranai	boring, uninteresting	**hima (na)**	free, not busy
muzukashii	difficult	**kurasu**	class
isogashii	busy		
kantan (na)	easy, simple		

EXERCISES

I Repeat the adjectives below and memorize their forms—present and past, affirmative and negative.

A. *Practice conjugating* **i**-*adjectives.*

	Present form		Past form	
	aff.	*neg.*	*aff.*	*neg.*
good, nice	ii desu	yokunai desu	yokatta desu	yokunakatta desu
hot	atsui desu	atsukunai desu	atsukatta desu	atsukunakatta desu
cold	samui desu	samukunai desu	samukatta desu	samukunakatta desu
interesting	omoshiroi desu	omoshirokunai desu	omoshirokatta desu	omoshirokunakatta desu
delicious	oishii desu	oishikunai desu	oishikatta desu	oishikunakatta desu
fun, enjoyable	tanoshii desu	tanoshikunai desu	tanoshikatta desu	tanoshikunakatta desu
boring	tsumaranai desu	tsumaranakunai desu	tsumaranakatta desu	tsumaranakunakatta desu
difficult	muzukashii desu	muzukashikunai desu	muzukashikatta desu	muzukashikunakatta desu
busy	isogashii desu	isogashikunai desu	isogashikatta desu	isogashikunakatta desu

B. *Practice conjugating* **na**-*adjectives.*

	Present form		Past form	
	aff.	*neg.*	*aff.*	*neg.*
pretty, clean, beautiful	kirei desu	kirei ja arimasen	kirei deshita	kirei ja arimasendeshita
lively	nigiyaka desu	nigiyaka ja arimasen	nigiyaka deshita	nigiyaka ja arimasendeshita
easy, simple	kantan desu	kantan ja arimasen	kantan deshita	kantan ja arimasendeshita
hard, tough	taihen desu	taihen ja arimasen	taihen deshita	taihen ja arimasendeshita
free, not busy	hima desu	hima ja arimasen	hima deshita	hima ja arimasendeshita

II Make up sentences following the patterns of the examples. Substitute the underlined parts with the alternatives given, using the same grammatical forms as in the examples.

A. *Comment about the weather yesterday.*

e.g. **Kinō wa samukatta desu.**

1. .... (atsui desu)

2. .... (atatakai desu)

B. *Comment about something you did.*

e.g. **Kinō no dēto wa tanoshikunakatta desu.**

1. .... (omoshiroi desu)

2. .... (ii desu)

| **dēto** date

C. *Comment about something you saw.*

e.g. **Kinō no o-matsuri wa <u>kirei deshita</u>.**

1. .... (nigiyaka desu)

D. *Comment about something you saw.*

e.g. **Kinō no o-matsuri wa <u>nigiyaka ja arimasendeshita</u>.**

1. .... (kirei desu)

Ⅲ Make up dialogues following the patterns of the examples. Substitute the underlined parts with the appropriate forms of the alternatives given.

A. *Ask and answer about something you experienced.*

e.g. **Nakamura:** **Eiga wa <u>omoshirokatta desu</u> ka.**

Ema: **Hai, <u>omoshirokatta desu</u>.**

Sumisu: **Iie, <u>omoshirokunakatta desu</u>.**

1. Nakamura: .... (sēru, yasui desu)

Ema: .... (yasui desu)

Sumisu: .... (yasui desu)

2. Nakamura: ....
(Nihon-go no kurasu, muzukashii desu)

Ema: .... (muzukashii desu)

Sumisu: .... (muzukashii desu)

VOCABULARY

sēru   sale

B. *Ask and answer about something you experienced.*

e.g. **Katō:**   <u>Pātī</u> wa dō deshita ka.

Ema: Totemo <u>tanoshikatta desu.</u>

Sumisu: Amari <u>tanoshikunakatta desu.</u>

1. Katō: .... (konsāto)

   Ema: .... (ii desu)

   Sumisu: .... (ii desu)

2. Nakamura: .... (tesuto)

   Ema: .... (kantan desu)

   Sumisu: .... (kantan desu)

IV *Contrast two things.* Make up sentences following the pattern of the example. Substitute the underlined parts with the appropriate forms of the alternatives given.

e.g. **Kinō wa <u>isogashikatta desu</u> ga, kyō wa <u>hima desu.</u>**

1. .... (hima desu, isogashii desu)

2. .... (atsui desu, suzushii desu)

3. .... (atatakai desu, samui desu)

V *Talk about something you did.* Make up dialogues following the pattern of the example. Substitute the underlined parts with the appropriate forms of the alternatives given.

e.g. **Nakamura:** Sumisu-san, shūmatsu ni nani o shimashita ka.

   Sumisu: <u>Hokkaidō</u> de <u>sukī o shimashita.</u>

   Nakamura: Dō deshita ka.

   Sumisu: Totemo <u>tanoshikatta desu.</u>

tesuto	test
sukī o shimasu	ski

1. Nakamura: ....

Sumisu: ....

(Asakusa, tenpura o tabemasu)

Nakamura: ....

Sumisu: ....

(oishii desu)

2. Nakamura: ....

Sumisu: ....

(Ginza, kabuki o mimasu)

Nakamura: ....

Sumisu: ....

(kirei desu)

VI Listen to the audio and fill in the blanks based on the information you hear. 114-116

1. O-matsuri wa totemo ....

2. Hokkaidō wa totemo ....

3. Sutēki wa amari ....

SPEAKING PRACTICE

1. Emma is visiting the Sasakis' home. 🔊 117

Ema: Sorosoro shitsureishimasu. Kyō wa dōmo arigatō gozaimashita.
Sasaki: Dō itashimashite.
Ema: Totemo tanoshikatta desu.
Sasaki: Watashi-tachi mo tanoshikatta desu. Mata kite kudasai.

Emma: I need to be going in a little while. Thank you very much [for today].
Sasaki: You're welcome.
Emma: I had a very nice time.
Sasaki: And we enjoyed having you. Please come again.

VOCABULARY

Sorosoro shitsureishimasu.	I need to be going in a little while.
sorosoro	in a little while
Dōmo arigatō gozaimashita.	(see NOTES 2, p. 112)
Dō itashimashite.	You're welcome.

watashi-tachi	we
Mata kite kudasai.	Please come again.
mata	again
kite kudasai	please come

2. On Monday morning, Smith and Nakamura are talking at the office. 🔊 118

> **Sumisu:** **Shūmatsu ni Hakone ni ikimashita. Kore, Hakone no o-miyage desu. Dōzo.**
>
> **Nakamura:** **Arigatō gozaimasu. Hakone wa dō deshita ka.**
>
> **Sumisu:** **Totemo yokatta desu.**

Smith: Over the weekend, I went to Hakone. This is a souvenir of Hakone. I hope you like it.

Nakamura: Thank you. How was Hakone?

Smith: It was very nice.

3. Nakamura received a souvenir from Smith the day before. 🔊 119

> **Nakamura:** **Sumisu-san, kinō wa o-miyage o arigatō gozaimashita. Totemo oishikatta desu.**
>
> **Sumisu:** **Sō desu ka. Yokatta desu.**

Nakamura: Thank you for the souvenir yesterday, Smith-san. It was really delicious.

Smith: Good. I'm glad to hear that.

NOTES

1. **Sorosoro shitsureishimasu.**

   Set phrase used when the time has come to leave a place you are visiting.

2. **Dōmo arigatō gozaimashita.**

   When expressing thanks for something that has ended, the past tense of **arigatō gozaimasu** is used.

3. **Kore, Hakone no o-miyage desu.**

   Kore wa Hakone no o-miyage desu is used when explaining what **kore** is in a situation where the listener's attention is already focused on **kore**. In contrast, the **kore** in **Kore, Hakone no o-miyage desu** is used to focus the listener's attention on something before explaining what it is.

4. **Yokatta desu.** (SPEAKING PRACTICE 3)

   This is used in the sense of "I'm glad to hear that," when hearing a positive response from someone to whom you have given a present or offered advice.

Active Communication

Ask people around you to give their impressions of places they have been, movies they have seen, and other experiences.

VOCABULARY

(o-) miyage	souvenir
Yokatta desu.	I'm glad to hear that. (see NOTES 4, above)

WEEKEND TRIPS

Tokyo is surrounded by a number of places to visit for pleasure within about two hours of the city. To the north is the historical site of Nikko; to the southwest are resort areas surrounding five large lakes in the foothills of Mt. Fuji; and to the south is Kamakura, the historic town that dates back to the twelfth century. The western part of the greater metropolitan area is the mountainous Okutama region known for its scenic rivers and gorges. Also close by is Yokohama, which preserves its heritage as a port first opened for world trade in the mid-nineteenth century, and Hakone, an easily accessible mountain vacation resort known for natural beauty, comfortable inns, and numerous hot-spring spas, called onsen.

Asking about Places: What Is at Nikko?

TARGET DIALOGUE

🔊 120

Nakamura and Raja are talking during their break.

Nakamura: **Do-yōbi ni Ema-san to Nikkō ni ikimasu.**

Raja: **Sō desu ka. Nikkō ni nani ga arimasu ka.**

Nakamura: **Ōkii o-tera ya jinja ga arimasu.**
Onsen mo arimasu.

Raja: **Onsen tte nan desu ka.**

Nakamura: (*Shows him a smartphone and points.*)
Kore desu. Nihon no supa desu yo.

Raja: **Ii desu ne.**

The Toshogu Shrine (Nikko)

■ **Nakamura-san wa do-yōbi ni Ema-san to Nikkō ni ikimasu.**
Nikkō ni ōkii o-tera ya jinja ga arimasu.

Nakamura: On Saturday, I'm going to Nikko with Emma-san.
Raja: Are you? What is there [to see] at Nikko?
Nakamura: There are large temples, shrines, and other sights. There are also onsen.
Raja: What is an "onsen"?
Nakamura: This is an onsen. It's a Japanese spa.
Raja: Oh, that's great.

■ Nakamura-san will go to Nikko with Emma-san on Saturday.
There are large temples, shrines, and other sights at Nikko.

VOCABULARY

ni	in, on, at (particle; see GRAMMAR 1, p. 115)	**jinja**	Shinto shrine
ga	(particle; see GRAMMAR 1, p. 115)	**onsen**	hot spring
arimasu	be, exist (see GRAMMAR 1, p. 115)	**... tte nan desu ka.**	What is a/an...?
(o-) tera	temple	**supa**	spa
ya	and, and so on (particle; see GRAMMAR 3, p. 115)	**yo**	(particle; see NOTES 2, p. 115)

NOTES

1. **Onsen tte nan desu ka.**

    ... tte nan desu ka is the way part of something one has heard may be repeated in order to ask what it means.

2. **Nihon no supa desu yo.**

    The particle **yo** is added to the end of a sentence to call attention to information the speaker thinks the other person does not know.

KEY SENTENCES

 121

1. **1-kai ni uketsuke ga arimasu.**

2. **Uketsuke ni onna no hito ga imasu.**

3. **Tēburu no ue ni hana ga arimasu.**

4. **Nikkō ni o-tera ya jinja ga arimasu.**

1. There is an information desk on the first floor.
2. There is a woman at the information desk.
3. There are flowers on the table.
4. At Nikko, there are temples, shrines, and other sights.

GRAMMAR

1. place **ni** noun **ga arimasu/imasu.**   (KS1, 2, 3, 4)

Both verbs **arimasu** and **imasu** express "being." **arimasu** is used for inanimate things (books, buildings, trees, etc.), and **imasu** for animate things (people, animals, insects, etc.). Existence in or at a place is indicated by the particle **ni**. When a subject is introduced for the first time, or when the speaker believes the information to be new to the listener, the subject marker **ga** is used after the noun. **ga** should be used, for instance, when stating that someone or something unknown to your listener is in or at a particular place.

2. Position words   (KS3)

When using words indicating position such as **ue** ("on," "above") and **shita** ("under"), use the following order: noun 1 (thing/person/place) **no** noun 2 (position).

3. noun 1 **ya** noun 2   (KS4)

The particle **ya** is used for "and" when listing two or more things or people and implying the existence of others. Another particle, **to**, also means "and" but it does not imply the existence of other people or things.

e.g. **1-kai ni ginkō to konbini ga arimasu.**

  There is a bank and a convenience store on the first floor (and nothing else).

Note that unlike "and" in English, both **ya** and **to** are used only to connect nouns. They cannot be used to connect verbs or clauses (see L4, GRAMMAR 4, p. 30).

VOCABULARY

onna no hito	woman		**ue**	on, above
onna	female, woman			
imasu	be, exist (see GRAMMAR 1, above)			
tēburu	table			

WORD POWER

Ⅰ Parts of a building
 122

①uketsuke ②yūbinkyoku ③kaigi-shitsu ④chūsha-jō

Ⅱ Things in a hotel room
 123

①heya ③denki-potto ⑤tsukue ⑦gomi-bako ⑨sofā
②reizōko ④beddo ⑥isu ⑧tēburu ⑩hana

VOCABULARY

yūbinkyoku	post office	**denki-potto**	electric kettle	**gomi-bako**	trash basket
kaigi-shitsu	meeting room	**beddo**	bed	**sofā**	sofa
chūsha-jō	parking lot	**tsukue**	desk		
heya	room	**isu**	chair		

Ⅲ Features of a tourist site

① (o-) tera

②jinja

③onsen

④taki

⑤mizuumi

Ⅳ Positions

①ue

②shita

③naka

④mae

⑤ushiro

⑥tonari

⑦chikaku

EXERCISES

Ⅰ *Practice conjugating verbs.* Repeat the verbs below and memorize their forms—present and past, affirmative and negative.

	Present form		Past form	
	aff.	*neg.*	*aff.*	*neg.*
be	arimasu	arimasen	arimashita	arimasendeshita
be	imasu	imasen	imashita	imasendeshita

VOCABULARY

taki	waterfall	**mae**	in front
mizuumi	lake	**ushiro**	behind
shita	under	**tonari**	next to
naka	inside	**chikaku**	vicinity, near

II Make up sentences following the patterns of the examples. Substitute the underlined part with the alternatives given.

A. *State what is at a particular place.*

e.g. **Nikkō ni o-tera ga arimasu.**

1. .... (jinja)

2. .... (mizuumi)

B. *State who is at a particular place.*

e.g. **Uketsuke ni onna no hito ga imasu.**

1. .... (otoko no hito)

2. .... (Tanaka-san)

III Make up dialogues following the patterns of the examples. Substitute the underlined parts with the alternatives given.

A. *Ask and answer what is at a particular place.*

e.g. **A: 1-kai ni nani ga arimasu ka.**

B: Ginkō ga arimasu.

1. A: .... (2-kai)

   B: .... (yūbinkyoku)

2. A: .... (4-kai)

   B: .... (kaigi-shitsu)

B. *Ask and answer who is at a particular place.*

e.g. **A: Uketsuke ni dare ga imasu ka.**

B: Tanaka-san ga imasu.

1. A: .... (chūsha-jō)

   B: .... (onna no hito)

2. A: .... (3-gai)

   B: .... (Sumisu-san)

VOCABULARY

otoko no hito	man
otoko	male, man

IV *State what is at a certain place.* Make up sentences following the pattern of the example. Substitute the underlined parts with the alternatives given.

e.g. **Tēburu no ue ni hana ga arimasu.**

1. .... (tsukue no shita, gomi-bako)

2. .... (reizōko no naka, mizu)

V *Ask and answer what is at a certain place.* Make up dialogues following the pattern of the example. Substitute the underlined parts with the alternatives given.

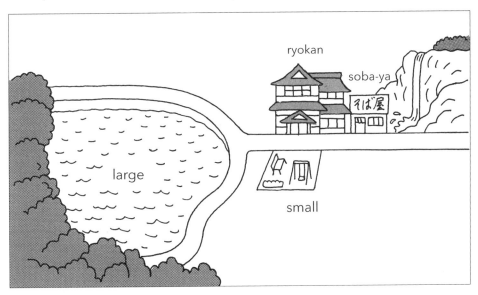

e.g. **A: Ryokan no chikaku ni nani ga arimasu ka.**

   B: Ōkii mizuumi ya taki ga arimasu.

1. A: .... (tonari)

   B: .... (soba-ya)

2. A: .... (mae)

   B: .... (chiisai kōen)

VOCABULARY

ryokan	Japanese inn
soba-ya	soba shop
soba	soba (buckwheat noodle)

VI Make up dialogues following the patterns of the examples. Substitute the underlined part with the alternatives given.

A. *Ask and answer what is at a certain place.*

e.g. **A: Hikidashi no naka ni nani ga arimasu ka.**

B: Nani mo arimasen.

1. A: .... (tsukue no ue)

   B: ....

2. A: .... (tēburu no shita)

   B: ....

3. A: .... (poketto no naka)

   B: ....

B. *Ask and answer who is at a certain place.*

e.g. **A: Tonari no heya ni dare ga imasu ka.**

B: Dare mo imasen.

1. A: .... (4-kai)

   B: ....

2. A: .... (kaigi-shitsu)

   B: ....

3. A: .... (konbini no mae)

   B: ....

VOCABULARY

hikidashi	drawer
poketto	pocket
daremo ... -masen	no one

VII *Talk about where you are going and what is there.* Make up dialogues following the pattern of the example. Substitute the underlined parts with the alternatives given.

e.g. **Katō:** **Nichi-yōbi ni kuruma de <u>Hakone</u> ni ikimasu.**

Sumisu: **Sō desu ka. <u>Hakone</u> ni nani ga arimasu ka.**

Katō: **<u>Mizuumi ya onsen</u> ga arimasu.**

Sumisu: **Ii desu ne.**

1. Katō: .... (Kamakura)

Sumisu: .... (Kamakura)

Katō: .... (jinja ya o-tera)

Sumisu: ....

2. Katō: .... (Odaiba)

Sumisu: .... (Odaiba)

Katō: .... (tēma-pāku ya onsen)

Sumisu: ....

VIII Listen to the audio and fill in the blanks based on the information you hear. 🔊 126-128

1. 1-kai ni .... ga arimasu.

2. 2-kai ni .... ga arimasu.

3. 3-gai ni .... ga arimasu.

VOCABULARY

Kamakura Kamakura (historic area south of Tokyo)
tēma-pāku theme park

SPEAKING PRACTICE

1. Nakamura and Raja are talking during their break.   🔊 129

   Nakamura: Raja-san no uchi wa Indo no doko desu ka.
   Raja: Goa desu.
   Nakamura: Donna tokoro desu ka.
   Raja: Shizukana tokoro desu.
   **   Furui kyōkai ya kireina bīchi ga arimasu.**
   Nakamura: Nani ga yūmei desu ka.
   Raja: Kashū-nattsu ga yūmei desu.

   Nakamura: Where is your home in India, Raja-san?
   Raja: I come from Goa.
   Nakamura: What kind of place is Goa?
   Raja: It's a quiet place. There are old churches, pretty beaches, and other sights.
   Nakamura: What is it famous for?
   Raja: It's famous for cashew nuts.

   NOTES

1. **Indo no doko desu ka.**
   No doko desu ka is used when asking for a more specific place within a larger area.

Active Communication   Ask people around you what is in their hometowns or nearby their houses.

VOCABULARY

Goa	Goa (state in India)
kyōkai	church
bīchi	beach
kashū-nattsu	cashew nuts

Asking for a Place: Where Is It?

TARGET DIALOGUE

🔊 130

Nakamura and Emma are in a souvenir shop in Nikko.

Nakamura:	Sumimasen. Kono chikaku ni oishii o-sobaya-san ga arimasu ka.
Mise no hito:	Ee. Sobaichi ga oishii desu yo.
Ema:	Doko ni arimasu ka.
Mise no hito:	Asoko ni o-tera ga arimasu ne. Sobaichi wa ano o-tera no mae desu.
Ema:	Sō desu ka. Sorekara, kono taki wa koko kara chikai desu ka.
	(*Shows a photo.*)
Mise no hito:	Iie, chotto tōi desu. Basu de 15-fun gurai desu.
Ema:	Sō desu ka. Dōmo arigatō gozaimasu.

■ **Sobaichi wa o-tera no mae ni arimasu.**

Nakamura:	Excuse me. Is there a good soba shop nearby?
Salesperson:	Yes, there is. The Sobaichi shop is good.
Emma:	Where is it?
Salesperson:	There is a temple over there, right? Sobaichi is in front of that temple.
Emma:	I see. Also, is this waterfall [in this photo] somewhere near here?
Salesperson:	No, it is a little far from here. About 15 minutes by bus.
Emma:	I see. Thank you very much.

■ Sobaichi is in front of the temple.

VOCABULARY

kono chikaku	vicinity, near here		**sorekara**	also
o-sobaya-san	soba shop (see NOTES 1, p. 124)		**chikai**	near, close
Sobaichi	Sobaichi (fictitious soba shop)		**tōi**	far
asoko	over there			

NOTES

1. **o-sobaya-san**

   Adding the suffix **-san** after the **-ya** denoting "shop" softens the tone.

2. **Sobaichi ga oishii desu yo.**

   When the particle **ga** is used, as in **... ga oishii desu**, the part preceding **ga** is information new to the listener. When the particle **wa** is used as in **... wa oishii desu**, the following part (**oishii desu**) is information new to the listener.

KEY SENTENCES

 131

1. Kaigi-shitsu ni isu ga muttsu arimasu.
2. Kaigi-shitsu ni o-kyaku-san ga 4-nin imasu.
3. Takushī-noriba wa eki no mae ni arimasu.
4. Sumisu-san wa 2-kai ni imasu.
5. Sumisu-san no uchi wa eki kara chikai desu.

1. There are six chairs in the meeting room.
2. There are four guests in the meeting room.
3. The taxi stand is in front of the station.
4. Smith-san is on the second floor.
5. Smith-san's house is near the station.

GRAMMAR

1. place ni noun ga number arimasu/imasu.   (KS1, 2)

When wanting to say how many of a noun are in a certain place, the word order is "place **ni** thing/person **ga** number **arimasu/imasu**." Also, there is no particle following the number (see L5, GRAMMAR 5, p. 39).

2. noun wa place ni arimasu/imasu.   (KS3, 4)

When stating that what or who is in a certain place, use **... ga arimasu/imasu**, as in **1-kai ni resutoran ga arimasu**. However, when stating where a certain thing or person is located, the thing or person becomes the topic of the sentence, and the particle **ga** changes to **wa**, as in **Resutoran wa 1-kai ni arimasu**.

①1-kai ni resutoran ga arimasu.   There is a restaurant on the first floor.
②Resutoran wa 1-kai ni arimasu.   The restaurant is on the first floor.

When the existence of a certain thing and its location is clear, as in ②, "place **ni arimasu**" at the end of the sentence can also be replaced with "place **desu**." (see L5, GRAMMAR 1, p. 39)

②'Resutoran wa 1-kai desu.

For ①, however, **ga arimasu** cannot be replaced with **desu**.

3. place 1 wa place 2 kara chikai/tōi desu.   (KS5)

This expression is used to describe subjectively the distance of one point and a different point.

VOCABULARY

o-kyaku-san	guest, customer
takushī-noriba	taxi stand

WORD POWER

I Things near a train station

①takushī-noriba   ③kōban   ⑤hon-ya   ⑦rāmen-ya

②basu-noriba   ④byōin   ⑥pan-ya

II Office supplies

①keshigomu   ③hasami   ⑤hikidashi

②enpitsu   ④kuria-fairu   ⑥kyabinetto

VOCABULARY

basu-noriba	bus terminal	**pan-ya**	bakery	**enpitsu**	pencil
kōban	police box	**pan**	bread	**hasami**	scissors
byōin	hospital, clinic	**rāmen-ya**	ramen shop	**kuria-fairu**	clear file
hon-ya	bookstore	**keshigomu**	eraser	**kyabinetto**	cabinet

III Demonstrative pronouns 134   IV i-adjectives 135

①koko   ②soko   ③asoko

①chikai

②tōi

EXERCISES

I Make up sentences following the patterns of the examples. Substitute the underlined parts with the alternatives given.

A. *State how many of a certain object are in a certain place.*

e.g. **Hikidashi no naka ni <u>pen</u> ga <u>5-hon</u> arimasu.**

1. .... (meishi, 6-mai)

2. .... (kurippu, mittsu)

3. .... (fairu, takusan)

B. *State how many people are in a certain place.*

e.g. **Kōen ni <u>onna no hito</u> ga <u>futari</u> imasu.**

1. .... (otoko no hito, 3-nin)

2. .... (onna no ko, hitori)

3. .... (otoko no ko, takusan)

II Make up dialogues following the patterns of the examples. Substitute the underlined parts with the alternatives given.

A. *Ask and answer how many of a certain object are on a certain place.*

e.g. **A: Tēburu no ue ni <u>ringo</u> ga ikutsu arimasu ka.**

   B: <u>Futatsu</u> arimasu.

1. A: .... (koppu, ikutsu)

   B: .... (yottsu)

VOCABULARY

soko	there	onna no ko	girl	ikutsu	how many
kurippu	paper clip	ko	child		
takusan	many, much	otoko no ko	boy		

2. A: .... (fōku, nan-bon)

   B: .... (10-pon)

3. A: .... (o-sara, nan-mai)

   B: .... (5-mai)

B. *Ask and answer how many people are in a certain place.*

e.g. **A: Resutoran ni** <u>otoko no hito</u> **ga nan-nin imasu ka.**

   B: <u>Hitori</u> **imasu.**

1. A: .... (onna no hito)

   B: .... (futari)

2. A: .... (onna no ko)

   B: .... (4-nin)

3. A: .... (otoko no ko)

   B: .... (takusan)

III *State where a facility or store is located.* Look at the illustrations and make up sentences following the pattern of the example. Substitute the underlined parts with the alternatives given.

e.g. **Chūsha-jō wa** <u>conbini no tonari</u> **ni arimasu.**

1. ....

   (takushī-noriba, eki no mae)

2. ....

   (hana-ya, byōin no tonari)

3. .... (kōban, asoko)

VOCABULARY	
fōku	fork
nan-bon	how many (long, thin objects)
nan-mai	how many (flat objects)
hana-ya	florist

127

Ⓘⓥ Make up dialogues following the patterns of the examples. Substitute the underlined parts with the alternatives given.

A. *Ask and answer where something is.*

e.g. **A: Chūsha-jō wa doko ni arimasu ka.**

B: Conbini no tonari ni arimasu.

1. A: .... (basu-noriba)

   B: .... (eki no mae)

2. A: .... (hon-ya)

   B: ....
   (rāmen-ya no tonari)

3. A: ....
   (Rondon Ginkō no fairu)

   B: .... (koko)

4. A: ....
   (kyabinetto no kagi)

   B: ....
   (ano hikidashi no naka)

B. *Ask and answer where someone is.*

e.g. **A: Sumisu-san wa doko ni imasu ka.**

B: 2-kai ni imasu.

1. A: .... (Tanaka-san)

   B: .... (shachō-shitsu)

2. A: .... (Gurīn-san)

   B: .... (3-gai)

3. A: .... (Sasaki-san)

   B: .... (kaigi-shitsu)

| **shachō-shitsu** | president's office |

Ⓥ *State whether the place you are now is near/distant from a certain place.* Make up sentences following the pattern of the example. Substitute the underlined parts with the alternatives given.

> e.g. **Toshokan wa eki kara chikai desu.**

1. .... (pan-ya, uchi, chikai)

2. .... (hoteru, kūkō, tōi)

3. ....
(Katō-san no uchi, kaisha, tōi)

ⅤⅠ *Talk about how close a certain place is to where you are now.* Make up dialogues following the pattern of the example. Substitute the underlined parts with the alternatives given.

> e.g. **Nakamura:**   **Taki wa koko kara chikai desu ka.**
>
> **Hoteru no hito:**   **Iie, chotto tōi desu.**
>
>   **Basu de 15-fun gurai desu.**
>
> **Nakamura:**   **Sō desu ka. Dōmo arigatō gozaimasu.**

1. Nakamura: .... (Kumano Jinja)

   Hoteru no hito: ....

   .... (iie, chotto tōi)

   .... (basu de 20-pun gurai)

   Nakamura: ....

2. Nakamura: .... (bōto-noriba)

   Hoteru no hito: .... (hai, chikai)

   .... (aruite 5-fun gurai)

   Nakamura: ....

3. Nakamura: .... (basutei)

   Hoteru no hito: .... (hai, chikai)

   .... (sugu soko)

   Nakamura: ....

VOCABULARY	
Kumano Jinja	Kumano Shrine
bōto-noriba	boat dock
basutei	bus stop
sugu soko	right [over] there

Ⅶ Listen to the audio and fill in the blanks based on the information you hear. 🔊 136-138

1. Chūsha-jō wa .... desu.

2. Kōban wa .... desu.

3. Nozomi Depāto no fairu wa .... desu.

SPEAKING PRACTICE

1. Kato and Emma are working.   🔊 139

   Katō: Nozomi Depāto no fairu wa doko ni arimasu ka.
   Ema: Koko ni arimasu. Dōzo.

   Kato: Where is the file for Nozomi Department Store?
   Emma: It's here. Here you go.

2. Kato telephones Suzuki, who is out of the office.   🔊 140

   Katō: Suzuki-san, ima doko desu ka.
   Suzuki: Ima Nozomi Depāto ni imasu.
   Katō: Nan-ji goro kaisha ni kaerimasu ka.
   Suzuki: 3-ji ni kaerimasu.

   Kato: Where are you now Suzuki-san?
   Suzuki: I'm at the Nozomi Department Store now.
   Kato: About what time will you get back to the office?
   Suzuki: I'll be back at 3 o'clock.

NOTES

1. **Nan-ji goro kaisha ni kaerimasu ka.**
   Goro is used when talking about approximate time. However, it cannot be used, like **gurai**, to mean an approximate period of time. (see L11, NOTES 1, p. 106)

Active Communication   If you are in Japan, go out on the street and ask various people if there is a station, department store, post office, etc. in the vicinity.

VOCABULARY

| ... **goro**   about (time) (see NOTES 1, above)

Giving and Receiving: I Received It from My Friend

TARGET DIALOGUE

141

Nakamura and Emma are in Nikko. They have gotten off the bus near the waterfall.

Ema:	Chotto samui desu ne.
Nakamura:	A, sukāfu ga arimasu yo.
	(Pulls a scarf out of her bag.)
	Kore, dōzo.
Ema:	E, ii n desu ka.
Nakamura:	Ee, watashi wa samukunai desu kara.
Ema:	Arigatō gozaimasu. Sutekina sukāfu desu ne.
Nakamura:	Ee, tanjōbi ni tomodachi ni moraimashita.

■ **Nakamura-san wa Ema-san ni sukāfu o kashimashita.**

Emma:	It's a bit cold here.
Nakamura:	Oh, I have a scarf. Here you go.
Emma:	Oh, are you sure?
Nakamura:	Certainly. [Because] I am not cold.
Emma:	Thank you very much. It's a lovely scarf!
Nakamura:	Thank you. I received it from a friend on my birthday.

■Nakamura-san lent her scarf to Emma-san.

VOCABULARY

sukāfu	scarf		suteki (na)	lovely, nice
arimasu	have		ni	from (particle; see GRAMMAR 1, p. 132)
Ii n desu ka.	Are you sure? (see NOTES 1, p. 132)		moraimasu	receive
kara	because (particle; see NOTES 2, p. 132)		kashimasu	lend, loan

1. **Ii n desu ka.**

    When someone makes an offer that is unexpected, this expression is used to confirm that he/she really meant it.

2. **Watashi wa samukunai desu kara.**

    Kara is added after an explanatory phrase, signaling a reason for something. Here, the expression is used out of Nakamura's consideration for Emma. She wants to give a reason, reassuring Emma that she is really willing to lend her scarf and make it easier for Emma to accept her offer.

KEY SENTENCES
 142

1. **Sumisu-san wa Nakamura-san ni hana o agemashita.**
2. **Nakamura-san wa Sumisu-san ni hana o moraimashita.**
3. **Sumisu-san wa ashita kaigi ga arimasu.**

1. Smith-san gave Nakamura-san some flowers.
2. Nakamura-san received flowers from Smith-san.
3. Smith-san has a meeting tomorrow.

GRAMMAR

1. **person 1 wa person 2 ni noun o agemasu.** (KS1)

The sentence construction using the verb **agemasu** is the same as the "person 1 **wa** person 2 **ni** noun **o** verb" construction explained in L9, GRAMMAR 2, p. 85. The particle **ni** follows the person who received the thing; the thing that changes hands takes the particle **o**.

NOTE: Agemasu cannot be used in a sentence meaning "someone gives something to me (the speaker)"; in that case the verb **kuremasu** is used.

2. **person 1 wa person 2 ni noun o moraimasu.** (KS2)

When using the verb **moraimasu** ("receive"), the referent of the particle **ni** is not the person receiving but the person giving. This **ni** means "from."

3. **person wa noun ga arimasu.** (KS3)

When using **arimasu** to mean "have" or "own," the noun takes the particle **ga**. When stating how many of the noun, the number follows "noun **ga**" and does not take a particle.

    e.g. **Sumisu-san wa ashita kaigi ga futatsu arimasu.**   Smith-san has two meetings tomorrow.

| **agemasu** | give |

WORD POWER

I Verbs

 143

①agemasu　②moraimasu

③arimasu　④kashimasu　⑤karimasu

II Gifts

 144

①iyaringu	⑤burausu	⑧sētā	⑪Kyōto no o-miyage
②nekkuresu	⑥baggu	⑨mafurā	
③yubiwa	⑦konsāto no chiketto	⑩nekutai	
④sukāfu			

III Words that can be used with **arimasu** ("have")

 145

①(o-) kane　　　　②yotei　　　　③yakusoku　　　　④jikan

VOCABULARY

karimasu (R2)	borrow	burausu	blouse	nekutai	tie	jikan	time
iyaringu	earrings	baggu	bag	(o-) kane	money		
nekkuresu	necklace	chiketto	ticket	yotei	schedule, plan		
yubiwa	ring	mafurā	muffler, scarf	yakusoku	appointment, promise		

EXERCISES

I *Practice conjugating verbs.* Repeat the verbs below and memorize their forms—present and past, affirmative and negative.

	Present form		Past form	
	aff.	*neg.*	*aff.*	*neg.*
give	**agemasu**	**agemasen**	**agemashita**	**agemasendeshita**
receive	**moraimasu**	**moraimasen**	**moraimashita**	**moraimasendeshita**
have	**arimasu**	**arimasen**	**arimashita**	**arimasendeshita**
lend	**kashimasu**	**kashimasen**	**kashimashita**	**kashimasendeshita**
borrow	**karimasu**	**karimasen**	**karimashita**	**karimasendeshita**

II *State what someone gave to or received from another.* Make up sentences following the pattern of the example and based on the information provided.

e.g. interesting

1. pretty

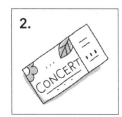

2.

3. Australian

e.g. **Sumisu-san wa Nakamura-san ni** <u>omoshiroi hon</u> **o agemashita.**

Nakamura-san wa Sumisu-san ni <u>omoshiroi hon</u> **o moraimashita.**

1. ....

....

2. ....

....

3. ....

....

III *State what someone lent to or borrowed from another.* Make up sentences following the pattern of the example. Substitute the underlined parts with the alternatives given.

e.g. **Nakamura-san wa Sumisu-san ni** <u>kasa</u> **o kashimashita.**

Sumisu-san wa Nakamura-san ni <u>kasa</u> **o karimashita.**

1. .... (kuruma)

.... (kuruma)

2. .... (o-kane)

.... (o-kane)

IV Make up dialogues following the patterns of the examples and based on the information provided.

A. *Ask and answer whom someone gave something to.*

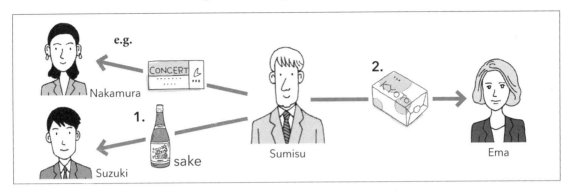

e.g. **A: Sumisu-san wa dare ni** <u>konsāto no chiketto</u> **o agemashita ka.**

  B: <u>Nakamura-san</u> **ni agemashita.**

1. A: ....

  B: ....

2. A: ....

  B: ....

B. *Ask and answer what someone received from another.*

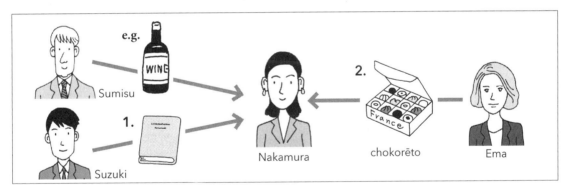

e.g. **A: Nakamura-san wa** <u>Sumisu-san</u> **ni nani o moraimashita ka.**

  B: <u>Wain</u> **o moraimashita.**

1. A: ....

  B: ....

2. A: ....

  B: ....

VOCABULARY

| **chokorēto** | chocolate |

V Make up sentences or dialogues following the patterns of the examples and based on the information provided.

	Kurisumasu	tanjōbi	Barentaindē
Risa → Sumisu	e.g. 1.	2.	e.g. 2. nothing
Sumisu → Risa	1. scarf pretty	3.	4. nothing

A. *State who gave what to whom, and who received what from whom, on a specific day.*

    e.g. 1. Risa-san wa Kurisumasu ni Sumisu-san ni nekutai o agemashita.

          Sumisu-san wa Kurisumasu ni Risa-san ni nekutai o moraimashita.

    1. ....

    ....

    2. ....

    ....

    3. ....

    ....

B. *Ask and answer what someone gave to another on a specific day.*

    e.g. 1. **A:** Risa-san wa Kurisumasu ni Sumisu-san ni nani o agemashita ka.

          B: Nekutai o agemashita.

    1. **A:** ....

        B: ....

    2. **A:** ....

        B: ....

VOCABULARY

Kurisumasu Christmas
Barentaindē Valentine's Day

3. A: ....

B: ....

C. *Ask and answer when someone received something from another.*

e.g. 1. A: **Sumisu-san wa itsu Risa-san ni nekutai o moraimashita ka.**

B: **Kurisumasu ni moraimashita.**

1. A: ....

B: ....

2. A: ....

B: ....

3. A: ....

B: ....

D. *Ask and answer what someone received from another on a specific day.*

e.g. 2. A: **Sumisu-san wa Barentaindē ni Risa-san ni nani o moraimashita ka.**

B: **Nani mo moraimasendeshita.**

4. A: ....

B: ....

VI *State someone's schedule.* Make up sentences following the pattern of the example. Substitute the underlined parts with the alternatives given.

e.g. Sumisu-san wa <u>ashita</u> <u>kaigi</u> ga arimasu.

1. ....

(konban, tomodachi to yakusoku)

2. ....

(asatte no gogo, jikan)

3. ....

(raishū, shutchō)

| **konban**　this evening

Ⅶ *Ask and answer someone's schedule.* Make up dialogues following the pattern of the example. Substitute the underlined parts with the alternatives given.

> **e.g. Tanaka:** **Sumisu-san, <u>ashita</u> wa isogashii desu ka.**
>
> **Sumisu:** **Hai, isogashii desu. <u>Kaigi</u> ga arimasu kara.**

1. Tanaka: .... (asatte)

   Sumisu: ....

   (ōkii purezen)

2. Tanaka: .... (kin-yōbi no yoru)

   Sumisu: ....

   (Nihon-go no kurasu)

Ⅷ *Talk about some item of a person's apparel.* Make up dialogues following the pattern of the example and based on the information provided.

e.g.   lovely

1.   kekkon-kinenbi   Wedding Anniversary   nice

2.   pretty

> **e.g. Nakamura:** **<u>Sutekina nekkuresu</u> desu ne.**
>
> **Ema:** **Ee, <u>tanjōbi</u> ni otto ni moraimashita.**
>
> **Nakamura:** **Yoku niaimasu ne.**
>
> **Ema:** **Arigatō gozaimasu.**

1. Nakamura: ....

   Ema: ....

   Nakamura: ....

   Ema: ....

2. Nakamura: ....

   Ema: ....

   Nakamura: ....

   Ema: ....

VOCABULARY

yoru	night	Yoku niaimasu ne.	It suits you well.
kekkon-kinenbi	wedding anniversary	yoku	well
kekkon	wedding, marriage	niaimasu	suit, look good on
kinenbi	anniversary		

IX Listen to the audio and answer the questions based on the information you hear. 🔊 146

    1. Sumisu-san wa tanjōbi ni nani o moraimashita ka.

....

    2. Dare ni moraimashita ka.

....

SPEAKING PRACTICE

1. The train lurches, and Emma steps on the foot of another person standing. 🔊 147

Onna no hito:	**Itai!**
Ema:	**Sumimasen. Daijōbu desu ka.**
Onna no hito:	**Ee, daijōbu desu.**
Ema:	**Dōmo sumimasendeshita.**

Woman: Ouch!
Emma: I'm sorry. Are you all right?
Woman: Yes, I'm fine.
Emma: I'm very sorry.

Active Communication

    1. Compliment someone around you on something he/she is wearing.

    2. Ask people around you if they have time tomorrow evening.

VOCABULARY

Itai!	Ouch!
Daijōbu desu ka.	Are you all right?
Sumimasendeshita.	I'm sorry (for what I did a while ago).

I Complete the sentences by choosing the most appropriate particle from the box below. The same particle may be used more than once. Some of the particles are not needed.

ga	o	ni	de	to

1. Sumisu-san wa Nakamura-san (   ) wain o agemashita.

2. Nakamura-san wa Sumisu-san (   ) wain o moraimashita.

3. Sumisu-san wa ima Kyōto (   ) imasu.

4. Kyōto ni furui o-tera (   ) arimasu.

5. Sumisu-san wa Kyōto (   ) o-tera o mimasu.

II Change the word in the parentheses to the form that is appropriate in the context of the sentence.

1. Kinō eiga o mimashita. Totemo _____. (omoshiroi)

2. Kono sandoitchi wa amari _____. (oishii)

3. Senshū no tesuto wa zenzen _____.

(muzukashii)

4. Kinō wa _____ ga, kyō wa isogashii desu. (hima)

5. Shūmatsu ni _____ resutoran de ban-gohan o tabemashita.

(yūmei)

III What do you say in the following situations?

1. You want to ask people who attended the party yesterday how the party was.

_____

2. You want to ask what there is to see at Nikko.

_____

3. You want to ask where the taxi stand is located.

_____

4. You want to ask what kind of place Shibuya is.

_____

5. You want to ask how many beers are in the refrigerator.

_____

MAKING LEISURE PLANS

Manga, anime, and computer games enjoyed by people from childhood to old age are now considered an important part of Japanese culture and have become quite popular around the world as well. The settings of these works are often real places or buildings around the country and they draw fans from around the country and the world. The photo is of buildings in Tokyo's Akihabara area, where numerous shops are clustered that sell figures and character goods relating to manga, anime, and games.

Talking about Preferences: I Like Japanese Anime

TARGET DIALOGUE

🔊 148

Smith's cousin Paul is visiting Japan.

Sumisu:	**Itoko no Pōru desu.**
Pōru:	**Hajimemashite. Pōru desu.**
	Yoroshiku onegaishimasu.
	Watashi wa Nihon no anime ga suki desu.
Suzuki:	**Donna anime ga suki desu ka.**
Pōru:	**Robotto no anime ga suki desu.**
Suzuki:	**A, watashi mo desu. Kaku no mo suki desu.**
	(Draws an illustration.)
Sumisu and Pōru:	**Wā! Sugoi! Jōzu desu ne!**

■ **Pōru-san to Suzuki-san wa robotto no anime ga suki desu.**

Smith: This is my cousin, Paul.
Paul: How do you do? I am Paul. Nice to meet you. I like Japanese anime.
Suzuki: What kind of anime do you like?
Paul: I like mecha anime.
Suzuki: Ah! I like them too.
         I also like drawing anime.
Smith and Paul: Wow!
         That's great. You're good!

■ Paul-san and Suzuki-san like
   mecha anime.

VOCABULARY

itoko	cousin	**kakimasu**	draw	**Sugoi!**	That's great!
anime	anime, animation	**no**	(nominalizer; see	**jōzu (na)**	skilled, be good at
suki (na)	like, favorite		GRAMMAR 3, p. 144)		
robotto	robot	**Wā!**	Wow! (exclamation of		
kaku	draw		surprise)		

142

1. **Donna anime ga suki desu ka.**

   When asking what someone likes from a specific category, use "**donna** noun **ga suki desu ka**."

2. **Watashi mo desu.**

   This means **Watashi mo robotto no anime ga suki desu**. The expression **Watashi mo desu** can be used when you want to say "I am the same [as the previous speaker]," whether it is affirmative or negative.

KEY SENTENCES

 149

1. **Chan-san wa wain ga suki desu.**
2. **Chan-san wa Nihon-go ga jōzu desu.**
3. **Sumisu-san wa sakkā o miru no ga suki desu.**

1. Chan-san likes wine.
2. Chan-san is good at Japanese.
3. Smith-san likes watching soccer matches.

GRAMMAR

1. **person wa** noun **ga suki desu.** (KS1)

   person wa noun **ga jōzu desu.** (KS2)

When using **suki desu** (**na**-adjective with equivalent meaning to "like") and **jōzu desu** ("be skilled"), the thing one likes or the skill takes the particle **ga**, and is followed by **suki desu** or **jōzu desu**.

NOTE: **Jōzu desu** is always used to describe others. Japanese almost never use it to describe themselves or members of their families because it sounds like boasting. People therefore rarely ask **jōzu desu ka** meaning "Are you good at [such-and-such]."

2. **Verb dictionary form** (KS3)

Japanese verbs are conjugated in various forms. Up to this point in this textbook, verbs have been introduced in the **masu**-form or its derivatives. In this lesson we will study a new form called the "dictionary form," which is so named because it is the form of the verb that is listed in dictionaries.

Japanese verbs are divided into three categories: Regular 1, Regular 2, and Irregular. The Irregular verbs are **kimasu** and **shimasu** or compound verbs formed with these verbs. The Regular 2 verbs introduced through Lesson 14 are: **tabemasu, mimasu, oshiemasu, misemasu, imasu, agemasu, karimasu**. Regular 2 verbs introduced from Lesson 15 onward will be included in VOCABULARY, marked (R2), for each lesson.

To obtain the dictionary form of a Regular 1 verb, the sound before the **masu** changes as shown in the chart on the following page. To obtain the dictionary form of Regular 2 verbs, the rule is simpler: change **masu** to **ru**. The dictionary form of Irregular verbs is shown in the chart on the following page.

sakkā	soccer, football
miru (R2)	see, watch

Regular 1			Regular 2		
	masu-form	Dictionary form		**masu**-form	Dictionary form
buy	kaimasu	kau	see, watch	mimasu	miru
go	ikimasu	iku	be	imasu	iru
swim	oyogimasu	oyogu	eat	tabemasu	taberu
lend	kashimasu	kasu	tell, teach	oshiemasu	oshieru
wait	machimasu	matsu	Irregular		
drink	nomimasu	nomu	come	kimasu	kuru
return, go home	kaerimasu	kaeru	do	shimasu	suru

3. person wa verb [dictionary form] no ga suki desu.　　　　　(KS3)

By adding the nominalizer **no** to the dictionary form of the verb in place of a noun in the sentence "person **wa** noun **ga suki desu**," you can express what someone likes to do. Likewise you can express what someone is skillful at doing with "person **wa** verb [dictionary form] **no ga jōzu desu**."

WORD POWER

I na-adjectives

 150

①suki (na)

①jōzu (na)

II Sports

 151

①sukī

②sakkā

③yakyū

④daibingu

VOCABULARY

sukī	skiing
yakyū	baseball
daibingu	scuba diving

III Dictionary form 🔊 152

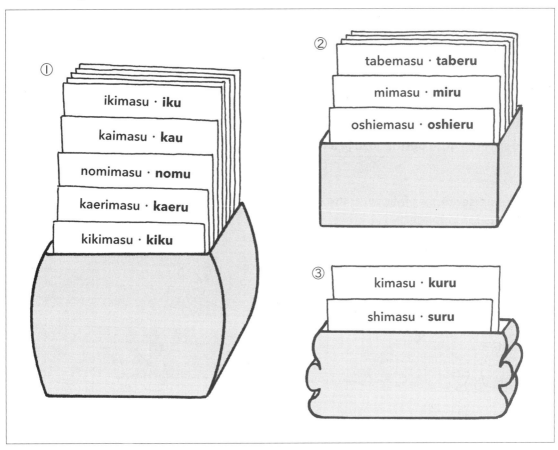

① ikimasu · **iku**
kaimasu · **kau**
nomimasu · **nomu**
kaerimasu · **kaeru**
kikimasu · **kiku**

② tabemasu · **taberu**
mimasu · **miru**
oshiemasu · **oshieru**

③ kimasu · **kuru**
shimasu · **suru**

IV Verbs 🔊 153

①kakimasu ②hanashimasu ③utaimasu ④oyogimasu ⑤hashirimasu

VOCABULARY

hanashimasu	talk, speak
utaimasu	sing
oyogimasu	swim
hashirimasu	run

EXERCISES

I *Practice conjugating* **na**-*adjectives.* Repeat the adjectives below and memorize their forms—present and past, affirmative and negative.

	Present form		Past form	
	aff.	*neg.*	*aff.*	*neg.*
like	**suki desu**	**suki ja arimasen**	**suki deshita**	**suki ja arimasendeshita**
be skilled	**jōzu desu**	**jōzu ja arimasen**	**jōzu deshita**	**jōzu ja arimasendeshita**

II Make up sentences following the patterns of the examples and based on the information provided.

gorufu	golf
dansu	dance
uta	song
uisukī	whiskey

A. *State what someone likes and is skilled at.*

e.g. <u>Katō-san</u> wa <u>nihonshu</u> ga suki desu. <u>Gorufu</u> ga jōzu desu.

1. ....

2. ....

3. ....

B. *State what someone dislikes and is unskilled at.*

e.g. <u>Katō-san</u> wa <u>kōhī</u> ga suki ja arimasen.

<u>Tenisu</u> ga jōzu ja arimasen.

1. ....
....

2. ....
....

3. ....
....

Ⅲ *Ask for and give more information about what one likes.* Make up dialogues following the pattern of the example. Substitute the underlined parts with the alternatives given.

e.g. **Ema:** Suzuki-san wa <u>supōtsu</u> ga suki desu ka.

Suzuki: Hai, suki desu.

Ema: Donna <u>supōtsu</u> ga suki desu ka.

Suzuki: <u>Yakyū</u> ga suki desu.

1. Ema: .... (kudamono)

   Suzuki: ....

   Ema: .... (kudamono)

   Suzuki: .... (ringo)

supōtsu sports
kudamono fruits

2. Ema: .... (Itaria-ryōri)

   Suzuki: ....

   Ema: .... (Itaria-ryōri)

   Suzuki: .... (piza)

3. Ema: .... (ongaku)

   Suzuki: ....

   Ema: .... (ongaku)

   Suzuki: .... (jazu)

Ⅳ *Practice conjugating verbs.* Repeat the verbs below and memorize their dictionary forms.

	masu-form	Dictionary form		**masu**-form	Dictionary form
go	ikimasu	iku	swim	oyogimasu	oyogu
sing	utaimasu	utau	talk, speak	hanashimasu	hanasu
run	hashirimasu	hashiru	eat	tabemasu	taberu
take	torimasu	toru	see	mimasu	miru
drink	nomimasu	nomu	come	kimasu	kuru
draw	kakimasu	kaku	do	shimasu	suru

Ⅴ *Practice making dictionary forms.* Change the following verbs to their dictionary forms.

e.g. **tabemasu** → **taberu**

1. utaimasu → ....

2. hashirimasu → ....

3. ikimasu → ....

4. shimasu → ....

5. oyogimasu → ....

6. hanashimasu → ....

7. mimasu → ....

8. kakimasu → ....

9. arukimasu → ....

10. yomimasu → ....

VOCABULARY

Itaria-ryōri	Italian cuisine
ryōri	food, dish, cooking, cuisine
piza	pizza
jazu	jazz

VI *State what a person likes to do.* Make up sentences following the pattern of the example and based on the information provided.

e.g. <u>Sakkā o miru</u> no ga suki desu.

1. ....

2. ....

3. ....

VII *Talk about what you like to do.* Make up dialogues following the pattern of the example. Substitute the underlined parts with the appropriate forms of the alternatives given.

e.g. **Katō:** Gurīn-san wa <u>ongaku o kiku</u> no ga suki desu ka.

Gurīn: Ee, suki desu. Katō-san wa?

Katō: Watashi mo suki desu. <u>Utau</u> no mo suki desu.

Gurīn: Sō desu ka. Ii desu ne.

1. Katō: .... (hashirimasu)

   Gurīn: ....

   Katō: ....

   .... (oyogimasu)

   Gurīn: ....

2. Katō: .... (e o kakimasu)

   Gurīn: ....

   Katō: ....

   .... (bijutsukan ni ikimasu)

   Gurīn: ....

VOCABULARY

| **bijutsukan** | art museum

VIII Listen to the audio and fill in the blanks based on the information you hear. 🔊 154, 155

1. Sumisu-san wa .... no ga suki desu.

2. Buraun-san wa .... no ga jōzu desu.

SPEAKING PRACTICE

1. Nakamura and Raja are talking during their break. 🔊 156

Nakamura: Raja-san wa supōtsu ga suki desu ka.
Raja: Hai, suki desu.
Nakamura: Donna supōtsu ga suki desu ka.
Raja: Sakkā ga suki desu. Demo, jōzu ja arimasen.

Nakamura: Do you like sports, Raja-san?
Raja: Yes, I do.
Nakamura: What sports do you like?
Raja: I like soccer. But I'm not good at playing it.

Active Communication Imagine you are at a party. Introduce people around you to one another and give details about their interests and skills.

VOCABULARY

| demo   but

Making an Invitation: Shall We Go Together?

TARGET DIALOGUE 157

Suzuki, Paul, and Smith are talking.

Suzuki: Tsugi no nichi-yōbi ni Akihabara de anime no ibento ga arimasu. Omoshiroi ibento desu kara, issho ni ikimasen ka.

Pōru: Ii desu ne. Zehi. Ibento wa nan-ji kara desu ka.

Suzuki: 1-ji kara desu. Hiru-gohan mo issho ni tabemashō. Sumisu-san mo issho ni dō desu ka.

Sumisu: Sumimasen. Anime wa chotto....

Suzuki: Sō desu ka.

■ **Suzuki-san to Pōru-san wa tsugi no nichi-yōbi ni anime no ibento ni ikimasu.**

Suzuki: Next Sunday there is an anime event in Akihabara. It's an interesting event, so shall we go [see it] together?
Paul: Sounds good. I'd love to. What time does the event start?
Suzuki: It starts at 1:00 p.m. Let's have lunch together too. Smith-san, how about you?
Smith: Sorry, anime is not really . . .
Suzuki: I see.

■ Next Sunday, Suzuki-san and Paul-san will go to the anime event.

VOCABULARY

tsugi	next	**kara**	because, so (particle; see GRAMMAR 4, p. 152)	**zehi**	I'd love to, by all means
Akihabara	Akihabara (district in Tokyo)			**tabemashō**	let's eat
ibento	event			**dō desu ka**	how about you?
arimasu	there is, take place (see GRAMMAR 1, p. 152)	**issho ni**	together	**chotto...**	(see GRAMMAR 2, p. 152)
		ikimasen ka	shall we go?		

NOTES

1. Sumisu-san mo issho ni dō desu ka.

Dō desu ka is the expression used to ask the listener's intention. Here Suzuki is asking whether Smith wants to come along on the visit to Akihabara.

KEY SENTENCES

 158

1. **Do-yōbi ni Asakusa de o-matsuri ga arimasu.**
2. **Shūmatsu ni issho ni eiga o mimasen ka.**
3. **Issho ni ikimashō.**
4. **Ii tenki desu kara, kōen de hiru-gohan o tabemasen ka.**

1. There is a festival in Asakusa on Saturday.
2. Shall we see a movie together on the weekend?
3. Let's go together.
4. The weather is nice, so shall we have lunch in the park?

GRAMMAR

1. place de event ga arimasu. (KS1)

Arimasu can also be used in the sense of "take place" or "happen." The place where the event happens takes the particle **de**.

2. verb[masu-form stem]masen ka. (KS2, 4)

When suggesting some action to someone, ask by changing the **masu** of the **masu**-form to **masen ka**. The ways of responding to that form of question are listed below.

(1) Agreeing
Ee/Hai, zehi.	Yes, I'd love to.
Ii desu ne. Zehi.	Sounds good. I'd love to.
Ee/Hai, sō shimashō.	Yes, let's do that.

(2) Declining
Sumimasen. noun wa chotto….	I'm sorry, but noun is not really [to my taste].
Zannen desu ga, noun wa chotto….	Unfortunately, noun is a little [inconvenient for me].

Wa chotto … is added when responding to an inconvenient date, time or day of the week, or to invitations you are reluctant to accept. The "is not really to my taste" or "is inconvenient for me" is omitted after **chotto** because of the Japanese tendency to avoid a clear refusal.

3. verb[masu-form stem]mashō. (KS3)

When making an invitation for the speaker and the listenter to do something together, the **masu** of the **masu**-form changes to **mashō**. This is generally expressed in English as "let's [verb] . . . ."

4. clause 1 kara, clause 2. (KS4)

Clause 1 ending with **kara** expresses the reason for clause 2.

mimasen ka	shall we see?	tabemasen ka	shall we eat?
ikimashō	let's go		

WORD POWER

I Events

🔊 159

①hanabi-taikai

②yuki-matsuri

③sakkā no shiai

II Parts of a train station

🔊 160

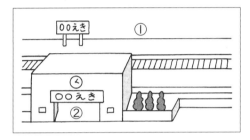

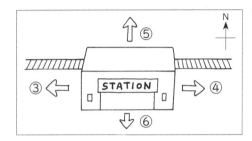

①hōmu ②deguchi ③nishi-guchi ④higashi-guchi ⑤kita-guchi ⑥minami-guchi

III Physical condition

🔊 161

①o-naka ga sukimashita

②nodo ga kawakimashita

③tsukaremashita

IV Variations on **masu**-form

🔊 162

	go	see	do	meet
V-masu	ikimasu	mimasu	shimasu	aimasu
V-masen ka	ikimasen ka	mimasen ka	shimasen ka	aimasen ka
V-mashō	ikimashō	mimashō	shimashō	aimashō

VOCABULARY

hanabi-taikai	fireworks festival	**deguchi**	exit	**minami-guchi**	south exit
hanabi	fireworks	**nishi-guchi**	west exit	**minami**	south
taikai	festival, event	**nishi**	west	**O-naka ga sukimashita.**	I'm hungry.
yuki-matsuri	snow festival	**higashi-guchi**	east exit	**Nodo ga kawakimashita.**	I'm thirsty.
yuki	snow	**higashi**	east	**Tsukaremashita.**	I'm tired.
shiai	game, match	**kita-guchi**	north exit		
hōmu	platform	**kita**	north		

EXERCISES

I *Invite someone to do something.* Make up sentences following the pattern of the example.

e.g. **Hiru-gohan o tabemasu.** → **Hiru-gohan o tabemasen ka.**

1. O-matsuri ni ikimasu. → ....

2. Eiga o mimasu. → ....

3. Shokuji o shimasu. → ....

4. Kōhī o nomimasu. → ....

II Make up dialogues following the patterns of the examples and based on the information provided.

A. *Invite someone to do something and accept one's invitation.*

e.g.	1. Nikkō	2. shokuji	3. sakkā no shiai

tomorrow	next month	this evening	next week

e.g. **A: Ashita issho ni eiga o mimasen ka.**

B: Ee, zehi.

1. A: ....

B: ....

2. A: ....

B: ....

3. A: ....

B: ....

VOCABULARY

| shokuji o shimasu   have a meal

B. *Invite someone to do something and refuse one's invitation.*

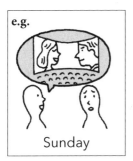

e.g.

Sunday

1. Hakone

Saturday

2. kabuki

Friday

3. hiru-gohan

weekend

e.g. A: <u>Nichi-yōbi</u> ni issho ni <u>eiga o mimasen</u> ka.

B: Zannen desu ga, <u>nichi-yōbi</u> wa chotto….

A: Sō desu ka. Ja, mata kondo.

1. A: ....

B: ....

A: ....

2. A: ....

B: ....

A: ....

3. A: ....

B: ....

A: ....

VOCABULARY

zannen desu	it is unfortunate
Mata kondo.	Next time., Another time.

Ⅲ Make up sentences or dialogues following the patterns of the examples and based on the information provided.

e.g. Asakusa	1. Sapporo	2.	3. Yokohama

Saturday	next month	this evening	Tuesday

A. *State when and where an event will take place.*

e.g. **Do-yōbi ni Asakusa de o-matsuri ga arimasu.**

1. ....

2. ....

3. ....

B. *Invite someone to an event and accept one's invitation.*

e.g. **A: Do-yōbi ni Asakusa de o-matsuri ga arimasu.**
      Issho ni ikimasen ka.
   B: Ii desu ne. Zehi.

1. A: ....

   ....

   B: ....

2. A: ....

   ....

   B: ....

3. A: ....

   ....

   B: ....

IV *Propose alternative options.* Make up dialogues following the pattern of the example. Substitute the underlined parts with the alternatives given.

e.g. A: Shūmatsu ni <u>Asakusa</u> de <u>o-matsuri</u> ga arimasu.

 <u>Do-yōbi</u> ni issho ni ikimasen ka.

 B: Zannen desu ga, <u>do-yōbi</u> wa chotto....

 A: Ja, <u>nichi-yōbi</u> wa dō desu ka.

 B: <u>Nichi-yōbi</u> wa jikan ga arimasu.

 A: Ja, <u>nichi-yōbi</u> ni ikimashō.

1. A: .... (Kamakura, o-matsuri)

 .... (nichi-yōbi)

 B: .... (nichi-yōbi)

 A: .... (do-yōbi)

 B: .... (do-yōbi)

 A: .... (do-yōbi)

2. A: .... (Shibuya, furī-māketto)

 .... (do-yōbi)

 B: .... (do-yōbi)

 A: .... (nichi-yōbi)

 B: .... (nichi-yōbi)

 A: .... (nichi-yōbi)

VOCABULARY

| ... wa dō desu ka   how about . . .

157

V *Give a reason and invite someone to do something.* Make up dialogues following the pattern of the example. Substitute the underlined parts with the appropriate forms of the alternatives given.

> e.g. **A: Ii tenki desu kara, kōen de hiru-gohan o tabemasen ka.**
>
> **B: Ii desu ne. Sō shimashō.**

1. A: ....
   (kono chikaku ni oishii soba-ya ga arimasu, issho ni ikimasu)

   B: ....

2. A: ....
   (nichi-yōbi wa Sumisu-san no tanjōbi desu, pātī o shimasu)

   B: ....

3. A: ....
   (chiketto ga 2-mai arimasu, konban eiga o mimasu)

   B: ....

VI *State a reason and invite someone to do something.* Make up dialogues following the pattern of the example. Substitute the underlined parts with the appropriate forms of the alternatives given.

> e.g. **A: O-naka ga sukimashita ne. Nani ka tabemasen ka.**
>
> **B: Ee, sō shimashō.**

1. A: ....
   (nodo ga kawakimashita, nani ka nomimasu)

   B: ....

2. A: ....
   (tsukaremashita, sukoshi yasumimasu)

   B: ....

VOCABULARY

pātī o shimasu	have a party	**yasumimasu**	rest
nani ka	something		
Sō shimashō.	Let's do that.		
sukoshi	a bit, a little		

Ⅶ *Invite someone to an event and propose a meeting time and place.* Make up dialogues following the pattern of the example. Substitute the underlined parts with the alternatives given.

> e.g. **Suzuki:** **Nichi-yōbi ni** <u>Yokohama</u> **de** <u>hanabi-taikai</u> **ga arimasu.**
>
> **Issho ni ikimasen ka.**
>
> **Sumisu:** **Ii desu ne. Zehi.** <u>Hanabi-taikai</u> **wa nan-ji kara desu ka.**
>
> **Suzuki:** <u>7-ji</u> **kara desu.** <u>6-ji</u> **ni** <u>Yokohama Eki no nishi-guchi</u> **de aimashō.**
>
> **Sumisu:** <u>6-ji</u> **ni** <u>Yokohama Eki no nishi-guchi</u> **desu ne. Wakarimashita.**

1. Suzuki: ....

   (Shibuya, konsāto)

   Sumisu: ....(konsāto)

   Suzuki: ....

   (6-ji han, 5-ji han, Shibuya Eki no higashi-guchi)

   Sumisu: ....

   (5-ji han, Shibuya Eki no higashi-guchi)

2. Suzuki: ....

   (Shinjuku, o-matsuri)

   Sumisu: ....(o-matsuri)

   Suzuki: ....

   (10-ji, 9-ji, Shinjuku Eki no minami-guchi)

   Sumisu: ....

   (9-ji, Shinjuku Eki no minami-guchi)

Ⅷ Listen to the audio and fill in the blanks based on the information you hear. 🔊 163, 164

1. Sumisu-san wa konban Suzuki-san to Shibuya de ....

2. 1) .... ni Asakusa de o-matsuri ga arimasu.

   2) Sumisu-san wa .... to o-matsuri ni ikimasu.

VOCABULARY

| **Shinjuku** | Shinjuku (district in Tokyo) |

SPEAKING PRACTICE

1. Sasaki is having a party at her home. 🔊 165

> **Sasaki:** **Sumisu-san, 15-nichi no nichi-yōbi ni uchi de pātī o shimasu.**
> **Kimasen ka.**
> **Sumisu:** **Arigatō gozaimasu. Zehi.**

Sasaki: Smith-san, I am having a party at my house on Sunday, the 15th. Would you like to come?
Smith: Thank you. I'd love to.

2. Nakamura is going to play tennis on Saturday. 🔊 166

> **Nakamura:** **Do-yōbi ni Sumisu-san to tenisu o shimasu.**
> **Ema-san mo issho ni shimasen ka.**
> **Ema:** **Arigatō gozaimasu. Zehi.**

Nakamura: On Saturday, I'm going to play tennis with Smith-san. Would you like to join us, Emma-san?
Emma: Thank you. I'd love to.

NOTES

1. 15-nichi no nichi-yōbi

This **no** expresses apposition. When giving the date and the day of the week, it is expressed by "date **no** day of the week." The date is stated first and then the day of the week. They are usually connected with **no**.

2. Kimasen ka.

When the speaker invites someone to his/her home or an event he/she plans, **Kimasen ka** is used.

3. Arigatō gozaimasu. Zehi.

When invited to the speaker's home, to an event the speaker has planned, or to join an event that is already decided, the affirmative response to the invitation is usually **Arigatō gozaimasu. Zehi**.

Active Communication

Invite someone around you to an event.

Stating a Wish: I Want to Buy a Souvenir

TARGET DIALOGUE 167

Paul and Suzuki are discussing what to do on Sunday.

Pōru:	Otōto mo anime ga suki desu kara, Akihabara de o-miyage o kaitai desu.
Suzuki:	Sō desu ka. Ja, hiru-gohan no mae ni, kaimono o shimashō.
Pōru:	Arigatō gozaimasu.
Suzuki:	Pōru-san, hoteru wa doko desu ka.
Pōru:	Shinjuku no Nozomi Hoteru desu.
Suzuki:	Ja, 10-ji ni hoteru no robī de aimashō.
Pōru:	10-ji desu ne. Wakarimashita.

■ **Suzuki-san to Pōru-san wa hiru-gohan o taberu mae ni kaimono o shimasu.**

Paul: My younger brother likes anime, too, so I'd like to buy him a souvenir at Akihabara.
Suzuki: I see. Before lunch, let's do some shopping.
Paul: Thank you.
Suzuki: Paul-san, where is your hotel?
Paul: It's the Nozomi Hotel in Shinjuku.
Suzuki: Then, let's meet at 10:00 in the lobby of your hotel.
Paul: At 10:00. I've got that.

■ Suzuki-san and Paul-san will do some shopping before they have lunch.

VOCABULARY

otōto	(my) younger brother		Nozomi Hoteru	Nozomi Hotel (fictitious hotel name)
kaitai desu	want to buy		robī	lobby
... no mae ni	before . . .		taberu mae ni	before eating
mae	before			

KEY SENTENCES

 168

1. **(Watashi wa) oishii o-sushi o tabetai desu.**
2. **Sumisu-san wa kaigi no mae ni shiryō o okurimasu.**
3. **Sumisu-san wa mainichi neru mae ni sutoretchi o shimasu.**

1. (I) want to eat some good sushi.
2. Smith-san will send the material before the meeting.
3. Smith-san does stretching exercises every day before going to bed.

GRAMMAR

1. **(Watashi wa)** verb **[masu**-form stem] **tai desu/takunai desu.**   (KS1)

When a speaker states a wish, the **masu** is removed from the **masu**-form and **tai desu** is added. The **-tai desu** is conjugated in the same way as **i**-adjectives.

e.g. **Ikitai desu.**   (I) want to go.

Ikitakunai desu.   (I) don't want to go.

Ikitakatta desu.   (I) wanted to go.

Ikitakunakatta desu.   (I) didn't want to go.

NOTE: Sometimes **ga** is used as the object marker in place of **o**.
e.g. **Wain o/ga nomitai desu.**   (I) want to drink wine.

-tai expresses the wish of the speaker and cannot be used to express the wish of anyone other than the speaker. **ka** may be added to the end of the sentence to change it into a question, but it is not appropriate for use when making an invitation. Also, it is considered impolite to use this expression when asking **-tai desu ka** ("do you want to do . . . ?") , especially to someone of higher status. When wishing to ask what someone wants to do, it is safer to attach **ka** to the **masu**-form of the verb (e.g., **nani o nomimasu ka**). Regarding future dreams or hopes, however, it is acceptable to ask, even of a person of higher status **-tai desu ka**.

2. person **wa** noun **no mae ni** verb.   (KS2)

Expresses what is/was done before the noun (event, action, etc.).

3. person **wa** verb 1 [dictionary form] **mae ni** verb 2.   (KS3)

Indicates that the verb 2 action comes before the verb 1 action.

tabetai desu	want to eat	**sutoretchi o shimasu**	do stretching exercises
shiryō	material, data, documents		
neru mae ni	before sleeping/going to bed		
nemasu (R2)	sleep, go to bed		

WORD POWER

Ⅰ Hobbies

🔊 169

①ikebana

②karate

③piano

④dansu

Ⅱ Verbs

🔊 170

①naraimasu

②ryōri o shimasu

③araimasu

④shawā o abimasu

⑤shokuji o shimasu

⑥hajimemasu

⑦kakimasu

⑧nemasu

VOCABULARY

ikebana	flower arrangement	**ryōri o shimasu**	cook	**hajimemasu** (R2)	start, begin
karate	karate	**araimasu**	wash	**kakimasu**	write
piano	piano	**shawā o abimasu** (R2)			
naraimasu	learn, take lessons in		take a shower		

EXERCISES

I *Practice conjugating verbs.* Repeat the verbs below and memorize their **tai**-forms—present and past, affirmative and negative.

	Present form		Past form	
	aff.	*neg.*	*aff.*	*neg.*
want to buy	kaitai desu	kaitakunai desu	kaitakatta desu	kaitakunakatta desu
want to eat	tabetai desu	tabetakunai desu	tabetakatta desu	tabetakunakatta desu
want to see	mitai desu	mitakunai desu	mitakatta desu	mitakunakatta desu
want to meet	aitai desu	aitakunai desu	aitakatta desu	aitakunakatta desu
want to go	ikitai desu	ikitakunai desu	ikitakatta desu	ikitakunakatta desu

II Make up sentences following the patterns of the examples.

A. *State what you want to do.*

e.g. **O-sushi o tabemasu.** → **O-sushi o tabetai desu.**

1. Terebi o mimasu. → ....

2. Tanaka-san ni aimasu. → ....

3. O-miyage o kaimasu. → ....

4. Onsen ni ikimasu. → ....

5. Tegami o kakimasu. → ....

B. *State what you don't want to do.*

e.g. **O-sushi o tabemasen.** → **O-sushi o tabetakunai desu.**

1. Terebi o mimasen. → ....

2. Tanaka-san ni aimasen. → ....

3. O-miyage o kaimasen. → ....

4. Onsen ni ikimasen. → ....

5. Tegami o kakimasen. → ....

VOCABULARY

tegami   letter

III Make up dialogues following the patterns of the examples. Substitute the underlined part(s) with the appropriate forms of the alternatives given.

A. *Ask and answer where one wants to live.*

e.g. **A: Shōrai donna tokoro ni sumitai desu ka.**

B: Umi no chikaku ni sumitai desu.

1. A: ....

   B: .... (atatakai tokoro)

2. A: ....

   B: .... (shizukana machi)

B. *Ask for information.*

e.g. **A: Nihon-go o benkyōshitai desu. Kono chikaku ni ii gakkō ga arimasu ka.**

B: Ee, AJALT Sukūru ga ii desu yo.

1. A: ....

   A: .... (o-hanami o shimasu, tokoro)

   B: .... (Sakura Kōen)

2. A: ....

   A: .... (tenisu o naraimasu, kurabu)

   B: .... (Minato Tenisu Kurabu)

3. A: ....

   A: .... (furui kagu o kaimasu, mise)

   B: .... (Antīku Tōkyō)

VOCABULARY

shōrai	in the future	**Sakura Kōen**	Sakura Park (fictitious park name)
sumimasu	live	**kurabu**	club
machi	town	**Minato Tenisu Kurabu**	Minato Tennis Club (fictitious club name)
benkyōshimasu	study (see APPENDIX D, p. 246)		
AJALT Sukūru	AJALT School (fictitious school name)	**kagu**	furniture
		Antīku Tōkyō	Antique Tokyo (fictitious shop name)
(o-) hanami o shimasu	view cherry blossoms	**antīku**	antiques

Ⅳ *State what someone will do before a particular event.* Look at the illustration and make up sentences following the patterns of the examples. Substitute the underlined part with the alternatives given.

e.g. 1.   **Gogo 1-ji kara kaigi ga arimasu.**

Kaigi no mae ni <u>shokuji o shimasu</u>.

1. ....

.... (shiryō o daunrōdoshimasu)

2. ....

.... (kōhī o kaimasu)

e.g. 2.   **Gogo 7-ji kara pātī ga arimasu.**

Pātī no mae ni <u>wain o kaimasu</u>.

3. ....

.... (biyōin ni ikimasu)

4. ....

.... (shawā o abimasu)

VOCABULARY

| daunrōdoshimasu | download |
| biyōin | hair dresser |

V Make up sentences following the patterns of the examples. Substitute the underlined part(s) with the appropriate forms of the alternatives given.

A. *State something that is done before doing something else.*

e.g. **Sumisu-san wa** <u>neru</u> **mae ni sutoretchi o shimasu.**

1. Sumisu-san wa .... mae ni nyūsu o chekkushimasu.
(shigoto o hajimemasu)

2. Sumisu-san wa .... mae ni shawā o abimasu.
(asa-gohan o tabemasu)

3. Sumisu-san wa .... mae ni te o araimasu.
(ryōri o shimasu)

B. *State something that was done before doing something else.*

e.g. **Sumisu-san wa** **Nihon ni kuru** **mae ni Nihon-go no benkyō o hajimemashita.**

1. .... wa .... mae ni mēru-adoresu o
(Suzuki-san, mēru o okurimasu)
chekkushimashita.

2. .... wa .... mae ni o-miyage o kaimashita.
(Pōru-san, kuni ni kaerimasu)

3. .... wa .... mae ni sutoretchi o shimashita.
(Ema-san, oyogimasu)

VI Listen to the audio and fill in the blanks based on the information you hear. 🔊171-173

1. Chan-san wa maiasa .... mae ni ....

2. Sumisu-san wa maiasa .... mae ni

....

3. Suzuki-san wa moku-yōbi ni .... mae ni

....

---

chekkushimasu	check
te	hand

SPEAKING PRACTICE

1. An event ended, and Suzuki takes Paul back to the hotel. 🔊 174

Suzuki:	Sui-yōbi no yoru wa isogashii desu ka.
Pōru:	Iie, isogashikunai desu.
Suzuki:	Ja, issho ni ban-gohan o tabemasen ka.
Pōru:	Ii desu ne. Zehi.
Suzuki:	Ja, mata sui-yōbi ni.

Suzuki: Are you busy on Wednesday evening?
Paul: No, I'm not busy.
Suzuki: Well then, how about going out for dinner together?
Paul: That would be very nice. I'd love to.
Suzuki: Then, I'll see you on Wednesday.

2. Paul and Suzuki are at a Japanese restaurant. A plate of sashimi has been served. 🔊 175

Pōru:	Kirei desu ne.
Suzuki:	Itadakimasu.
Pōru:	Chotto matte kudasai. Taberu mae ni shashin o toritai desu.

Paul: Doesn't that look nice!
Suzuki: Let's eat!
Paul: Please wait a minute! Before we eat it, I want to take a picture.

NOTES

1. **Ja, mata sui-yōbi ni.**

   Sui-yōbi ni is a shortened version of **sui-yōbi ni aimashō**. When people part, they rarely say **sayōnara**, usually using a phrase that refers to the next time they will meet.

   e.g. **Ja, mata ashita.**   See you tomorrow.

Active
Communication

1. Get information about schools and teachers, or about a subject you want to take a lesson in.

2. Get information about things you want to buy and places you want to visit.

VOCABULARY

| **Itadakimasu.** | [said before eating] |

CASUAL STYLE 1

WHAT IS THE CASUAL STYLE?

Japanese has a number of speech levels or styles that are used depending on degree of familiarity and status in vertical relationships. The style studied so far in this textbook is the so-called **desu/masu** style that is most widely used in adult conversation.

Conversations in families or among friends follow the "casual style." People sometimes change their style of speech according to the circumstances, even when speaking to the same person, and a number of complex elements go into judging when and with whom to use casual style. Casual style, if used inappropriately, sounds very rude, and it should never be used carelessly where it does not belong. Here we introduce the casual style mainly for the purpose of hearing comprehension.

SAMPLE DIALOGUE 1 ———————————————————— 🔊 176

A student in a university classroom finds a pen on the floor and speaks to her classmates:

Hayashi:	Kore, dare no pen?	Hayashi:	Whose pen is this?
Yamada:	Sā. (*Turning toward Abe*) **Abe no?**	Yamada:	I don't know. Is it yours, Abe?
Abe:	Uun, ore no ja nai.	Abe:	No, it's not mine.
Hayashi:	Raja-san, kore tte Raja-san no?	Hayashi:	Raja, is this yours?
Raja:	Un, boku no. Arigatō.	Raja:	Yes, it is. Thanks.

desu/masu style	Casual style
noun 1 **wa** noun 2 **desu.**	noun 1 **wa** noun 2. **Desu** is omitted. When **ne** or **yo** is added, they become **da ne, da yo.**
noun 1 **wa** noun 2 **desu ka.**	noun 1 **wa** noun 2? **Ka** is omitted, and the question is expressed by rising intonation. **Wa** is often omitted and sometimes becomes **tte.**
Hai, noun 2 **desu.**	**Un,** noun 2.
Iie, noun 2 **ja arimasen.**	**Uun,** noun 2 **ja nai.**
last name + **san** first name + **san**	"Last name + **san**" and "first name + **san**" can be used, but sometimes **san** is replaced by **kun** or **chan**. The first name or last name without a title, as well as nicknames, are also used.
watashi	Males often use **boku** or **ore**. Females sometimes use **atashi**.

SAMPLE DIALOGUE 2 177

Nakamura is talking to a friend named Chiba on the phone.

Nakamura: **Ashita no pātī, iku?**	Nakamura: Are you going to tomorrow's party?
Chiba: **Un, iku.**	Chiba: Yes, I am.

desu/masu style	Casual style
Ikimasu.	**Iku.** The present affirmative form of verbs is expressed by the dictionary form.
Pātī ni ikimasu ka.	**Pātī, iku?** The particle **ni** is often omitted when indicating a destination, but when the sentence involves someone relating to a benefactive expression, or when it indicates current location, it is not omitted. **Wa** and **o** are often omitted. **De, to,** and **ya** are not omitted.

SAMPLE DIALOGUE 3 178

Nakamura attended yesterday's party, but her friend Ono did not.

Ono: **Kinō no pātī, dō datta?**	Ono: How was yesterday's party?
Nakamura: **Sugoku nigiyaka datta.**	Nakamura: It was very lively.
Ono: **Ryōri wa?**	Ono: How about the food?
Nakamura: **Oishikatta yo.**	Nakamura: It was good.

Adjectives as predicates in casual style				
	Present form		Past form	
	aff.	*neg.*	*aff.*	*neg.*
i-adj.	ōkii	ōkikunai	ōkikatta	ōkikunakatta
	ii	yokunai	yokatta	yokunakatta
na-adj.	kirei *	kirei ja nai	kirei datta	kirei ja nakatta

*In cases when **ne** or **yo** is added, in casual speech, they become **kirei da ne** and **kirei da yo**.

BUSINESS TRIPS

Even in times when teleconferencing has become quite common, people in business recognize the value of face-to-face communication and travel frequently to meet in person with clients and associates. The Japanese archipelago stretches over a distance of 3,000 kilometers and the climate varies widely from Hokkaido in the north to Okinawa in the south. That diversity makes for great variety in the specialties of each area, whether fruit, vegetables, seafood, dairy or other products. Souvenirs sold in each part of the country feature local specialties, such as cookies made with butter from Hokkaido's famous dairy industry or sweets made with Okinawa-grown pineapple. People who go on business trips often purchase such souvenirs to share with their families or office mates.

Explaining Plans: I Will Go to Osaka and See Her

TARGET DIALOGUE

🔊 179

Emma speaks to Kato while he is working.

Ema: Katō-san, chotto yoroshii desu ka.

Katō: Hai.

Ema: Ashita Ōsaka ni ikimasu.

Katō: A, pakkēji-fea desu ne.

Ema: Ee. Fea no ato, shisha ni itte, Chan-san ni aimasu.
Asatte kōjō o mite, 4-ji no hikōki de Tōkyō ni kaerimasu.

Katō: Wakarimashita. Ki o tsukete.

■ **Ema-san wa ashita Ōsaka ni ikimasu.**
Asatte kōjō o mite, Tōkyō ni kaerimasu.

Emma: Kato-san. May I have a moment of your time?
Kato: Yes.
Emma: Tomorrow, I will go to Osaka.
Kato: Ah, to the package fair, right?
Emma: Yes. After the fair, I will go to the branch office and see Chan-san.
The day after tomorrow I will see the factory, and then I will take a 4:00
flight back to Tokyo.
Kato: I understand. Please take care.

■ Emma-san will go to Osaka tomorrow.
The day after tomorrow she will see the
factory and then come back to Tokyo.

VOCABULARY

yoroshii	be all right (polite expression of **ii**; see NOTES 1, p. 173)	**fea**	fair	**mite**	see (**te**-form of **mimasu**)
		... no ato	after . . .	**Ki o tsukete.**	Take care. (see NOTES 2, p. 173)
		ato	after		
pakkēji-fea	package fair	**itte**	go (**te**-form of **ikimasu**)		
pakkēji	package	**kōjō**	factory		

NOTES

1. **Chotto yoroshii desu ka.**

   This expression is used when addressing someone of higher status who is busy with something.

2. **Ki o tsukete.**

   This means "take care" or "be careful" but when spoken to a person leaving on a trip, it is often used to hold the meaning of "Have a safe trip!"

KEY SENTENCES

 180

1. **Ema-san wa ashita Ōsaka-shisha ni itte, Chan-san ni aimasu.**
2. **Sumisu-san wa kaigi no ato, repōto o kakimashita.**

1. Emma-san will go to the Osaka branch office tomorrow and see Chan-san.
2. Smith-san wrote a report after the meeting.

GRAMMAR

1. Verb **te**-form (KS1)

Japanese verbs are divided into three categories: Regular 1, Regular 2, and Irregular (see L15, GRAMMAR 2, p. 143). For Regular 1 verbs the **te**-form is obtained according to the sound immediately before **masu** as shown in the chart below. For Regular 2 verbs, the rule is simpler: change **masu** to **te**. The **te**-form of Irregular verbs is the same as for Regular 2 verbs.

Regular 1				Regular 2		
	masu-form	**te**-form			**masu**-form	**te**-form
buy	kaimasu	katte	eat		tabemasu	tabete
wait	machimasu	matte	tell, teach		oshiemasu	oshiete
return, go home	kaerimasu	kaette	show		misemasu	misete
go	ikimasu	itte*	see, watch		mimasu	mite
draw, write	kakimasu	kaite	be		imasu	ite
swim	oyogimasu	oyoide		Irregular		
drink	nomimasu	nonde	come		kimasu	kite
lend	kashimasu	kashite	do		shimasu	shite

*Exceptional inflection

2. person **wa** verb 1 [**te**-form], verb 2. (KS1)

The **te**-form is used when stating several consecutive actions/acts. In this case the subject of the first action and of the next action is the same. Using the **te**-form, it is possible to link together two or three clauses; in that case the first and second verbs will be in the **te**-form. However, if the moods and tenses of the clauses are not the same, they cannot be linked using the **te**-form. For example, sentences such as the following cannot be linked using the **te**-form.

1. Statement: **(Watashi wa) chiketto ga 2-mai arimasu.** I have two tickets.
2. Suggestion: **Ashita issho ni eiga o mimasen ka.**

   Shall we see a movie together tomorrow?

VOCABULARY

| **repōto** | report |

Further, when the first clause uses a verb of movement such as **ikimasu**, **kimasu**, or **kaerimasu**, the location of the action of the second clause is assumed to be the same, even if not stated explicitly. For example: **Kinō Ginza ni itte, hiru-gohan o tabemashita.** ("Yesterday I went to Ginza and ate lunch [there]") The place where I ate lunch was Ginza.

3. person wa noun no ato, verb. (KS2)

This expression is used when talking about an action following a noun (event, action, etc.). When emphasizing that the action comes after, not before, the particle **de** is added after **ato**.

WORD POWER

❶ te-form

🔊 181

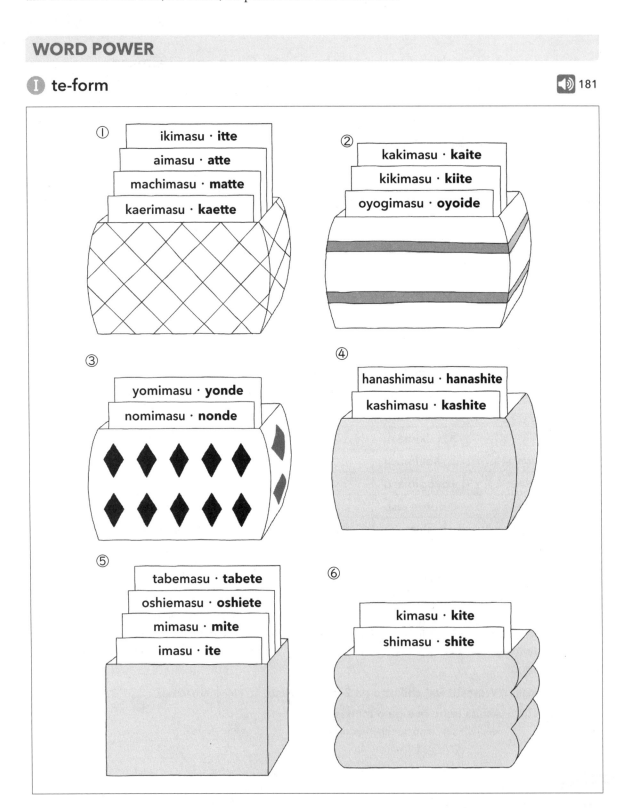

① ikimasu · **itte**
aimasu · **atte**
machimasu · **matte**
kaerimasu · **kaette**

② kakimasu · **kaite**
kikimasu · **kiite**
oyogimasu · **oyoide**

③ yomimasu · **yonde**
nomimasu · **nonde**

④ hanashimasu · **hanashite**
kashimasu · **kashite**

⑤ tabemasu · **tabete**
oshiemasu · **oshiete**
mimasu · **mite**
imasu · **ite**

⑥ kimasu · **kite**
shimasu · **shite**

EXERCISES

I *Practice making **te**-forms.* Change the following verbs to their **te**-forms.

e.g. **tabemasu** → **tabete**

1. kimasu → ....
2. nomimasu → ....
3. kakimasu → ....
4. aimasu → ....
5. kaerimasu → ....

6. yomimasu → ....
7. mimasu → ....
8. kikimasu → ....
9. shimasu → ....
10. ikimasu → ....

II *State a sequence of actions.* Make up sentences following the pattern of the example and based on the information provided.

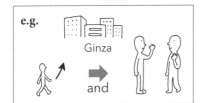
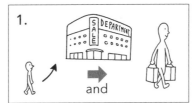

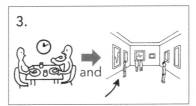

e.g. **Ginza ni ikimasu. Tomodachi ni aimasu.**

→ **Ginza ni itte, tomodachi ni aimasu.**

1. Depāto ni ikimasu. Kaimono o shimasu.

→ ....

2. Tomodachi ni aimasu. Eiga o mimasu.

→ ....

3. Resutoran de hiru-gohan o tabemasu. Bijutsukan ni ikimasu.

→ ....

III *Ask and answer what one will do.* Make up dialogues following the pattern of the example. Substitute the underlined parts with the appropriate forms of the alternatives given.

　　e.g. A: Ashita nani o shimasu ka.

　　　　B: Hakone ni itte, tenisu o shimasu.

　　1. A: ....

　　　　B: ....

　　　　　　　　　　　　　(Ginza de kaimono o shimasu, eiga o mimasu)

　　2. A: ....

　　　　B: ....

　　　　　　　　　　　　　(Yokohama ni ikimasu, sakkā no shiai o mimasu)

IV *Ask and answer what one did.* Make up dialogues following the pattern of the example. Substitute the underlined parts with the appropriate forms of the alternatives given.

　　e.g. A: Kinō nani o shimashita ka.

　　　　B: Ōsaka-shisha ni itte, purezen o shimashita.

　　1. A: ....

　　　　B: ....

　　　　　　　　　　　　　(kuruma o karimasu, doraibu o shimasu)

　　2. A: ....

　　　　B: ....

　　　　　　　　　　　　　(tomodachi ni aimasu, issho ni sumō o mimasu)

---

purezen o shimasu	give a presentation
doraibu o shimasu	go for a drive
sumō	sumo [wrestling]

Ⅴ *Invite someone to do something.* Combine the sentences following the pattern of the example.

    e.g. **Uchi ni kimasen ka. Hiru-gohan o tabemasen ka.**

      → **Uchi ni kite, hiru-gohan o tabemasen ka.**

  1. Sandoitchi o kaimasen ka. Kōen de tabemasen ka.

    → ....

  2. Nikkō ni ikimasen ka. Yūmeina jinja o mimasen ka.

    → ....

Ⅵ *State what someone will do after a particular event.* Look at the illustrations and make up sentences following the patterns of the examples. Substitute the underlined parts with the appropriate forms of the alternatives given.

  e.g. 1 **Gogo 1-ji kara kaigi ga arimasu.**

      Kaigi no ato, <u>repōto o kakimasu</u>.

  1. ....

    .... (Yamamoto-san ni aimasu)

  e.g. 2 **Kinō pātī ga arimashita.**

      Pātī no ato, <u>takushī de uchi ni kaerimashita</u>.

  2. ....

    .... (bā ni itte, uisukī o nomimasu)

VOCABULARY

| **Yamamoto** Yamamoto (surname)

VII *Describe a schedule.* Make up sentences following the pattern of the example and based on the information provided in the schedule of Smith's business trip.

e.g.	Thursday	Osaka	Meeting	→ Call Green-san
1.	Friday	Kobe	Golf	→ Go to a friend's house
2.	Saturday	Kyoto	Have a meal with Yamamoto-san	→ See old temples and shrines

e.g. Sumisu-san wa moku-yōbi ni Ōsaka ni itte, kaigi o shimasu.

Kaigi no ato, Gurīn-san ni denwa o shimasu.

1. ....

....

2. ....

....

VIII *Talk about a plan.* Make up dialogues following the pattern of the example. Substitute the underlined parts with the alternatives given.

e.g. Katō: Ema-san, fea no ato, nani o shimasu ka.

Ema: Kōbe ni itte, tomodachi ni aimasu.

Katō: Sō desu ka.

1. Katō: ....

Ema: ....

(Nara, furui o-tera o mimasu)

Katō: ....

2. Katō: ....

Ema: ....

(shisha, Chan-san to uchiawase o shimasu)

Katō: ....

VOCABULARY

kaigi o shimasu	have a meeting
Kōbe	Kobe (city near Osaka)
Nara	Nara (old city in western Japan)
uchiawase o shimasu	have a preparatory meeting

IX Listen to the audio and fill in the blanks based on the information you hear. 182

Ema-san wa do-yōbi ni Shinjuku ni _____,

terebi o _____.

SPEAKING PRACTICE

1. A meeting at the Osaka branch office has ended and Chan comes to talk to Emma. 🔊 183

Chan: Ema-san, sutēki wa suki desu ka.

Ema: Hai, suki desu.

Chan: Ja, Kōbe ni itte, Kōbe Bīfu o tabemasen ka.

Ema: Arigatō gozaimasu. Zehi.

Chan: Emma-san, do you like steak?
Emma: Yes, I do.
Chan: How would you like to go to Kobe and have some Kobe Beef?
Emma: Thank you very much. I'd love to.

2. Smith and Nakamura are talking at the office. 🔊 184

Sumisu: Gogo 6-ji kara kaigi ga arimasu.

**   Ban-gohan wa kaigi no mae ni tabemasu ka. Ato de tabemasu ka.**

Nakamura: Kaigi no ato de tabemasu.

Smith: There is a meeting from 6:00 P.M. Are you going to eat supper before the meeting? After the meeting?
Nakamura: I'll eat after the meeting.

NOTES

1. **Sutēki wa suki desu ka.**
   The use of **wa** here indicates that of various kinds of food, the topic that has been brought up is "steak." When the word that is the topic has the particles **ga** or **o**, they change to **wa**. When the particle is other than **ga** or **o**, **wa** is added.

2. **Ban-gohan wa kaigi no mae ni tabemasu ka.**
   Ban-gohan has been made the topic, so the particle **o** has changed to **wa**, and **ban-gohan** comes at the head of the sentence.

 Tell people around you what you did yesterday. Then talk about your plans for the coming weekend.

VOCABULARY

| **Kōbe Bīfu**   Kobe Beef (famous, high-quality beef)

Making a Request: Please Give Her My Regards

TARGET DIALOGUE

🔊 185

After the package fair, Emma is in a taxi talking to Kato on the phone.

Katō: Fea wa dō deshita ka.

Ema: Omoshiroi pakkēji ga takusan arimashita.

Iroirona sanpuru o moraimashita kara,

takuhaibin de okurimashita.

Katō: Sō desu ka. Ja, getsu-yōbi no kaigi de hōkokushite kudasai.

Ema: Hai, wakarimashita.

Katō: Ima kara Ōsaka-shisha desu ka.

Ema: Hai, sō desu.

Katō: Chan-san ni yoroshiku tsutaete kudasai.

Ema: Hai, tsutaemasu.

■ **Ema-san wa getsu-yōbi no kaigi de pakkēji-fea ni tsuite hōkokushimasu.**

Kato: How was the fair?

Emma: There were many interesting packages. I received various samples, so I sent them [back] by parcel delivery service.

Kato: Okay. Then, at the meeting on Monday, please report on your visit.

Emma: Yes, I understand.

Kato: Are you now headed to the Osaka branch office?

Emma: Yes, that's right.

Kato: Please give my regards to Chan-san.

Emma: Yes, I will relay your message.

■ Emma-san will report on the package fair at the meeting on Monday.

VOCABULARY

iroiro(na)	various	hōkokushimasu	report
sanpuru	sample	Yoroshiku tsutaete kudasai.	Please give him/her my regards.
takuhaibin	parcel delivery service	tsutaemasu (R2)	relay a message
hōkokushite kudasai	please report	... ni tsuite	about . . .

NOTES

1. Yoroshiku tsutaete kudasai.

    This is a set phrase requesting someone to relay your regards/greetings to someone who is not present.

KEY SENTENCES

 186

1. Chotto matte kudasai.
2. Ema-san wa Chan-san ni mēru de shiryō o okurimashita.
3. Tsugi no shingō o migi ni magatte kudasai.

1. Please wait a moment.
2. Emma-san sent Chan-san the material by e-mail.
3. Turn right at the next traffic light.

GRAMMAR

1. verb [te-form] kudasai. (KS1, 3)

Adding **kudasai** after the **te**-form makes the polite form of an imperative.

2. means de (KS2)

When stating a means of communication or transportation, add the particle **de**.

3. place/space o (KS3)

In a sentence expressing a movement passing or moving through a place/space, the place/space is followed by the particle **o**.

WORD POWER

I Verbs 187

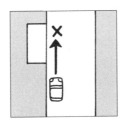

①magarimasu

②tomemasu

③iimasu

④mottekimasu

⑤todokemasu

⑥machimasu

VOCABULARY					
shingō	traffic light	magarimasu	turn	mottekimasu	bring
migi	right	tomemasu (R2)	stop	todokemasu (R2)	deliver
magatte kudasai	please turn	iimasu	say		

Ⅱ Positions and directions

🔊 188

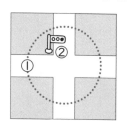

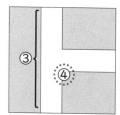

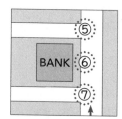

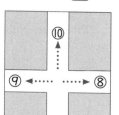

①kōsaten
②shingō

③michi
④kado

⑤saki
⑥mae
⑦temae

⑧migi
⑨hidari
⑩massugu

Ⅲ Means of delivery

🔊 189

①takuhaibin

②yūbin

③baikubin

EXERCISES

Ⅰ *Practice conjugating verbs.* Repeat the verbs below and memorize their **te**-forms.

	masu-form	**te**-form
say	iimasu	itte
wait	machimasu	matte
turn	magarimasu	magatte
take	torimasu	totte
lend, loan	kashimasu	kashite
show	misemasu	misete
stop	tomemasu	tomete
tell, teach	oshiemasu	oshiete
deliver	todokemasu	todokete
bring	mottekimasu	mottekite

VOCABULARY

kōsaten	intersection		temae	just before		baikubin	motorbike courier service
michi	road		hidari	left			
kado	corner		massugu	straight			
saki	beyond		yūbin	mail			

II *Make a request.* Make up sentences following the pattern of the example.

e.g. **Namae o kakimasu.** → **Namae o kaite kudasai.**

1. Chotto machimasu. → ....

2. Shashin o torimasu. → ....

3. Mō ichi-do iimasu. → ....

4. Pen o kashimasu. → ....

5. Pasokon o todokemasu. → ....

III Make up sentences or dialogues following the patterns of the examples. Substitute the underlined parts with the appropriate forms of the alternatives given.

A. *Make a request.*

e.g. **Sumimasen. <u>Ano resutoran no namae</u> o <u>oshiete</u> kudasai.**

1. .... (mēru-adoresu, kakimasu)

2. .... (menyū, misemasu)

3. ....
.... (kaigi no shiryō, mottekimasu)

B. *Make and accept a request to send something by a certain means.*

e.g. **A: <u>Sumisu-san</u> ni <u>mēru</u> de <u>shiryō</u> o okutte kudasai.**

   B: Hai, wakarimashita.

1. A: ....
   (Nozomi Depāto, yūbin, shorui)

   B: ....

2. A: ....
   (Ōsaka-shisha no Chan-san, takuhaibin, kono nimotsu)

   B: ....

3. A: ....
   (Yokohama-shisha, baikubin, katarogu)

   B: ....

VOCABULARY

menyū	menu
shorui	documents
nimotsu	package, luggage
katarogu	catalog

IV *Give directions to a taxi driver.* Make up sentences following the patterns of the examples. Substitute the underlined part(s) with the alternatives given.

A. e.g. <u>Ginkō no mae</u> de tomete kudasai.

    1. .... (kōsaten no temae)

    2. .... (shingō no saki)

B. e.g. <u>Tsugi no kōsaten</u> o massugu itte kudasai.

    1. .... (kono michi)

    2. .... (Ginza Dōri)

C. e.g. <u>Depāto no temae</u> o magatte kudasai.

    1. .... (sūpā no temae)

    2. .... (gakkō no saki)

D. e.g. <u>Tsugi no shingō</u> o <u>hidari</u> ni magatte kudasai.

    1. .... (tsugi no kōsaten, hidari)

    2. .... (futatsu-me no kado, migi)

    3. .... (hashi no temae, migi)

V *Give directions to a taxi driver.* Tell the driver the route indicated by the arrows or to stop at the point indicated by the X.

e.g. **Tsugi no kōsaten o migi ni magatte kudasai.**

    1. ....

    2. ....

    3. ....

    4. ....

    5. ....

VOCABULARY

Ginza Dōri	Ginza Street
futatsu-me	second
-me	(suffix that attaches to a number and turns it into ordinal number)
hashi	bridge

VI Make up dialogues following the patterns of the examples. Substitute the underlined parts with the alternatives given.

A. *Request that a purchase be delivered.*

e.g. **Sumisu:** Sumimasen. Kono <u>reizōko</u> o todokete kudasai.

Mise no hito: Hai.

Sumisu: <u>Ashita no gogo</u> onegaishimasu.

Mise no hito: Hai. Wakarimashita. Dewa, o-namae to go-jūsho o onegaishimasu.

1. Sumisu: .... (denshi-renji)

   Mise no hito: ....

   Sumisu: .... (kin-yōbi ni)

   Mise no hito: ....

   ....

2. Sumisu: .... (sofā)

   Mise no hito: ....

   Sumisu: ....
   (nichi-yōbi no 2-ji made ni)

   Mise no hito: ....

   ....

VOCABULARY

| go-jūsho | your address |
| made ni | by [specified time] |

B. *Give directions to a taxi driver.*

e.g. Ema: **Tōkyō Tawā** no chikaku made onegaishimasu.

Untenshu: **Hai.**

(after a while)

Ema: **Tsugi no shingō o <u>hidari</u> ni magatte kudasai.**

Untenshu: **Hai.**

Ema: **Ano <u>shiroi biru no mae</u> de tomete kudasai.**

Untenshu: **Hai, wakarimashita.**

(They have reached her destination.)

Untenshu: **4,000-en desu.**

Ema: **Hai.**

Untenshu: **Arigatō gozaimashita.**

Ema: **Dōmo.**

1. Ema: .... (Ebisu Eki)

   Untenshu: ....

   Ema: .... (migi)

   Untenshu: ....

   Ema: .... (manshon no mae)

   Untenshu: ....

   Ema: ....

   Untenshu: ....

   Ema: ....

VII Listen to the audio and fill in the blanks based on the information you hear. 🔊 190-192

Kato and Emma are talking.

1. Ema-san wa tonari no heya kara isu o ....

2. Ema-san wa Tanaka-san ni kaigi no shiryō o ....

3. Ema-san wa Katō-san ni pen o ....

   Katō-san wa Ema-san ni pen o ....

VOCABULARY

Tōkyō Tawā	Tokyo Tower		**Ebisu Eki**	Ebisu Station
made	to, as far as (particle)		**Ebisu**	Ebisu (district in Tokyo)
biru	building		**manshon**	condominium

SPEAKING PRACTICE

1. Emma is staying at a hotel.

🔊 193

> **Hoteru no hito:** Hai, rūmu-sābisu desu.
> **Ema:** Sumimasen. Mōfu o onegaidekimasu ka.
> **Hoteru no hito:** Hai, shōchishimashita.

> Hotel employee: Hello. This is room service.
> Emma: Excuse me. May I ask for a blanket?
> Hotel employee: Yes, certainly.

2. Emma checks out of the hotel.

🔊 194

> **Ema:** Sumimasen. Nimotsu o 5-ji made azukatte kudasai.
> **Furonto no hito:** Hai, shōchishimashita.

> Emma: Excuse me. Please keep my bag [here] until 5:00 P.M.
> Front desk clerk: Yes, certainly.

NOTES

1. **Mōfu o onegaidekimasu ka.**
   The expression "noun **o onegaidekimasu ka**" is more polite than the expression "noun **o onegaishimasu**."

2. **Shōchishimashita.**
   When asked to do something or relay information, **shōchishimashita** ("certainly") is a more polite way of saying **wakarimashita** ("I understand").

Active Communication If you're in Japan, give directions to a taxi driver or ask to have a package delivered in Japanese.

VOCABULARY

rūmu-sābisu	room service		**azukarimasu**	keep, take care of
mōfu	blanket			
Onegaidekimasu ka.	May I ask [you to do this]?			
Shōchishimashita.	Yes, certainly.			

Quiz 4 (Units 7-8)

I Change the word in the parentheses to the form that is appropriate in the context of the sentence.

1. Depātō de kēki o _____, tomodachi no uchi ni ikimashita.

   (kaimasu)

2. Tonari no heya kara isu o _____ kudasai. (mottekimasu)

3. Kuni ni _____ mae ni o-miyage o kaimasu. (kaerimasu)

4. Watashi wa e o _____ no ga suki desu. (kakimasu)

5. Nodo ga kawakimashita. Bīru o _____ tai desu. (nomimasu)

II Look at the illustrations and complete the dialogue by filling in the blanks with the appropriate forms of the words given in the box. You may use the same word more than once.

shimasu	jōzu desu	suki desu

Takahashi: Sumisu-san wa tenisu ga (**1.**) ka.

Sumisu: Ee, demo amari (**2.**).

Takahashi: Ashita tomodachi to tenisu o (**3.**).

            Sumisu-san mo issho ni (**4.**) ka.

Sumisu: Arigatō gozaimasu. Zehi.

188

AT THE MUSEUM

Japan has many different kinds of museums showing everything from Western fine arts to Japanese ukiyoe prints and from state-of-the-art technology to yōkai fantasy creatures. Museums in the Tokyo area include the Tokyo National Museum, featuring historic and cultural treasures from Japan and other parts of Asia; the Ghibli Museum, Mitaka designed and supervised by genius anime creator Hayao Miyazaki; and the National Museum of Emerging Science and Innovation, where visitors can experience science and space through stereoscopic films and get a real sense of the technologies of the future. The photo shows part of the exhibits at the Edo-Tokyo Museum tracing the architecture and culture of Tokyo from the seventeenth century to the present.

Going Places (3): How Do You Go There?

TARGET DIALOGUE

🔊 195

Smith and Suzuki are meeting at the museum. Smith receives a phone call from Suzuki.

Suzuki: Sumisu-san, sumimasen.

             Nebōshimashita. Ima uchi o demashita.

Sumisu: Koko made donokurai kakarimasu ka.

Suzuki: 30-pun gurai kakarimasu.

Sumisu: Sō desu ka. Ja, 1-kai no kafe ni imasu.

Suzuki: Sumimasen.

■ **Suzuki-san no uchi kara hakubutsukan made 30-pun gurai kakarimasu.**

Suzuki: I'm sorry, Smith-san. I've overslept. I've just now left home.
Smith: How long will it take you to get here?
Suzuki: It will take about 30 minutes.
Smith: I see. Then I'll be in the café on the first floor.
Suzuki: I'm sorry.

■ It takes about 30 minutes from Suzuki-san's house to the museum.

VOCABULARY

nebōshimasu	oversleep	**kafe**	café
o	(particle; see GRAMMAR 2, p. 191)	**hakubutsukan**	museum
demasu (R2)	leave		
kakarimasu	take [time]		

KEY SENTENCES
 196

1. Sumisu-san wa Tōkyō Eki de shinkansen ni norimasu.
2. Sumisu-san wa Hiroshima Eki de shinkansen o orimasu.
3. Tōkyō kara Hiroshima made shinkansen de 4-jikan kakarimasu.
4. Sumisu-san wa Hiroshima ni 1-shūkan imasu.

1. Smith-san will take the Shinkansen from Tokyo Station.
2. Smith-san will get off the Shinkansen at Hiroshima Station.
3. It takes four hours from Tokyo to Hiroshima by Shinkansen.
4. Smith-san will be in Hiroshima for a week.

GRAMMAR

1. person **wa** place **de** transportation **ni norimasu.** (KS1)

When using **norimasu** ("get on"), the means of transportation toward which the action is taken takes the particle **ni**. Likewise, the point of arrival for **tsukimasu** ("arrive") takes **ni**.

e.g. **Sumisu-san wa 8-ji ni kaisha ni tsukimashita.**

Smith-san arrived at the office at 8:00.

2. person **wa** place **de** transportation **o orimasu.** (KS2)

When using **orimasu** ("get off"), the means of transportation that is the point of departure of the action takes the particle **o**. Likewise, the point of departure of **demasu** ("leave") takes the particle **o**.

e.g. **Sumisu-san wa 7-ji han ni uchi o demashita.**

Smith-san left home at 7:30.

3. place 1 **kara** place 2 **made** (transportation **de**) period **kakarimasu.** (KS3)

The verb **kakarimasu** means "take time" and is used when the speaker considers the time to be long. When the speaker does not feel the time to be long, "period **desu**" is used. The amount of time is placed immediately before the verb **kakarimasu** and no particle is needed after it. When the time given is approximate, **gurai** may be added.

e.g. **Uchi kara kaisha made 40-pun gurai kakarimasu.**

It takes about 40 minutes from my home to the office.

4. person **wa** place **ni** period **imasu.** (KS4)

The period spent in a certain place is placed immediately before the verb **imasu**, with no particle after it. When the time given is approximate, **gurai** may be added.

e.g. **Tanaka-san wa Rondon ni 3-nen gurai imashita.**

Tanaka-san stayed in London for about three years.

VOCABULARY

norimasu	get on, take [train, bus, etc.]	**1-shūkan (isshūkan)**	one week
Hiroshima Eki	Hiroshima Station	**imasu** (R2)	stay, be
Hiroshima	Hiroshima (city in western Japan)		
orimasu (R2)	get off		

WORD POWER

I Verbs

 197

    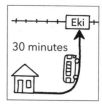

①norimasu　②orimasu　③demasu　④tsukimasu　⑤kakarimasu

II Periods

 198

	Minutes		Hours
5	go-fun (kan)	1	ichi-jikan
10	juppun (kan)	2	ni-jikan
15	jūgo-fun (kan)	3	san-jikan
20	nijuppun (kan)	4	yo-jikan
25	nijūgo-fun (kan)	5	go-jikan
30	sanjuppun (kan)	6	roku-jikan

	Days	Weeks	Months	Years
1	ichi-nichi	isshūkan	ikkagetsu (kan)	ichi-nen (kan)
2	futsuka (kan)	ni-shūkan	ni-kagetsu (kan)	ni-nen (kan)
3	mikka (kan)	san-shūkan	san-kagetsu (kan)	san-nen (kan)
4	yokka (kan)	yon-shūkan	yon-kagetsu (kan)	yo-nen (kan)
5	itsuka (kan)	go-shūkan	go-kagetsu (kan)	go-nen (kan)
6	muika (kan)	roku-shūkan	rokkagetsu (kan)	roku-nen (kan)

(see also APPENDIX G, pp. 248, 249)

NOTE 1: The **kan** in parentheses in the charts above can be added or omitted, but **kan** is often added when the speaker wants to clearly state a period of time.

NOTE 2: When **han** ("half") is added, the **han** comes after the counter. **Kan** indicated in parentheses is not added in this case.

e.g. **san-jikan han**　　three and a half hours
　　ichi-nen han　　one and a half years

VOCABULARY

tsukimasu	arrive	**-kagetsu (kan)**	...months
-fun/pun (kan)	...minutes	**-nen (kan)**	...years
-ka/nichi (kan)	...days		
-shūkan	...weeks		

EXERCISES

I *Practice conjugating verbs.* Repeat the verbs below and memorize their dictionary forms and **te**-forms.

	masu-form	Dictionary form	**te**-form
get on, take	norimasu	noru	notte
get off	orimasu	oriru	orite
leave	demasu	deru	dete
arrive	tsukimasu	tsuku	tsuite
take (time)	kakarimasu	kakaru	kakatte

II *State where someone will get on and get off a means of public transportation.* Make up sentences following the pattern of the example and based on the information provided.

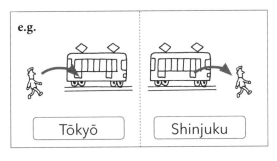
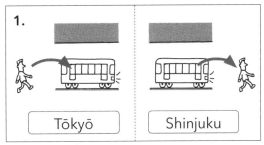
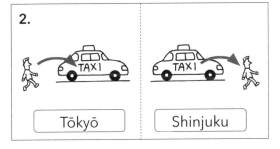

e.g. **Sumisu-san wa Tōkyō Eki de <u>densha</u> ni norimasu.**

Shinjuku Eki de <u>densha</u> o orimasu.

1. ....

2. ....

3. ....

III *State a person's departure and arrival time.* Make up sentences following the pattern of the example. Substitute the underlined parts with the alternatives given.

e.g. **Katō-san wa 7-ji ni uchi o demashita. 8-ji ni kaisha ni tsukimashita.**

1. ....

(10-ji ni hoteru, 11-ji ni kūkō)

2. ....

(asa Tōkyō, 1-ji goro Kyōto)

IV Make up dialogues following the patterns of the examples and based on the information provided.

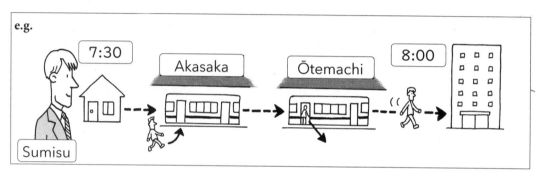

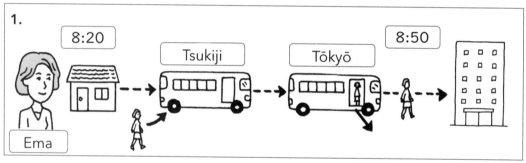

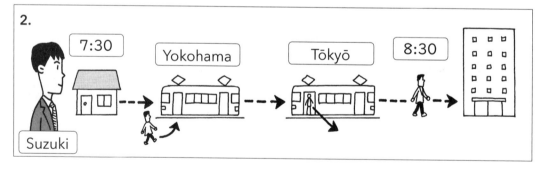

VOCABULARY

Akasaka	Akasaka (district in Tokyo)
Ōtemachi	Otemachi (district in Tokyo)
Tsukiji	Tsukiji (district in Tokyo)

A. *Ask and answer how one commutes to work.*

e.g. **Tanaka:** Sumisu-san wa dōyatte kaisha ni ikimasu ka.

Sumisu: Akasaka Eki de chikatetsu ni notte, Ōtemachi Eki de orimasu.
Eki kara kaisha made arukimasu.

1. Tanaka: Ema-san wa ....

Ema: ....

....

2. Tanaka: Suzuki-san wa ....

Suzuki: ....

....

B. *Ask and answer what time one leaves home and what time one arrives at the office.*

e.g. **Tanaka:** Mainichi nan-ji ni uchi o demasu ka.

Sumisu: 7-ji han ni demasu.

Tanaka: Nan-ji ni kaisha ni tsukimasu ka.

Sumisu: 8-ji ni tsukimasu.

1. Tanaka: ....

Ema: ....

Tanaka: ....

Ema: ....

2. Tanaka: ....

Suzuki: ....

Tanaka: ....

Suzuki: ....

dōyatte   how, in what way

195

V *Ask and answer how long it takes to get a particular place.* Make up dialogues following the pattern of the example and based on the information provided.

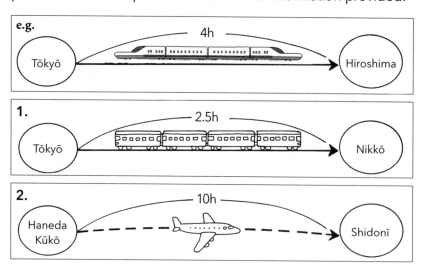

e.g. A: **Tōkyō** kara **Hiroshima** made donokurai kakarimasu ka.

B: **Shinkansen** de **4-jikan** gurai kakarimasu.

1. A: ....

   B: ....

2. A: ....

   B: ....

VI *Ask and answer how long one stayed in a particular place.* Make up dialogues following the pattern of the example. Substitute the underlined parts with the alternatives given.

e.g. Sumisu: Tanaka-san wa donokurai <u>Nyūyōku</u> ni imashita ka.

Tanaka: <u>Yokka</u> imashita.

1. Sumisu: .... (Honkon)

   Tanaka: .... (2-shūkan)

2. Sumisu: .... (Sapporo)

   Tanaka: .... (5-kagetsu)

3. Sumisu: .... (Rondon)

   Tanaka: .... (3-nen)

VOCABULARY

| **Haneda Kūkō** | Haneda Airport |
| **Nyūyōku** | New York |

VII *Talk about a vacation plan.* Make up dialogues following the pattern of the example. Substitute the underlined parts with the alternatives given.

> e.g. **Suzuki:** **Natsu-yasumi ni nani o shimasu ka.**
>
> **Nakamura:** <u>**Nyūyōku ni itte**</u>, <u>**myūjikaru o mimasu**</u>.
>
> **Suzuki:** **Sō desu ka. Donokurai** <u>**Nyūyōku**</u> **ni imasu ka.**
>
> **Nakamura:** <u>**1-shūkan**</u> **imasu.**
>
> **Suzuki:** **Ii desu ne.**

1. Suzuki: ....

   Nakamura: ....

   (Okinawa, daibingu o shimasu)

   Suzuki: ....

   (Okinawa)

   Nakamura: ....

   (muika)

   Suzuki: ....

2. Suzuki: ....

   Nakamura: ....

   (Kyōto, o-tera o mimasu)

   Suzuki: ....

   (Kyōto)

   Nakamura: ....

   (itsuka)

   Suzuki: ....

VIII Listen to the audio and fill in the blanks based on the information you hear. 🔊 199-201

1. Chan-san wa .... ni uchi o dete, ... ni kaisha ni tsukimasu.

2. Tōkyō kara Kamakura made .... de .... gurai kakarimasu.

3. Ema-san wa Hokkaidō ni .... imasu.

VOCABULARY

myūjikaru	musical
daibingu o shimasu	scuba dive

SPEAKING PRACTICE

1. Paul is at Akihabara Station. 🔊 202

> **Pōru:** Tōkyō Dōmu ni ikitai n desu ga.
> **Ekiin:** 5-bansen no densha ni notte, Suidōbashi de orite kudasai.
> **Pōru:** Sui... nan desu ka.
> **Ekiin:** Suidōbashi desu. Koko kara futatsu-me desu.
> **Pōru:** Arigatō gozaimasu.

Paul:	I would like to go to Tokyo Dome.
Station employee:	Take the train at Platform 5 and get off at Suidobashi.
Paul:	Sui . . . what?
Station employee:	Suidobashi. It's the second station from here.
Paul:	Thank you very much.

NOTES

1. **Tōkyō Dōmu ni ikitai n desu ga.**

   Tōkyō Dōmu ni ikitai desu indicates that the speaker wants to go to Tokyo Dome, but when changed to **Tōkyō Dōmu ni ikitai n desu ga**, the implication is that the speaker seeks advice and information about what train to take and from where. This **...n desu ga** is actually a preliminary, which would be followed by a question such as "which train should I take?" However, since it is clear to the listener from the situation what the speaker is asking for, the question part is omitted.

2. **Sui... nan desu ka.**

   When you have been unable to make out completely what the speaker said and you want it to be repeated, state the part that was audible and, after a brief pause, add **nan desu ka.**

 **Active Communication** If you're in Japan, ask a station employee the route and time required to get to a place you want to go to.

VOCABULARY

Tōkyō Dōmu	Tokyo Dome	**5-bansen**	Platform 5
ikitai n desu ga	I'd like to go	**-bansen**	platform...
ekiin	station employee	**Suidōbashi**	Suidobashi (station in Tokyo)

Asking Permission: May I Have It?

TARGET DIALOGUE

🔊 203

Smith and Suzuki are at at the museum.

Sumisu:	**Kore wa mukashi no o-kane desu ka.**
Suzuki:	**Ee, sō desu.**
	A, koko ni Eigo no panfuretto ga arimasu yo.
Sumisu:	**Sō desu ne.**
	(Going over to a museum staff.) **Sumimasen.**
	Kono panfuretto o moratte mo ii desu ka.
Hakubutsukan no hito:	**Hai, dōzo.**

(Smith and Suzuki look around the exhibit.)

Suzuki:	**Tsukaremashita ne.**
Sumisu:	**Sō desu ne. Ashi ga itai desu.**
	(Sees an object that looks like a chair, and asks the museum staff.)
	Sumimasen. Koko ni suwatte mo ii desu ka.
Hakubutsukan no hito:	**Hai, dōzo.**

■ **Sumisu-san wa hakubutsukan de Eigo no panfuretto o moraimashita.**

Smith:	Are these coins from a long time ago?
Suzuki:	Yes, that's right. Oh, there are English-language pamphlets over here.
Smith:	I see. Excuse me, may I have a copy of this pamphlet?
Museum staff:	Yes, please.
Suzuki:	It's tiring, isn't it?
Smith:	Yes, my legs hurt.
	Excuse me. Is it all right to sit down here?
Museum staff:	Yes, that's fine.

■ Smith-san got an English pamphlet at the museum.

VOCABULARY

mukashi	a long time ago	**ashi**	foot, leg	**suwatte mo ii desu ka**	May I sit [here]?
Eigo	English	**itai**	hurt, sore, painful	**suwarimasu**	sit down
panfuretto	pamphlet	**ni**	on (particle; see		
moratte mo ii desu ka	May I have . . . ?		GRAMMAR 2, p. 200)		

199

KEY SENTENCES

 204

1. Kono e no shashin o totte mo ii desu ka.
2. Koko ni suwatte mo ii desu ka.
3. (Watashi wa) atama ga itai desu.

1. May I take a photo of this painting?
2. May I sit here?
3. I have a headache.

GRAMMAR

1. verb [**te**-form] **mo ii desu ka.** (KS1, 2)

This expression is used when asking permission for something. When responding affirmatively, one says **Hai, dōzo**; when responding negatively, one says **Sumimasen ga, chotto....**

2. place/thing **ni** (KS2)

Actions such as **kakimasu** ("write, draw"), **suwarimasu** ("sit down"), **okimasu** ("put"), or **tomemasu** ("park") are performed with reference to a place or thing. When there is some result of the action, the noun indicating the place or thing takes the particle **ni**.

> e.g. **Koko ni namae o kaite kudasai.**
>
>   Please write your name here.

3. (**Watashi wa**) body part **ga itai desu.** (KS3)

This expression is used when stating that some part of the body hurts. The painful part of the body takes the particle **ga**. The subject of the sentence is always the speaker, and **watashi wa** is usually omitted.

(shashin o) totte mo ii desu ka	May I take [photos]?
atama	head

WORD POWER

❶ Verbs

🔊 205

①tsukaimasu

②suwarimasu

③hairimasu

④okimasu

⑤akemasu

⑥shimemasu

⑦tsukemasu

⑧keshimasu

❷ Parts of the body

🔊 206

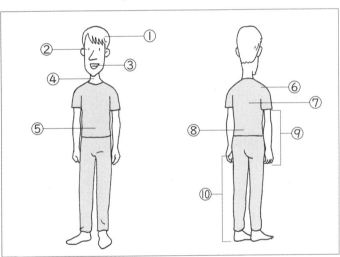

①atama	③ha	⑤onaka	⑦senaka	⑨te
②me	④nodo	⑥kata	⑧koshi	⑩ashi

❸ Symptoms

🔊 207

①Atama ga itai desu.

②Kibun ga warui desu.

③Netsu ga arimasu.

VOCABULARY

tsukaimasu	use	**tsukemasu** (R2)	turn on	**onaka**	stomach, belly	**kibun ga warui**	feel sick, unwell
hairimasu	enter	**keshimasu**	turn off	**kata**	shoulder	**kibun**	feeling
okimasu	put, place	**me**	eye	**senaka**	back	**netsu ga arimasu**	have a fever
akemasu (R2)	open	**ha**	tooth	**koshi**	lower back	**netsu**	fever
shimemasu (R2)	close	**nodo**	throat				

EXERCISES

I *Practice conjugating verbs.* Repeat the verbs below and memorize their **te**-forms.

	masu-form	te-form
use	tsukaimasu	tsukatte
sit down	suwarimasu	suwatte
enter	hairimasu	haitte
put, place	okimasu	oite
open	akemasu	akete
close	shimemasu	shimete
turn on	tsukemasu	tsukete
turn off	keshimasu	keshite

II *Ask permission to do something.* Make up sentences following the pattern of the example.

e.g. **Kono panfuretto o moraimasu.**

→ **Kono panfuretto o moratte mo ii desu ka.**

1. Mado o akemasu.

   → ....

2. Kāten o shimemasu.

   → ....

3. Denki o tsukemasu.

   → ....

4. Ashita yasumimasu.

   → ....

5. Kono heya ni hairimasu.

   → ....

6. Koko ni nimotsu o okimasu.

   → ....

VOCABULARY

mado	window
kāten	curtain
denki	lights
yasumimasu	take a day off

III *Ask and grant permission to do something.* Make up dialogues following the pattern of the example and based on the information provided.

e.g. **Suzuki:** <u>**Shiryō o kopīshite** mo ii desu ka.**</u>

Toshokan no hito: Hai, dōzo.

1. Suzuki: ....

   Toshokan no hito: ....

2. Suzuki: ....

   Toshokan no hito: ....

3. Suzuki: ....

   Toshokan no hito: ....

4. Suzuki: ....

   Toshokan no hito: ....

VOCABULARY

kopīshimasu	make a copy
jūdenshimasu	recharge

IV *Ask and refuse permission to do something.* Make up dialogues following the pattern of the example and based on the information provided.

e.g. **Sumisu:**   <u>Koko de shokuji o shite</u> mo ii desu ka.

O-tera no hito: Sumimasen ga, chotto....

1. Sumisu: ....

    O-tera no hito: ....

2. Sumisu: ....

    O-tera no hito: ....

3. Sumisu: ....

    O-tera no hito: ....

V *Ask permission to do something.* Make up dialogues following the pattern of the example. Substitute the underlined parts with the alternatives given.

e.g. **Sumisu:**   Sumimasen. Kaigi-shitsu de <u>benkyōshite</u> mo ii desu ka.

Uketsuke no hito: Hai, dōzo.

Sumisu: <u>4-ji</u> made tsukatte mo ii desu ka.

Uketsuke no hito: Hai, dōzo.

Sumisu: Arigatō gozaimasu.

VOCABULARY

niwa   garden, yard

1. Sumisu: ....
(hiru-gohan o tabemasu)

Uketsuke no hito: ....

Sumisu: .... (1:30)

Uketsuke no hito: ....

Sumisu: ....

2. Sumisu: ....
(hon o yomimasu)

Uketsuke no hito: ....

Sumisu: .... (7:30)

Uketsuke no hito: ....

Sumisu: ....

Ⅵ *State a request of another person.* Look at the illustrations and make up sentences following the pattern of the example. Substitute the underlined parts with the appropriate forms of the alternatives given.

e.g. <u>Tēburu no ue ni</u> <u>nimotsu o oite</u> kudasai.

1. .... (koko, namae o kakimasu)

2. .... (sono isu, suwarimasu)

3. ....
(ano chūsha-jō, kuruma o tomemasu)

VOCABULARY

tomemasu (R2)   park

VII *Ask for permission to borrow a pen.* Make up a dialogue based on the information provided.

1. Mise no hito: ....

2. Sumisu: ....

3. Sumisu: ....

4. Mise no hito: ....

5. Sumisu: ....

VIII *State which part of your body hurts.* Make up sentences following the pattern of the example. Substitute the underlined part with the alternatives given.

e.g. **(Watashi wa)** <u>atama</u> **ga itai desu.**

1. .... (ha)

2. .... (onaka)

3. .... (ashi)

IX *Tell a doctor one's symptoms.* Make up dialogues following the pattern of the example and based on the information provided.

e.g. **Isha:**   **Dō shimashita ka.**

Chan: **Kibun ga warui desu.**

1. Isha: ....

   Chan: ....

2. Isha: ....

   Chan: ....

3. Isha: ....

   Chan: ....

X Listen to the audio and fill in the blanks based on the information you hear. 🔊 208, 209

1. Sumisu-san wa .... kara .... o tsukaimasu.

2. Smith came to the Japanese-language school.

   Sumisu-san wa Nihon-go no kurasu no panfuretto o ....

VOCABULARY	
38-do	38 degrees
-do	...degree
isha	medical doctor
Dō shimashita ka.	What seems to be the problem? (see NOTES 2, p. 208)

SPEAKING PRACTICE

1. Green is at the home appliances store.
🔊 210

Gurīn:	Sumimasen. Kono terebi o todokete kudasai.
Mise no hito:	Hai, koko ni go-jūsho to o-namae o onegaishimasu.
Gurīn:	Rōmaji de kaite mo ii desu ka.
Mise no hito:	Hai.

Green:	Excuse me. Please deliver this TV [for me].
Salesperson:	Yes. Please fill in your address and name here.
Green:	May I write it in romaji?
Salesperson:	Yes.

2. Green is at the clinic.
🔊 211

Isha:	Dō shimashita ka.
Gurīn:	Sumimasen. Eigo de hanashite mo ii desu ka.
Isha:	Hai, dōzo.

Doctor:	What seems to be the problem?
Green:	Excuse me. May I speak in English?
Doctor:	Yes. Go ahead.

NOTES

1. Rōmaji de kaite mo ii desu ka.

When indicating the means of communication for writing or speaking (characters or language), use the particle **de**.

2. Dō shimashita ka.

This is a doctor's standard query to a patient to learn what symptoms he/she has, meaning "what seems to be the problem?" It is also used when asking people in need and means "what is the matter?"

Active Communication

If you're in Japan, go to various stores or public institutions and ask permission to do something—to take a photograph, for example.

VOCABULARY

rōmaji	romaji, romanized Japanese

Forbidding Actions: Please Don't Take Photos

TARGET DIALOGUE

🔊 212

Smith and Suzuki are at the museum.

Sumisu:	**Kireina kimono desu ne.**
Suzuki:	**Hontō ni kirei desu ne.**
	Kore wa 300-nen gurai mae no kimono desu.
Sumisu:	**Sō desu ka. Imōto ni misetai desu.**
	(Takes a photo.)
Hakubutsukan no hito:	**Sumimasen. Koko de shashin o toranaide kudasai.**
Sumisu:	**Wakarimashita. Sumimasen.**
Suzuki:	**Sumisu-san, asoko ni mo kireina kimono ga arimasu yo.**
Sumisu:	**A, sō desu ne. Ikimashō.**

Smith:	Isn't that a beautiful kimono.
Suzuki:	Yes, it certainly is beautiful.
	This is a kimono from about 300 years ago.
Smith:	Is that so? I want to show this to my sister.
Museum staff:	Excuse me. Please do not take photos here.
Smith:	I understand. I'm sorry.
Suzuki:	Smith-san, over there, too, is another beautiful kimono.
Smith:	Ah, I see. Let's go.

VOCABULARY

kimono	kimono
... mae	. . . ago
imōto	(my) younger sister
toranaide kudasai	please don't take [photos]

KEY SENTENCES

 213

1. Koko wa deguchi desu kara, kuruma o tomenaide kudasai.
2. Wasabi o irenaide kudasai.
3. Eki no mae ni konbini ga arimasu.
   Eki no naka ni mo (konbini ga) arimasu.

1. This is the exit, so please do not park your car here.
2. Please do not add wasabi.
3. There is a convenience store in front of the station. There is another (convenience store) inside the station.

GRAMMAR

1. Verb **nai**-form
(KS1, 2)

To form the **nai**-form of Regular 1 verbs, change the sound before **masu**, as shown in the chart below and add **nai**. The rule for Regular 2 verbs is simple; simply remove **masu** and add **nai**. The rule for Irregular verbs is irregular, as shown in the chart below.

	Regular 1			Regular 2	
	masu-form	**nai**-form		**masu**-form	**nai**-form
buy	kaimasu	kawanai	see	mimasu	minai
go	ikimasu	ikanai	be	imasu	inai
swim	oyogimasu	oyaganai	eat	tabemasu	tabenai
lend	kashimasu	kasanai	tell, teach	oshiemasu	oshienai
wait	machimasu	matanai		Irregular	
drink	nomimasu	nomanai	come	kimasu	konai
return, go home	kaerimasu	kaeranai	do	shimasu	shinai

2. verb [**nai**-form] **de kudasai.**
(KS1, 2)

This is the sentence pattern used when stating "please do not [do such and such]." This is a fairly strong expression which is used by managers or officials when giving instructions to people. When wishing to soften the expression, in most cases it is used along with some reason the action should not be taken (KS1). This expression can also be used when asking that a certain ingredient not be used in a dish (KS2).

3. place **ni mo** noun **ga arimasu.**
(KS3)

When the particle **mo** is attached to a noun phrase indicating the location of something, the particle **ni** is retained and **mo** is added after it. Generally, when desiring to add the meaning of "also," the particles **ga, wa, o** can be replaced by **mo** but for other particles, the **mo** is simply added.

VOCABULARY

tomenaide kudasai	please don't park
wasabi	wasabi
irenaide kudasai	please don't add/put in
iremasu (R2)	put in, add

WORD POWER

I Verbs

🔊 214

① tachimasu

② sawarimasu

③ iremasu

④ tabako o suimasu

II nai-form

🔊 215

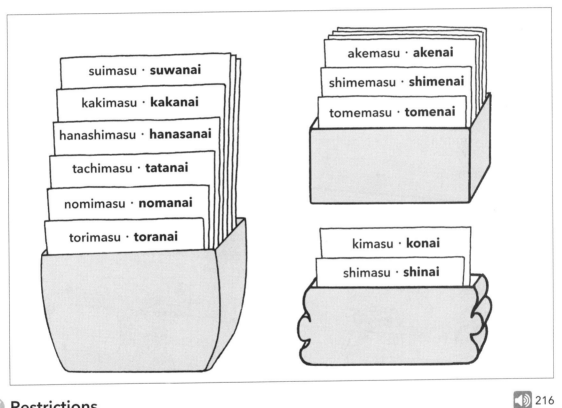

suimasu · **suwanai**

kakimasu · **kakanai**

hanashimasu · **hanasanai**

tachimasu · **tatanai**

nomimasu · **nomanai**

torimasu · **toranai**

akemasu · **akenai**

shimemasu · **shimenai**

tomemasu · **tomenai**

kimasu · **konai**

shimasu · **shinai**

III Restrictions

🔊 216

① tachiiri-kinshi

② chūsha-kinshi

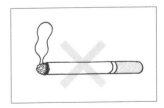

③ kin'en

VOCABULARY

tachimasu	stand up	chūsha-kinshi	no parking
sawarimasu	touch	kin'en	no smoking
tabako o suimasu	smoke a cigarette		
tachiiri-kinshi	no entry		

Ⅳ Adjective

 217

abunai

EXERCISES

Ⅰ *Practice making **nai**-forms.* Change the following verbs to their **nai**-forms.

e.g. **aimasu** → **awanai**

1. hanashimasu → ....
2. misemasu → ....
3. sawarimasu → ....
4. oyogimasu → ....
5. kaimasu → ....

6. agemasu → ....
7. tachimasu → ....
8. kikimasu → ....
9. kimasu → ....
10. shimasu → ....

Ⅱ *Forbid someone to do something.* Make up sentences following the pattern of the example and based on the illustration provided.

e.g. **Mado o akemasu.** → **Mado o akenaide kudasai.**

1. Shashin o torimasu. → ....
2. Doa o shimemasu. → ....
3. Denki o keshimasu. → ....
4. Kabin ni sawarimasu. → ....

VOCABULARY

abunai	dangerous
doa	door
kabin	vase

III *Forbid someone to park with a reason.* Make up sentences following the pattern of the example. Substitute the underlined part with the alternatives given.

e.g. **Koko wa** <u>iriguchi</u> **desu kara, kuruma o tomenaide kudasai.**

1. .... (deguchi)

2. .... (mise no mae)

3. .... (chūsha-kinshi)

IV *Forbid someone to do something with a reason.* Make up dialogues following the pattern of the example. Substitute the underlined parts with the appropriate forms of the alternatives given.

e.g. **A:** <u>**Koko wa tachiiri-kinshi**</u> **desu kara,** <u>**hairanaide**</u> **kudasai.**

B: Hai, wakarimashita. Sumimasen.

1. A: ....
   (koko wa kin'en, tabako o suimasu)

   B: ....

2. A: ....
   (abunai, tachimasu)

   B: ....

| iriguchi   entrance

V *State that the same thing is found in two places.* Make up sentences following the pattern of the example. Substitute the underlined parts with the alternatives given.

    e.g. **<u>Nikkō</u> ni <u>onsen</u> ga arimasu.**

        <u>Hakone</u> ni mo arimasu.

Nikkō   Hakone

1. ....

(2-kai, kaigi-shitsu, 3-gai)

2. ....

(tēburu no ue, bīru, reizōko no naka)

VI *Ask and answer that there is the same thing in two places.* Make up dialogues following the pattern of the example. Substitute the underlined parts with the alternatives given.

    e.g. **A: Sumimasen. Kono chikaku ni <u>konbini</u> ga arimasu ka.**

        B: Ee, <u>eki no mae</u> ni arimasu.

        Sorekara, <u>eki no naka</u> ni mo arimasu yo.

        A: Sō desu ka. Arigatō gozaimasu.

1. A: .... (kōen)

   B: ....

   B: .... (byōin no mae, gakkō no tonari)

   A: ....

2. A: .... (chūsha-jō)

   B: ....

   B: .... (ano biru no tonari, depāto no chika)

   A: ....

VII *At a restaurant, ask that a specific ingredient not be put into the food.* Make up dialogues following the pattern of the example. Substitute the underlined parts with the alternatives given.

    e.g. **Chan:**   <u>Hanbāgā</u> o onegaishimasu.

    Mise no hito: Hai.

    Chan: Sumimasen ga, <u>kechappu</u> o irenaide kudasai.

    Mise no hito: Hai, wakarimashita.

1. Chan: .... (o-sushi)

   Mise no hito: ....

   Chan: .... (wasabi)

   Mise no hito: ....

2. Chan: .... (sandoitchi)

   Mise no hito: ....

   Chan: .... (mayonēzu)

   Mise no hito: ....

3. Chan: .... (chīzu-bāgā)

   Mise no hito: ....

   Chan: .... (tomato)

   Mise no hito: ....

VIII Listen to the audio and fill in the blanks based on the information you hear. 🔊 218-220

1. .... to .... ni otearai ga arimasu.

2. .... to .... ni konbini ga arimasu.

3. 3-ji kara .... ga arimasu kara, Nakamura-san wa kaigi-shitsu no

   eakon o ....

VOCABULARY

hanbāgā	hamburger		**tomato**	tomato
kechappu	ketchup			
mayonēzu	mayonnaise			
chīzu-bāgā	cheese burger			

SPEAKING PRACTICE

1. Smith got tipsy at Sasaki's house yesterday and spilled red wine on her carpet. 🔊 221

    Sumisu: Sasaki-san, ohayō gozaimasu.
    Sasaki: Ohayō gozaimasu.
    Sumisu: Kinō wa sumimasendeshita.
    Sasaki: Iie, dōzo ki ni shinaide kudasai.

    Smith: Good morning, Sasaki-san.
    Sasaki: Good morning.
    Smith: I'm very sorry about yesterday.
    Sasaki: Oh, that's all right. Please don't worry about it.

2. Smith has a pain in his stomach and is being examined by a doctor. 🔊 222

    Isha: Kyō wa o-sake o nomanaide kudasai.
    Sumisu: Hai, wakarimashita.

    Doctor: Please do not have any alcohol today.
    Smith: Yes. I understand.

Active Communication

A stranger is trying to park in front of your house. What would you say?

Ki ni shinaide kudasai.	Please don't worry about it.
ki ni shimasu	worry about
(o-) sake	alcoholic drink, sake

AT WORK AND AFTER WORK

Businesspeople in Japan often go out to enjoy eating and drinking in the evening after work. This custom is a product of the belief that when they can get to know each other better it is easier to work together. There are also various traditional events that bring people together to savor some seasonal highlight. Among such events, people look forward especially to the "cherry blossom viewing" parties held to eat and drink beneath the cherry trees in spring, and these parties are held as regular annual events in some companies.

Explaining Actions: What Are You Doing Now?

TARGET DIALOGUE

🔊 223

Kato has asked Smith to prepare for a meeting.

Katō: Mō kaigi no junbi wa dekimashita ka.

Sumisu: Sumimasen. Mada desu. Kaigi-shitsu wa yoyakushimashita ga, shiryō wa ima tsukutte imasu.

Katō: Sō desu ka. 3-ji made ni owarimasu ka.

Sumisu: Hai, mō sugu dekimasu.

(15 minutes later)

Sumisu: Katō-san, shiyrō ga dekimashita.

          Chekku o onegaishimasu.

Katō: Hai.

Kato: Have you finished preparing for the meeting?
Smith: I'm sorry. I have not finished yet. I reserved the meeting room,
         but I am now preparing the materials.
Kato: I see. Will you finish by three o'clock?
Smith: Yes, I will be ready soon.
Smith: Kato-san, the materials are ready. Please check them.
Kato: All right.

mō	already	**yoyakushimasu**	make a reservation	**mō sugu**	soon
junbi	preparation	**tsukutte imasu**	be making	**chekku**	check
dekimasu (R2)	be done	**tsukurimasu**	make		
mada desu	not yet	**owarimasu**	finish		

218

> NOTES

1. **Mō kaigi no junbi wa dekimashita ka.**
   Shiryō ga dekimashita.
   When the information about what is done or finished in using the verb **dekimasu/owarimasu** is new to the listener, the pattern of the second sentence is used: noun **ga dekimashita/owarimashita**. In the first sentence, Kato has already taken up the topic **kaigi no junbi**, so the particle **ga** is replaced with **wa**. The **mō** ("already") can be placed at the beginning or later in the sentence.

KEY SENTENCES

 224

1. **Sumisu-san wa ima hiru-gohan o tabete imasu.**
2. **Sumisu-san wa Nihon-go o naratte imasu.**
3. **Mō repōto o yomimashita ka.**
4. **Gurīn-san wa tenpura wa suki desu ga, o-sushi wa suki ja arimasen.**

1. Smith-san is eating his lunch now.
2. Smith-san is taking Japanese lessons.
3. Have you already read the report?
4. Green-san likes tempura, but he does not like sushi.

> GRAMMAR

1. **person wa verb [te-form] imasu. (1)**   (KS1, 2)

The present progressive form ("is doing") is formed by adding **imasu** to the verb **te**-form. (KS1)
The **te**-form **imasu** can also be used to express an action intentionally repeated over a certain period of time. (KS2)

2. **Mō verb [masu-form stem] mashita ka.**   (KS3)

The past form of a verb may express not just the simple past but the completion of an action. Here, by adding **mō**, the speaker asks whether the action has already been completed.
To respond, the listener says:

> **Hai,** verb [**masu**-form stem] **mashita.**   Yes, I have . . . .
> **Iie, mada desu.**   No, not yet.

3. **wa for contrast**   (KS4)

When contrasting two things, the particle **wa** is added after both words. When the particle of the word with which the contrast is made is **ga** or **o**, it is replaced with **wa**. When the particle is any other than **ga** or **o**, the particle **wa** is added.

> e.g. **Wain o nomimasu. Bīru o nomimasen.**   (I) drink wine. (I) don't drink beer.
>   →**Wain wa nomimasu ga, bīru wa nomimasen.**   (I) drink wine, but not beer.
>
>   **Tanaka-san ni aimashita. Yamada-san ni aimasendeshita.**
>   (I) met Tanaka-san. (I) didn't meet Yamada-san.
>   →**Tanaka-san ni wa aimashita ga, Yamada-san ni wa aimasendeshita.**
>   (I) met Tanaka-san, but not Yamada-san.

> VOCABULARY

tabete imasu	be eating
naratte imasu	be taking lessons in

WORD POWER

Ⅰ Verbs

 225

①setsumei o shimasu

②sōji o shimasu

③owarimasu

④tsukurimasu

⑤dekimasu

Ⅱ Lessons

 226

①shodō

②gitā

③Furansu-go

VOCABULARY

setsumei o shimasu	explain	**Furansu-go**	French
sōji o shimasu	clean		
shodō	calligraphy		
gitā	guitar		

EXERCISES

I *Practice conjugating verbs.* Repeat the verbs below and memorize their **te imasu**-forms—affirmative and negative.

	masu-form	te imasu-form	
		aff.	*neg.*
explain	setsumei o shimasu	setsumei o shite imasu	setsumei o shite imasen
make	tsukurimasu	tsukutte imasu	tsukutte imasen
drink	nomimasu	nonde imasu	nonde imasen
talk	hanashimasu	hanashite imasu	hanashite imasen

II *State what someone is doing now.* Change the sentences following the pattern of the example.

e.g. **Sumisu-san wa sōji o shimasu.**

→ **Sumisu-san wa sōji o shite imasu.**

1. Sumisu-san wa shinbun o yomimasu.

→ ....

2. Sumisu-san wa mēru o kakimasu.

→ ....

3. Sumisu-san wa kopī o shimasu.

→ ....

4. Sumisu-san wa Tanaka-san to hanashimasu.

→ ....

5. Sumisu-san wa onrain-kaigi o shimasu.

→ ....

6. Sumisu-san wa purojekuto no setsumei o shimasu.

→ ....

VOCABULARY

shinbun	newspaper
kopī o shimasu	make a copy
onrain-kaigi o shimasu	have an online meeting
purojekuto	project

Ⅲ Make up dialogues following the patterns of the examples and based on the information provided.

A. *Ask and answer what one is doing now.*

e.g. 1. A: Gurīn-san wa ima nani o shite imasu ka.

B: Denwa o shite imasu.

1. A: ....

B: ....

2. A: ....

B: ....

3. A: ....

B: ....

4. A: ....

B: ....

5. A: ....

B: ....

B. *Answer what one is doing now.*

    e.g. 2. **A: Katō-san wa ima shiryō o tsukutte imasu ka.**

        B: Iie, purojekuto no setsumei o shite imasu.

6. A: Sasaki-san wa ima kōhī o nonde imasu ka.

    B: ....

7. A: Ema-san wa ima Sasaki-san to hanashite imasu ka.

    B: ....

8. A: Nakamura-san wa ima denwa o shite imasu ka.

    B: ....

IV *State what someone does every week.* Make up sentences following the pattern of the example. Substitute the underlined parts with the alternatives given.

    e.g. Sumisu-san wa maishū Nihon-go o naratte imasu.

1. ....

                                                 (Nakamura-san, ikebana)

2. ....

                                                   (Katō-san, gitā)

3. ....

                                                   (Ema-san, shodō)

4. ....

                                              (Suzuki-san, Furansu-go)

V Make up dialogues following the patterns of the examples. Substitute the underlined parts with the appropriate forms of the alternatives given.

A. *Ask and answer whether one has completed an action.*

    e.g. A: Mō hiru-gohan o tabemashita ka.

        B: Hai, tabemashita.

1. A : .... (resutoran, yoyakushimasu)

    B : .... (yoyakushimasu)

2. A : .... (repōto, kakimasu)

    B : .... (kakimasu)

B. *Ask and answer whether one has completed an action.*

e.g. **A:** <u>Sōji</u> wa mō owarimashita ka.

     B: Iie, mada desu.

1. A: .... (daunrōdo)

     B: ....

2. A: .... (kanji no benkyō)

     B: ....

C. *State that one is in the midst of something.*

e.g. **A:** <u>Kaigi no shiryō</u> wa mō dekimashita ka.

     B: Ima <u>tsukutte</u> imasu. **Mō sukoshi matte kudasai.**

1. A: .... (repōto)

     B: .... (kakimasu)

2. A: .... (purezen no junbi)

     B: .... (shimasu)

3. A: .... (hiru-gohan)

     B: .... (tsukurimasu)

Ⅵ *State two contrasting things.* Make up sentences following the pattern of the example and based on the information provided.

suki desu

yasumi desu

shimasu

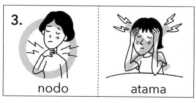

itai desu

VOCABULARY

daunrōdo	download
kanji	kanji
mō sukoshi	a little longer
sunōbōdo o shimasu	snowboard

e.g. **Kōcha wa suki desu ga, kōhī wa suki ja arimasen.**

1. ....

2. ....

3. ....

Ⅶ *Talk about what someone is doing where.* Make up dialogues following the pattern of the example. Substitute the underlined parts with the appropriate forms of the alternatives given.

e.g. **Chan:** **Nakamura-san, Ema-san wa doko desu ka.**

Nakamura: **3-gai no kaigi-shitsu desu.**

Chan: **Sō desu ka.**

Nakamura: **Ima Nozomi Depāto no Tanaka-san ni atarashii shōhin no setsumei o shite imasu.**

Chan: **Wakarimashita. Arigatō.**

1. Chan: .... (Suzuki-san)

   Nakamura: .... (1-kai no kafe)

   Chan: ....

   Nakamura: ....
   .... (o-kyaku-san to hanashimasu)

   Chan: ....

2. Chan: .... (Sumisu-san)

   Nakamura: .... (6-kai no kaigi-shitsu)

   Chan: ....

   Nakamura: ....
   .... (purezen no junbi o shimasu)

   Chan: ....

| shōhin | product, goods |
| junbi o shimasu | prepare |

VIII Listen to the audio and fill in the blanks based on the information you hear. 🔊227-229

1. Sumisu-san wa _____ ni Nihon-go o _____.

2. Sumisu-san wa ima _____ de o-kyaku-san to
_____.

3. Ema-san wa ima purezen no _____ o _____.

SPEAKING PRACTICE

1. Smith is at the dry cleaners.   🔊230

Sumisu: **Kore, onegaishimasu. Itsu dekimasu ka.**
Mise no hito: Sui-yōbi no yūgata dekimasu.

Smith: Here [is what I have today]. When will it be ready?
Laundry staff: It will be ready Wednesday evening.

2. On a holiday, Chan calls Emma.   🔊231

Ema: Moshimoshi.
Chan: Chan desu. Ima ii desu ka.
Ema: Sumimasen. Ima ryōri o shite imasu.
Chan: Ja, mata ato de denwashimasu.
Ema: Onegaishimasu.

Emma: Hello?
Chan: This is Chan. Can you talk now?
Emma: I'm sorry. I'm cooking now.
Chan: Okay. I'll call you back later.
Emma: Please do!

VOCABULARY

yūgata	evening	**ato de**	later
Moshimoshi.	Hello. (greeting when making or answering a telephone call) (see NOTES 1, p. 227)	**denwashimasu**	telephone, call (see APPENDIX D, p. 246)

3. Kato and Smith are talking during their break.

🔊 232

Katō: Sumisu-san, nani ka undō o shite imasu ka.
Sumisu: Ee, tokidoki jogingu o shite imasu.
Katō: Shigoto no ato desu ka.
Sumisu: Iie, asa hashitte imasu.

Kato: Smith-san, are you doing any kind of exercise?
Smith: Yes, sometimes I go jogging.
Kato: You do that after work?
Smith: No, I go running in the morning.

NOTES

1. **Moshimoshi.**

   When calling on the phone, this expression is used as a greeting by both the caller and the recipient of the call. It is not much used in a business environment.

2. **Ima ii desu ka.**

   This is the expression used to ask whether the person called is free to speak.

3. **Nani ka undō o shite imasu ka.**

   When **nani ka** is used by itself, it means "something," but when it is used together with a noun, as in "**nani ka** + noun," it means "some/any noun." **nani ka undō** means "any [kind of] exercise."

Active Communication

Imagine that you are involved in some activity that you can't break away from, and a call comes in on your cell phone. Explain to the person on the phone why it is inconvenient for you to talk at the moment.

VOCABULARY

undō o shimasu	do exercise
jogingu o shimasu	jog

Work and Interests: I Work for an Apparel Maker

TARGET DIALOGUE

🔊 233

The staff of the office are together at an *izakaya* drinking place. Smith's younger sister Lisa, who is visiting Japan, joins them.

Suzuki: Sumisu-san, imōto-san wa Nihon-go ga wakarimasu ka.

Sumisu: Hai, sukoshi wakarimasu yo.

(Lisa arrives and is talking as they are drinking.)

Suzuki: Risa-san, o-shigoto wa?

Risa: Dezainā desu. Nyūyōku no apareru-mēkā ni tsutomete imasu.

Suzuki: O-shigoto wa tanoshii desu ka.

Risa: Ee, totemo tanoshii desu.
　　　　Watashi no yume wa jibun no burando o tsukuru koto desu.

Suzuki: Sō desu ka. Ganbatte kudasai.

Risa: Hai, arigatō gozaimasu.

■ Risa-san wa Nyūyōku no apareru-mēkā ni tsutomete imasu.
　Yume wa jibun no burando o tsukuru koto desu.

Suzuki: Smith-san, does your sister understand Japanese?
Smith: Yes, she understands a little.
Suzuki: Lisa-san, may I ask what work you are doing?
Lisa: I am a designer. I work for an apparel maker in New York.
Suzuki: Do you enjoy your work?
Lisa: Yes, I really enjoy my work. My dream is to create my own brand.
Suzuki: Really. I hope it works out.
Lisa: Yes, thank you.

■ Lisa-san works for an apparel maker in New York. Her dream is to create her own brand of apparel.

VOCABULARY

imōto-san	(another person's) younger sister	**apareru**	apparel	**burando**	brand
		mēkā	maker	**koto**	(nominalizer; see GRAMMAR 4, p. 229)
wakarimasu	understand	**tsutomete imasu**	work for, be employed		
o-shigoto	your work			**Ganbatte kudasai.**	I hope it works out.
dezainā	designer	**yume**	dream	**ganbarimasu**	do one's best
apareru-mēkā	apparel maker	**jibun no**	one's own		

234

KEY SENTENCES

1. Sumisu-san wa Tōkyō ni sunde imasu.
2. Sumisu-san wa Nihon-go ga wakarimasu.
3. Sumisu-san wa Chan-san o shitte imasu.
4. Sumisu-san no shumi wa hon o yomu koto desu.

1. Smith-san lives in Tokyo.
2. Smith-san understands Japanese.
3. Smith-san knows Chan-san.
4. Smith-san's hobby is reading.

GRAMMAR

1. person wa verb [te-form] imasu. (2) (KS1, 3)

Sunde imasu, tsutomete imasu, and shitte imasu are in the "te-form imasu" and express a present state.

2. person wa noun ga wakarimasu. (KS2)

Following the noun that is the object of the verb **wakarimasu** ("understand"), the particle **ga** is added, as in the case of **suki desu**, **jōzu desu**, **itai desu** (see L15, GRAMMAR 1, p. 143).

3. person wa noun o shitte imasu. (KS3)

The verb **shirimasu** ("know") is always used, not in the **masu**-form but in the form **shitte imasu**. As distinct from other verbs, the possible replies to the question **shitte imasu ka** ("do you know [about so-and-so]?") are as follows:

e.g. **Chan-san o shitte imasu ka.**   Do you know Chan-san?

Hai, shitte imasu.   Yes, (I) know (her).

Iie, shirimasen.   No, (I) don't know (her).

Shirimasen is appropriate when someone wants to know whether or not you know someone/something. The negative answer, when someone asks for further information, would be **wakarimasen**.

4. noun wa verb [dictionary form] koto desu. (KS4)

When you talk about your hobbies or dreams, the sentence pattern "noun 1 **wa** noun 2 **desu**" or "noun **wa** verb [dictionary form] **koto desu**" can be used.

VOCABULARY

sunde imasu	live
shitte imasu	know
shumi	hobby, pastime

WORD POWER

Ⅰ Verbs

🔊 235

①sunde imasu

②tsutomete imasu

③shitte imasu

④wakarimasu

Ⅱ Family

🔊 236

	Related to the speaker	Related to others
child	kodomo	okosan
son	musuko	musuko-san
daughter	musume	ojōsan/musume-san
older brother	ani	onīsan
older sister	ane	onēsan
younger brother	otōto	otōto-san
younger sister	imōto	imōto-san

EXERCISES

Ⅰ

Practice conjugating verbs. Repeat the verbs below and memorize their **te imasu**-forms—affirmative and negative.

	masu-form	te imasu-form	
		aff.	neg.
live	sumimasu	sunde imasu	sunde imasen
be employed	tsutomemasu	tsutomete imasu	tsutomete imasen
know	—*	shitte imasu	shirimasen**

*__masu__-form is hardly ever used.

The negative **te imasu-form is **shitte imasen**, but this form is not used.

VOCABULARY

kodomo	child	**ojōsan**	(another person's) daughter	**ane**	(my) older sister
okosan	(another person's) child	**musume-san**	(another person's) daughter	**onēsan**	(another person's) older sister
musuko	(my) son	**ani**	(my) older brother	**otōto-san**	(another person's) younger brother
musuko-san	(another person's) son	**onīsan**	(another person's) older brother		
musume	(my) daughter				

Ⅱ *State where someone lives.* Make up sentences following the pattern of the example. Substitute the underlined parts with the alternatives given.

> e.g. **Yamamoto-san** wa **Kyōto** ni sunde imasu.

1. .... (Gurīn-san, Shibuya)

2. .... (Nakamura-san, Shinjuku)

Ⅲ *Ask and answer where someone lives.* Make up dialogues following the pattern of the example. Substitute the underlined parts with the alternatives given.

> e.g. **A: Suzuki-san** wa doko ni sunde imasu ka.
>
> **B: Yokohama** ni sunde imasu.

1. A: .... (Yamada-san)

   B: .... (Shibuya)

2. A: .... (Howaito-san)

   B: .... (Roppongi)

Ⅳ *State where someone is employed.* Make up sentences following the pattern of the example. Substitute the underlined parts with the alternatives given.

> e.g. **Tanaka-san** wa **depāto** ni tsutomete imasu.

1. .... (Yamada-san, ginkō)

2. .... (Sumisu-san, ABC Fūzu)

Ⅴ *Ask and answer where someone is employed.* Make up dialogues following the pattern of the example. Substitute the underlined parts with the alternatives given.

> e.g. **A: Buraun-san** wa doko ni tsutomete imasu ka.
>
> **B: Rondon Ginkō** ni tsutomete imasu.

1. A: .... (Howaito-san)

   B: .... (JBP Japan)

2. A: .... (Suzuki-san no onīsan)

   B: .... (ryokō-gaisha)

VOCABULARY

Howaito	White (surname)
JBP Japan	JBP Japan (fictitious company name)
ryokō-gaisha	travel agency

VI Make up sentences following the patterns of the examples and based on the information provided.

	Person	Residence	Employer
e.g.	Andō-san	Shinagawa	JBP Japan
1.	Gurīn-san	Shibuya	ABC Fūzu
2.	Nakamura-san no imōto-san	Sapporo	ginkō
3.	Chan-san no onēsan	Honkon	depāto

A. *State where someone lives.*

e.g. **Andō-san wa Shinagawa ni sunde imasu.**

1. ....

2. ....

3. ....

B. *State where someone is employed.*

e.g. **Andō-san wa JBP Japan ni tsutomete imasu.**

1. ....

2. ....

3. ....

VII Make up dialogues following the patterns of the examples. Substitute the underlined part with the alternatives given.

A. *Ask and answer whether someone knows someone or something.*

e.g. A: <u>Sasaki-san</u> o shitte imasu ka.

B: Hai, shitte imasu.

1. A: .... (Buraun-san)

B: Hai, ...

2. A: .... (Tanaka-san no jūsho)

B: Hai, ...

Andō	Ando (surname)
Shinagawa	Shinagawa (district in Tokyo)

B. *Ask and answer whether someone knows someone or something.*

e.g. **A: Howaito-san o shitte imasu ka.**

B: Iie, shirimasen.

1. A: ....

(Chan-san no mēru-adoresu)

B: Iie, ...

2. A: ....

(Suzuki-san no denwa-bangō)

B: Iie, ...

Ⅷ Make up dialogues following the patterns of the examples. Substitute the underlined parts with the alternatives given.

A. *Talk about your work and whether you know a particular person.*

Smith meets various people for the first time at a party.

e.g. **Sumisu: Andō-san, o-shigoto wa?**

Andō: Enjinia desu. JBP Japan ni tsutomete imasu.

Sumisu: Sō desu ka. Ja, Yokohama-shisha no Itō-san o shitte imasu ka.

Andō: Hai, shitte imasu.

1. Sumisu: .... (Kojima-san)

Kojima: .... (kaishain)

Sumisu: ....

(Ōsaka-shisha no Yamashita-san)

Kojima: ....

2. Sumisu: .... (Kobayashi-san)

Kobayashi: .... (bengoshi)

Sumisu: ....

(Honkon-shisha no Wan-san)

Kobayashi: ....

VOCABULARY			
enjinia	engineer	**Yamashita**	Yamashita (surname)
Itō	Ito (surname)	**Kobayashi**	Kobayashi (surname)
Kojima	Kojima (surname)	**bengoshi**	lawyer
kaishain	company employee	**Wan**	Wang (surname)

B. *Talk about whether one knows someone and something.*

e.g. **Sumisu:** JBP Japan no <u>Itō-san</u> o shitte imasu ka.

Nakamura: Hai, shitte imasu.

Sumisu: Ja, <u>Itō-san no denwa-bangō</u> o shitte imasu ka.

Nakamura: Sumimasen. Wakarimasen.

1. Sumisu: .... (Wan-san)

   Nakamura: ....

   Sumisu: ....

   (Wan-san no mēru-adoresu)

   Nakamura: ....

2. Sumisu: .... (Andō-san)

   Nakamura: ....

   Sumisu: ....

   (Andō-san no keitai no bangō)

   Nakamura: ....

IX *State what language someone understands.* Make up sentences following the pattern of the example. Substitute the underlined part with the alternatives given.

e.g. **Sumisu-san wa <u>Nihon-go</u> ga wakarimasu.**

1. .... (Furansu-go)

2. .... (kanji)

X *Talk about knowing other languages.* Make up dialogues following the pattern of the example and based on the information provided.

e.g. Sumisu	1. Katō	2. Sasaki
O Furansu-go × Doitsu-go	O Eigo × Chūgoku-go	O Chūgoku-go × Kankoku-go

VOCABULARY

keitai	mobile phone
Doitsu-go	German
Chūgoku-go	Chinese
Kankoku-go	Korean

e.g. Tanaka: Sumisu-san wa Furansu-go ga wakarimasu ka.

Sumisu: Hai, wakarimasu.

Tanaka: Doitsu-go mo wakarimasu ka.

Sumisu: Iie, wakarimasen.

1. Tanaka: ....

Katō: ....

Tanaka: ....

Katō: ....

2. Tanaka: ....

Sasaki: ....

Tanaka: ....

Sasaki: ....

XI *Ask and answer about someone's pastime.* Make up dialogues following the pattern of the example. Substitute the underlined parts with the appropriate forms of the alternatives given.

e.g. Tanaka: <u>Sumisu-san</u> no shumi wa nan desu ka.

Sumisu: <u>Hon o yomu</u> koto desu.

1. Tanaka: .... (Ema-san)

Ema: .... (shasin o torimasu)

2. Tanaka: .... (Nakamura-san)

Nakamura: .... (kēki o tsukurimasu)

3. Tanaka: .... (Suzuki-san)

Suzuki: .... (e o kakimasu)

XII Listen to the audio and fill in the blanks based on the information you hear. 🔊 237, 238

1. Nakamura-san no .... wa Sapporo ni

.... Ginkō ni ....

2. Sumisu-san wa .... wa wakarimasu ga,

.... wa wakarimasen.

SPEAKING PRACTICE

1. Kato is talking with Raja. 🔊 239

Katō: Raja-san wa Tōkyō Daigaku desu yo ne.
Raja: Hai.
Katō: Senkō wa nan desu ka.
Raja: Baiotekunorojī desu.
Katō: Ja, Mori-sensei o shitte imasu ka.
Raja: Hai, yoku shitte imasu.

Kato: You are studying at the University of Tokyo, right?
Raja: That's right.
Kato: What is your specialty?
Raja: My specialty is biotechnology.
Kato: Then do you know Professor Mori?
Raja: Yes, I know him well.

2. Smith wants to call Tanaka right away. 🔊 240

Sumisu: Nakamura-san, Tanaka-san no keitai no bangō o shitte imasu ka.
Nakamura: Sumimasen. Wakarimasen. Suzuki-san ni kiite kudasai.

Smith: Nakamura-san, do you know Tanaka-san's mobile phone number?
Nakamura: I'm sorry. I don't know. Please ask Suzuki-san.

NOTES

1. Tōkyō Daigaku desu yo ne.
Kato knows that Raja is a student, so he has omitted the word **gakusei** from his question, but his question is intended to confirm that Raja is a student at the University of Tokyo. **Yo ne** is attached to a question when the speaker thinks that the listener has the correct information.

Active Communication

1. Next time you meet a Japanese person, tell him/her where you live and where you are employed. Then ask that person where he/she lives and is employed.

2. Talk about your hobbies.

VOCABULARY

yo ne	. . . right? (confirming expression) (combination of particles; see NOTES 1, above)	**baiotekunorojī**	biotechnology
		Mori-sensei	Professor Mori
senkō	specialty, major	**Mori**	Mori (surname)
		sensei	(honorific used for teachers, doctors, etc.)

I Complete the sentences by choosing the most appropriate particle from the box below. The same particle may be used more than once. Some of the particles are not needed.

ga	o	ni	de	to

1. Ane wa ginkō (   ) tsutomete imasu.

2. Koko (   ) nimotsu o oite kudasai.

3. Maiasa nan-ji ni uchi (   ) demasu ka.

4. Tōkyō Eki de shinkansen (   ) norimashita.

5. Risa-san wa Nihon-go (   ) sukoshi wakarimasu.

II Change the word in the parentheses to the form that is appropriate in the context of the sentence.

1. A: Sumimasen. Kono pen o .... mo ii desu ka.   (tsukaimasu)

   B: Hai, dōzo.

2. A: Koko wa tachiiri-kinshi desu kara, ... de kudasai.

   (hairimasu)

   B: Hai. Wakarimashita.

3. Sasaki-san wa ima o-kyaku-san to .... imasu.   (hanashimasu)

4. Watashi no shumi wa eiga o .... koto desu.   (mimasu)

5. A: Repōto wa mō kakimashita ka.

   B: Ima .... imasu. Mō sukoshi matte kudasai.   (kakimasu)

III What do you say in the following situations?

1. You want to ask how long it takes to go from Tokyo to Okinawa by air.

   ....

2. You want to ask that tomato not be put into the sandwich.

   ....

3. You want to ask what Smith-san is doing now.

   ....

4. You want to ask Smith-san where his sister lives.

   ....

CASUAL STYLE 2

SAMPLE DIALOGUE 1 — 🔊 241

A notebook with experimental data is sitting on Hayashi's desk.

Raja:	Sore, mite mo ii?
Hayashi:	Un, ii yo. Hai. *(Hands to Raja.)*
Raja:	Kore, karite mo ii?
Hayashi:	Ē, chotto....

Raja:	Can I have a look at that?
Hayashi:	Yeah, sure. Here.
Raja:	Can I borrow this?
Hayashi:	Well, that's not quite . . .

desu/masu style	Casual style
Mite mo ii desu ka.	**Mite mo ii?**
	Expressions seeking permission for something are formed using the "**te**-form **mo ii?**" (rising intonation). When permission is granted, the response is **ii yo** ("All right." "Sure.") or **dōzo**. When wishing to gently refuse, the more vague **Ē, chotto...** is used. A firm refusal is expressed by saying **dame** ("No." "That can't happen.").

SAMPLE DIALOGUE 2 — 🔊 242

Tomorrow the university club will have a party.

Yamada:	Ashita no pātī, iku?
Raja:	Un, iku.
Hayashi:	Atashi wa ikanai.
	Baito aru kara.

Yamada:	Are you going to tomorrow's party?
Raja:	Yes. I'm going.
Hayashi:	I'm not going.
	Because I have a part-time job.

desu/masu style	Casual style
Ikimasen.	**Ikanai.**
	The present negative form of verbs is expressed by the **nai**-form.

Hayashi is planning to hold a party at her home next Saturday.

Hayashi: Kondo no doyō, uchi konai?	Hayashi: Why don't you come over to my house next Saturday?
Raja: Un, iku. Arigatō.	Raja: Sure. I'll be there. Thanks!

desu/masu style	Casual style
Kimasen ka.	**Konai?** Express an invitation by using the **nai**-form with rising intonation.

Hayashi brought along the latest edition of a really popular manga series.

Hayashi: Mō kore, yonda?	Hayashi: Have you already read this?
Raja: Un, yonda.	Raja: Yeah. I read it.
Abe: Ore wa mada. Kashite.	Abe: I haven't. Can I borrow it? [lit. Lend me that.]
Hayashi: Ii yo.	Hayashi: Sure.

desu/masu style	Casual style
Yomimashita.	**Yonda.** The past affirmative form of verbs is expressed by the **ta**-form. See the APPENDIX D (pp. 244, 245) for the **ta**-form. For the past negative form, the **i** of the **nai**-form changes to **katta**.
Kashite kudasai.	**Kashite.** A request or instruction is expressed using the **te**-form alone. When agreeing to a request or instruction, respond with **ii yo**, **wakatta** ("Got it."), **arigatō** or something similar. When gently declining a request, say **Ē, chotto….** When refusing outright, **iya (da)** ("I don't want to") is often used.

APPENDIXES

List of Grammar Points

A. Particles

Particles	Examples	Unit	Lesson
no	Kochira wa Nozomi Depāto no Tanaka-san desu.	1	1
	Kore wa dare no pen desu ka.	1	2
	Sore wa watashi no ja arimasen.	1	2
	Kaigi wa ashita no 4-ji kara desu.	2	3
	Kore wa Furansu no wain desu.	2	5
	Kochira wa intān no Raja-san desu.	3	6
o	Tanaka-san o onegaishimasu.	1	1
	Kore o kudasai.	2	4
	Shūmatsu ni nani o shimasu ka.	4	8
	Tsugi no shingō o migi ni magatte kudasai.	8	19
	Hiroshima Eki de shinkansen o orimasu.	9	20
ka	Nozomi Depāto no Tanaka-san desu ka.	1	1
	Kaigi wa yokka desu ka, yōka desu ka.	3	7
wa	Sumisu-san wa Amerika-jin desu.	1	1
	Tenpura wa suki desu ga, o-sushi wa suki ja arimasen.	10	23
kara	Kaigi wa ashita no 4-ji kara desu.	2	3
	Sumisu-san wa kyonen Amerika kara kimashita.	3	6
	Ashita wa isogashii desu. Kaigi ga arimasu kara.	6	14
	Ii tenki desu kara, kōen de hiru-gohan o tabemasen ka.	7	16
made	Shigoto wa 9-ji kara 5-ji made desu.	2	3
	Tōkyō Tawā no chikaku made onegaishimasu.	8	19
mo	Kore wa 3,000-en desu. Are mo 3,000-en desu.	2	4
	Ema-san wa pātī de nani mo tabemasendeshita.	4	8
	Eki no mae ni konbini ga arimasu. Eki no naka ni mo arimasu.	9	22
to	Karē to sarada o onegaishimasu.	2	4
	Tomodachi to resutoran ni ikimashita.	3	6
de	Kādo de onegaishimasu.	2	4
	Hitori de kimasu ka.	3	6
	Sumisu-san wa shinkansen de Ōsaka ni ikimasu.	3	7
	Resutoran de ban-gohan o tabemashita.	4	8
	Do-yōbi ni Asakusa de o-matsuri ga arimasu.	7	16
	Ban-gohan wa kaigi no ato de tabemasu.	8	18
ni	Sumisu-san wa ashita ginkō ni ikimasu.	3	6
	Ema-san wa 4-gatsu ni Nihon ni kimashita.	3	7
	Sumisu-san wa ashita Tanaka-san ni aimasu.	4	9
	Sumisu-san wa Suzuki-san ni resutoran no basho o oshiemashita.	4	9

	1-kai ni uketsuke ga arimasu.	6	12
	Nakamura-san wa Sumisu-san ni hana o moraimashita.	6	14
	Kaigi no mae ni shiryō o okurimasu.	7	17
	Tōkyō Eki de shinkansen ni norimasu.	9	20
	Koko ni suwatte mo ii desu ka.	9	21
	Nyūyōku no apareru-mēkā ni tsutomete imasu.	10	24
ga	Dono basu ga ikimasu ka.	3	6
	Depāto ni ikimashita ga, nani mo kaimasendeshita.	5	11
	1-kai ni uketsuke ga arimasu.	6	12
	Sumisu-san wa ashita kaigi ga arimasu.	6	14
	Chan-san wa wain ga suki desu.	7	15
	Tōkyō Dōmu ni ikitai n desu ga.	9	20
	(Watashi wa) atama ga itai desu.	9	21
	Sumisu-san wa Nihon-go ga wakarimasu.	10	24
ya	Ōkii o-tera ya jinja ga arimasu.	6	12
ne	Kaigi wa 1-ji kara desu ne.	3	6
	Ii mise desu ne.	4	9
yo	Nihon no supa desu yo.	6	12
yo ne	Raja-san wa Tōkyō Daigaku desu yo ne.	10	24

B. Sentence patterns

N=noun, V=verb, A=adjective

Sentence patterns	Examples	Unit	Lesson
N wa N desu	Sumisu-san wa Amerika-jin desu.	1	1
	Shigoto wa 9-ji kara 5-ji made desu.	2	3
	Resutoran wa 5-kai desu.	2	5
	Kaigi wa yokka desu ka, yōka desu ka.	3	7
N o kudasai	Kore o kudasai.	2	4
	Sono wain o 2-hon kudasai.	2	5
N o onegaishimasu	Tanaka-san o onegaishimasu.	1	1
	Karē to sarada o onegaishimasu.	2	4
N wa N ni/e V	Sumisu-san wa ashita ginkō ni/e ikimasu.	3	6
N wa N kara V	Sumisu-san wa kyonen Amerika kara kimashita.	3	6
N wa N o V	Sumisu-san wa ashita tenisu o shimasu.	4	8
	Sumisu-san wa Hiroshima Eki de shinkansen o orimasu.	9	20
N wa N ni V	Sumisu-san wa ashita Tanaka-san ni aimasu.	4	9
	Sumisu-san wa Tōkyō Eki de shinkansen ni norimasu.	9	20
N wa N ni N o V	Sumisu-san wa Suzuki-san ni resutoran no basho o oshiemashita.	4	9
	Sumisu-san wa Nakamura-san ni hana o agemashita.	6	14
	Nakamura-san wa Sumisu-san ni hana o moraimashita.	6	14

N wa A desu	Kono hon wa omoshiroi desu.	5	10
N ni N ga arimasu /imasu	1-kai ni uketsuke ga arimasu.	6	12
	Uketsuke ni onna no hito ga imasu.	6	12
N wa N ni arimasu /imasu	Takushī-noriba wa eki no mae ni arimasu.	6	13
	Sumisu-san wa 2-kai ni imasu.	6	13
	Sumisu-san wa Hiroshima ni 1-shūkan imasu.	9	20
N wa N ga V	Sumisu-san wa ashita kaigi ga arimasu.	6	14
	Sumisu-san wa Nihon-go ga wakarimasu.	10	24
N wa N ga A	Chan-san wa wain ga suki desu.	7	15
	(Watashi wa) atama ga itai desu.	9	21
N wa V no ga A	Sumisu-san wa sakkā o miru no ga suki desu.	7	15
N de N ga arimasu	Do-yōbi ni Asakusa de o-matsuri ga arimasu.	7	16
V masen ka	Shūmatsu ni issho ni eiga o mimasen ka.	7	16
V mashō	Issho ni ikimashō.	7	16
V tai desu	(Watashi wa) oishii o-sushi o/ga tabetai desu.	7	17
V te, V	Ema-san wa Ōsaka-shisha ni itte, Chan-san ni aimasu.	8	18
V te kudasai	Chotto matte kudasai.	8	19
V te mo ii desu ka	Kono e no shashin o totte mo ii desu ka.	9	21
V naide kudasai	Wasabi o irenaide kudasai.	9	22
V te imasu	Sumisu-san wa ima hiru-gohan o tabete imasu.	10	23
	Sumisu-san wa Nihon-go o naratte imasu.	10	23
	Sumisu-san wa Tōkyō ni sunde imasu.	10	24
	Sumisu-san wa Chan-san o shitte imasu.	10	24
N wa V koto desu	Sumisu-san no shumi wa hon o yomu koto desu.	10	24

C. Interrogatives

Interrogatives	Examples	Unit	Lesson
ikutsu	Tēburu no ue ni ringo ga ikutsu arimasu ka.	6	13
ikura	Kore wa ikura desu ka.	2	4
itsu	Kaigi wa itsu desu ka.	2	3
	Natsu-yasumi wa itsu kara itsu made desu ka.	3	7
	Katō-san wa itsu Ōsaka-shisha ni ikimasu ka.	3	6
dare	Kore wa dare no pen desu ka.	1	2

	Sumisu-san wa ashita dare to Nozomi Depāto ni ikimasu ka.	3	6
	Sumisu-san wa dare ni denwa o shimasu ka.	4	9
	Uketsuke ni dare ga imasu ka.	6	12
dō	Fujisan wa dō deshita ka.	5	11
	Sumisu-san mo issho ni dō desu ka.	7	16
	Dō shimashita ka.	9	21
dōyatte	Sumisu-san wa dōyatte kaisha ni ikimasu ka.	9	20
doko	Kore wa doko no bīru desu ka.	2	5
	Wain-shoppu wa doko desu ka.	2	5
	Sumisu-san wa ashita doko ni ikimasu ka.	3	6
	Doko kara kimashita ka.	3	6
	Doko de ban-gohan o tabemashita ka.	4	8
dochira	Sumisu-san, o-kuni wa dochira desu ka.	1	1
donata	Hai, donata desu ka.	5	10
dono	Dono basu ga ikimasu ka.	3	6
donokurai	Donokurai arukimashita ka.	5	11
dore	A: Ano T-shatsu wa ikura desu ka. B: Dore desu ka.	2	5
donna	Nikkō wa donna tokoro desu ka.	5	10
nani	Shūmatsu ni nani o shimasu ka.	4	8
	Nikkō ni nani ga arimasu ka.	6	12
nan	Kore wa nan desu ka.	1	2
	Sumisu-san wa nan de Ōsaka ni ikimasu ka.	3	7
nan-ji	Kaigi wa nan-ji kara nan-ji made desu ka.	2	3
	Ima nan-ji desu ka.	2	3
	Nan-ji ni ikimasu ka.	3	7
nan-gatsu	O-matsuri wa nan-gatsu desu ka.	3	7
nan-nichi	O-matsuri wa nan-nichi desu ka.	3	7
nan-yōbi	O-matsuri wa nan-yōbi desu ka.	3	7
nan-nin	Resutoran ni otoko no hito ga nan-nin imasu ka.	6	13
nan-mei	Nan-mei sama desu ka.	4	8
nan-bon	Tēburu no ue ni fōku ga nan-bon arimasu ka.	6	13
nan-mai	Tēburu no ue ni o-sara ga nan-mai arimasu ka.	6	13

D. Verbs

This textbook introduces the **masu**-form, dictionary form, **te**-form, and **nai**-form for the conjugated forms of verbs. Other forms are the **ta**-form, conditional form, volitional form, and imperative form, which will be introduced in Volume II and III.

	Regular 1	Regular 2	Irregular	
masu-form	kakimasu	tabemasu	kimasu	shimasu
Dictionary form	kaku	taberu	kuru	suru
te-form	kaite	tabete	kite	shite
nai-form	kakanai	tabenai	konai	shinai
ta-form	kaita	tabeta	kita	shita
Conditional form	kakeba	tabereba	kureba	sureba
Volitional form	kakō	tabeyō	koyō	shiyō
Imperative form	kake	tabero	koi	shiro

Regular 1 verbs					
-masu	Dictionary	**-te**	**-nai**	**-ta**	Meaning
aimasu	au	atte	awanai	atta	meet
azukarimasu	azukaru	azukatte	azukaranai	azukatta	keep
araimasu	arau	aratte	arawanai	aratta	wash
arimasu	aru	atte	nai	atta	exist, have, take place
arukimasu	aruku	aruite	arukanai	aruita	walk
iimasu	iu	itte	iwanai	itta	say
ikimasu	iku	itte	ikanai	itta	go
utaimasu	utau	utatte	utawanai	utatta	sing
okimasu	oku	oite	okanai	oita	put, place
okurimasu	okuru	okutte	okuranai	okutta	send
oyogimasu	oyogu	oyoide	oyoganai	oyoida	swim
owarimasu	owaru	owatte	owaranai	owatta	finish
kaimasu	kau	katte	kawanai	katta	buy
kaerimasu	kaeru	kaette	kaeranai	kaetta	return, come back
kakarimasu	kakaru	kakatte	kakaranai	kakatta	take [time]
kakimasu	kaku	kaite	kakanai	kaita	write, draw
kashimasu	kasu	kashite	kasanai	kashita	lend, loan
ganbarimasu	ganbaru	ganbatte	ganbaranai	ganbatta	do one's best
kikimasu	kiku	kiite	kikanai	kiita	listen to, ask
keshimasu	kesu	keshite	kesanai	keshita	turn off
sawarimasu	sawaru	sawatte	sawaranai	sawatta	touch
shirimasu*	shiru	shitte	shiranai	shitta	know
(tabako o) suimasu	suu	sutte	suwanai	sutta	smoke
sumimasu	sumu	sunde	sumanai	sunda	live
suwarimasu	suwaru	suwatte	suwaranai	suwatta	sit down
tachimasu	tatsu	tatte	tatanai	tatta	stand up
tsukaimasu	tsukau	tsukatte	tsukawanai	tsukatta	use
tsukimasu	tsuku	tsuite	tsukanai	tsuita	arrive
tsukurimasu	tsukuru	tsukutte	tsukuranai	tsukutta	make
(shashin o) torimasu	toru	totte	toranai	totta	take (a photo)
naraimasu	narau	naratte	narawanai	naratta	learn, take lessons in
niaimasu	niau	niatte	niawanai	niatta	suit, look good on
noborimasu	noboru	nobotte	noboranai	nobotta	climb

244

nomimasu	nomu	nonde	nomanai	nonda	drink
norimasu	noru	notte	noranai	notta	get on, take
hairimasu	hairu	haitte	hairanai	haitta	enter
hashirimasu	hashiru	hashitte	hashiranai	hashitta	run
hanashimasu	hanasu	hanashite	hanasanai	hanashita	talk, speak
magarimasu	magaru	magatte	magaranai	magatta	turn
machimasu	matsu	matte	matanai	matta	wait
moraimasu	morau	moratte	morawanai	moratta	receive
yasumimasu	yasumu	yasunde	yasumanai	yasunda	rest, take a day off
yomimasu	yomu	yonde	yomanai	yonda	read
wakarimasu	wakaru	wakatte	wakaranai	wakatta	understand

* This form is hardly ever used. Instead, **shitte imasu** (the **te**-form) is used.

Regular 2 verbs					
-masu	Dictionary	**-te**	**-nai**	**-ta**	Meaning
akemasu	akeru	akete	akenai	aketa	open
agemasu	ageru	agete	agenai	ageta	give
(shawā o) abimasu	abiru	abite	abinai	abita	take a shower
imasu	iru	ite	inai	ita	be, exist, stay
iremasu	ireru	irete	irenai	ireta	put in, add
oshiemasu	oshieru	oshiete	oshienai	oshieta	tell, teach
orimasu	oriru	orite	orinai	orita	get off
karimasu	kariru	karite	karinai	karita	borrow
shimemasu	shimeru	shimete	shimenai	shimeta	close
tabemasu	taberu	tabete	tabenai	tabeta	eat
tsukaremasu	tsukareru	tsukarete	tsukarenai	tsukareta	get tired
tsukemasu	tsukeru	tsukete	tsukenai	tsuketa	turn on
(ki o) tsukemasu	tsukeru	tsukete	tsukenai	tsuketa	be careful
tsutaemasu	tsutaeru	tsutaete	tsutaenai	tsutaeta	relay a message
tsutomemasu	tsutomeru	tsutomete	tsutomenai	tsutometa	work for, be employed
dekimasu	dekiru	dekite	dekinai	dekita	be done
demasu	deru	dete	denai	deta	leave
todokemasu	todokeru	todokete	todokenai	todoketa	deliver
tomemasu	tomeru	tomete	tomenai	tometa	stop, park
nemasu	neru	nete	nenai	neta	sleep, go to bed
hajimemasu	hajimeru	hajimete	hajimenai	hajimeta	start, begin
misemasu	miseru	misete	misenai	miseta	show
mimasu	miru	mite	minai	mita	see, watch

Irregular verbs					
-masu	Dictionary	**-te**	**-nai**	**-ta**	Meaning
kimasu	kuru	kite	konai	kita	come
mottekimasu	mottekuru	mottekite	mottekonai	mottekita	bring
shimasu	suru	shite	shinai	shita	do
ki ni shimasu	ki ni suru	ki ni shite	ki ni shinai	ki ni shita	worry about
jūdenshimasu	jūdensuru	jūdenshite	jūdenshinai	jūdenshita	recharge
daunrōdoshimasu	daunrōdosuru	daunrōdoshite	daunrōdoshinai	daunrōdoshita	download
chekkushimasu	chekkusuru	chekkushite	chekkushinai	chekkushita	check
nebōshimasu	nebōsuru	nebōshite	nebōshinai	nebōshita	oversleep
hōkokushimasu	hōkokusuru	hōkokushite	hōkokushinai	hōkokushita	report
yoyakushimasu	yoyakusuru	yoyakushite	yoyakushinai	yoyakushita	make a reservation

The verb **shimasu** ("do") takes various nouns and expresses many meanings. The particle **o** is added to some nouns, and in other cases such as **benkyōshimasu**, **kopīshimasu**, **denwashimasu** introduced in this textbook, they are used without attaching **o**.

uchiawase o shimasu	have a preparatory meeting	sutoretchi o shimasu	do stretching exercises
undō o shimasu	do exercise	sunōbōdo o shimasu	snowboard
(o-) hanami o shimasu	view cherry blossoms	setsumei o shimasu	explain
kaigi o shimasu	have a meeting	sōji o shimasu	clean
kaimono o shimasu	shop	daibingu o shimasu	scuba dive
kopī o shimasu	make a copy	tenisu o shimasu	play tennis
gorufu o shimasu	play golf	denwa o shimasu	telephone, call
sanpo o shimasu	take a walk	doraibu o shimasu	go for a drive
shigoto o shimasu	work	pātī o shimasu	have a party
junbi o shimasu	prepare	purezen o shimasu	give a presentation
jogingu o shimasu	jog	benkyō o shimasu	study
shokuji o shimasu	have a meal	ryōri o shimasu	cook
sukī o shimasu	ski		

E. Adjectives

i-adjectives

aoi	blue	samui	cold
akai	red	shiroi	white
atatakai	warm	suzushii	cool
atarashii	new, fresh	takai	expensive
atsui	hot	tanoshii	fun, pleasant, enjoyable
abunai	dangerous	chiisai	small
ii	nice, good	chikai	near, close
isogashii	busy	tsumaranai	boring, uninteresting
itai	hurt, sore, painful	tōi	far
oishii	delicious, tasty	furui	old
ōkii	large, big	muzukashii	difficult
omoshiroi	interesting	yasui	inexpensive
kuroi	black	warui	bad

na-adjectives

iroiro (na)	various	suteki (na)	lovely, nice
kantan (na)	easy, simple	taihen (na)	hard, tough
kirei (na)	pretty, beautiful, clean	nigiyaka (na)	lively
shizuka (na)	quiet	hima (na)	free, not busy
jōzu (na)	skilled, be good at	benri (na)	convenient
suki (na)	like, favorite	yūmei (na)	famous

F. Ko-so-a-do words

<Basic>

	ko-words	so-words	a-words	do-words
thing	**kore** this one	**sore** that one	**are** that one over there	**dore** which one (of three or more) **dochira** which one (of the two)
+ noun	**kono pen** this pen	**sono pen** that pen	**ano pen** that pen over there	**dono pen** which pen (of three or more) **dochira no pen** which pen (of the two)
place	**koko** here	**soko** there	**asoko** over there	**doko** where
direction	**kochira** this way	**sochira** that way	**achira** that way over there	**dochira** which way
people	----	----	----	**dare** who

<Polite>

	ko-words	so-words	a-words	do-words
thing	**kochira** this one	**sochira** that one	**achira** that one over there	**dochira** which one
+ noun	**kochira no pen** this pen	**sochira no pen** that pen	**achira no pen** that pen over there	**dochira no pen** which pen
place	**kochira** here	**sochira** there	**achira** over there	**dochira** where
direction	**kochira** this way	**sochira** that way	**achira** that way over there	**dochira** which way
people	**kochira** this (person)	**sochira** that (person)	**achira** that (person) over there	**dochira** who

G. Time expressions

Relative time

Day

ototoi	day before yesterday
kinō	yesterday
kyō	today
ashita	tomorrow
asatte	day after tomorrow

Morning

kinō no asa	yesterday morning
kyō no asa	this morning
kesa	this morning
ashita no asa	tomorrow morning

Evening

kinō no ban/yoru	yesterday evening/night
yūbe	yesterday evening
konban	this evening
kon'ya	tonight
ashita no ban/yoru	tomorrow evening/night

Week

sensenshū	week before last
senshū	last week
konshū	this week
raishū	next week
saraishū	week after next

Month

sensengetsu	month before last
sengetsu	last month
kongetsu	this month
raigetsu	next month
saraigetsu	month after next

Year

ototoshi	year before last
kyonen	last year
kotoshi	this year
rainen	next year
sarainen	year after next

Every: **mai-**

maiasa	every morning
maiban	every evening, every night
mainichi	every day
maishū	every week
maitsuki/maigetsu	every month
maitoshi/mainen	every year

Specific time

ichi-ji ippun	1:01	**shichi-ji nana-fun**	7:07
ni-ji ni-fun	2:02	**hachi-ji happun**	8:08
san-ji san-pun	3:03	**ku-ji kyū-fun**	9:09
yo-ji yon-pun	4:04	**jū-ji juppun**	10:10
go-ji go-fun	5:05	**jūichi-ji jūippun**	11:11
roku-ji roppun	6:06	**jūni-ji jūni-fun**	12:12

Refer to p. 63 for years, days of the week, months, and days of the month.

Periods

Minutes: -fun/pun

ippun (kan)	(for) 1 minute	**happun (kan)**	(for) 8 minutes
ni-fun (kan)	(for) 2 minutes	**hachi-fun (kan)**	//
san-pun (kan)	(for) 3 minutes	**kyū-fun (kan)**	(for) 9 minutes
yon-pun (kan)	(for) 4 minutes	**juppun (kan)**	(for) 10 minutes
go-fun (kan)	(for) 5 minutes	**jūippun (kan)**	(for) 11 minutes
roppun (kan)	(for) 6 minutes	**jūni-fun (kan)**	(for) 12 minutes
nana-fun (kan)	(for) 7 minutes		

nan-pun (kan)	how many minutes

Hours: -jikan

ichi-jikan	(for) 1 hour	**hachi-jikan**	(for) 8 hours
ni-jikan	(for) 2 hours	**ku-jikan**	(for) 9 hours
san-jikan	(for) 3 hours	**jū-jikan**	(for) 10 hours
yo-jikan	(for) 4 hours	**jūichi-jikan**	(for) 11 hours
go-jikan	(for) 5 hours	**jūni-jikan**	(for) 12 hours
roku-jikan	(for) 6 hours		
nana-jikan	(for) 7 hours		
shichi-jikan	//		

nan-jikan	how many hours

Days: -nichi (kan)

ichi-nichi	(for) 1 day	**nanoka (kan)**	(for) 7 days
futsuka (kan)	(for) 2 days	**yōka (kan)**	(for) 8 days
mikka (kan)	(for) 3 days	**kokonoka (kan)**	(for) 9 days
yokka (kan)	(for) 4 days	**tōka (kan)**	(for) 10 days
itsuka (kan)	(for) 5 days	**jūichi-nichi (kan)**	(for) 11 days
muika (kan)	(for) 6 days	**jūni-nichi (kan)**	(for) 12 days

nan-nichi (kan)	how many days

Weeks: -shūkan

isshūkan	(for) 1 week	**nana-shūkan**	(for) 7 weeks
ni-shūkan	(for) 2 weeks	**hasshūkan**	(for) 8 weeks
san-shūkan	(for) 3 weeks	**kyū-shūkan**	(for) 9 weeks
yon-shūkan	(for) 4 weeks	**jusshūkan**	(for) 10 weeks
go-shūkan	(for) 5 weeks	**jūisshūkan**	(for) 11 weeks
roku-shūkan	(for) 6 weeks	**jūni-shūkan**	(for) 12 weeks

nan-shūkan	how many weeks

Months: -kagetsu (kan)

ikkagetsu (kan)	(for) 1 month	hachi-kagetsu (kan)	(for) 8 months
ni-kagetsu (kan)	(for) 2 months	hakkagetsu (kan)	//
san-kagetsu (kan)	(for) 3 months	kyū-kagetsu (kan)	(for) 9 months
yon-kagetsu (kan)	(for) 4 months	jukkagetsu (kan)	(for) 10 months
go-kagetsu (kan)	(for) 5 months	jūikkagetsu (kan)	(for) 11 months
rokkagetsu (kan)	(for) 6 months	jūni-kagetsu (kan)	(for) 12 months
nana-kagetsu (kan)	(for) 7 months		

nan-kagetsu (kan)   how many months

Years: -nen (kan)

ichi-nen (kan)	(for) 1 year	hachi-nen (kan)	(for) 8 years
ni-nen (kan)	(for) 2 years	kyū-nen (kan)	(for) 9 years
san-nen (kan)	(for) 3 years	jū-nen (kan)	(for) 10 years
yo-nen (kan)	(for) 4 years	jūichi-nen (kan)	(for) 11 years
go-nen (kan)	(for) 5 years	jūni-nen (kan)	(for) 12 years
roku-nen (kan)	(for) 6 years		
nana-nen (kan)	(for) 7 years		
shichi-nen (kan)	//		

nan-nen (kan)   how many years

NOTE: Except for with **jikan** and **shūkan**, the suffix **kan** may be considered optional and need be added only when specificity is called for.

Seasons

haru	spring	aki	autumn
natsu	summer	fuyu	winter

H. Counters

The abstract numbers (**ichi, ni, san**) are given on p. 11 (0-9), p. 22 (10-30; 40, 50, ...), and p. 31 (100, 200, ...). For an explanation of very large numbers, see PLUS ONE on p. 31.

Hitotsu, futatsu, mittsu system

hitotsu	one	itsutsu	five	kokonotsu	nine
futatsu	two	muttsu	six	tō	ten
mittsu	three	nanatsu	seven	jūichi	eleven
yottsu	four	yattsu	eight	jūni	twelve

ikutsu   how many

Thin, flat objects: -mai

ichi-mai	one	go-mai	five	kyū-mai	nine
ni-mai	two	roku-mai	six	jū-mai	ten
san-mai	three	nana-mai	seven	jūichi-mai	eleven
yon-mai	four	hachi-mai	eight	jūni-mai	twelve

nan-mai   how many

Long, slender objects: -hon/pon/bon

ippon	one	go-hon	five	kyū-hon	nine
ni-hon	two	roppon	six	juppon	ten
san-bon	three	nana-hon	seven	jūippon	eleven
yon-hon	four	happon	eight	jūni-hon	twelve

nan-bon   how many

People: **-nin**

hitori	1 person	**roku-nin**	6 people	**kyū-nin**	9 people
futari	2 people	**nana-nin**	7 people	**ku-nin**	//
san-nin	3 people	**shichi-nin**	//	**jū-nin**	10 people
yo-nin	4 people	**hachi-nin**	8 people	**jūichi-nin**	11 people
go-nin	5 people			**jūni-nin**	12 people

nan-nin　　how many people

Floors of a house or building: **-kai/gai**

ikkai	1st floor	**go-kai**	5th floor	**jukkai**	10th floor
ni-kai	2nd floor	**rokkai**	6th floor	**jūikkai**	11th floor
san-gai	3rd floor	**nana-kai**	7th floor	**jūni-kai**	12th floor
san-kai	//	**hachi-kai**	8th floor		
yon-kai	4th floor	**kyū-kai**	9th floor		

nan-gai/nan-kai　　how many floors, which floor

Also: **chika ikkai**, 1st floor basement, **chika ni-kai**, 2nd floor basement, etc.

I. Extent, frequency, quantity

Extent

totemo	very
amari ... -nai desu/-masen	not very
zenzen ... -nai desu/-masen	not at all

e.g. **Kono kēki wa totemo oishii desu.**	This cake is very good.
Kono kēki wa amari oishikunai desu.	This cake is not very good.
Kono kēki wa zenzen oishikunai desu.	This cake is not good at all.

Frequency

itsumo	always
yoku	often
tokidoki	sometimes
tama ni	occasionally
amari ... -masen	not often
zenzen ... -masen	not at all

e.g. **Itsumo ryōri o shimasu.**	(I) always cook.
Yoku ryōri o shimasu.	(I) often cook.
Tokidoki ryōri o shimasu.	(I) sometimes cook.
Tama ni ryōri o shimasu.	(I) occasionally cook.
Amari ryōri o shimasen.	(I) don't often cook.
Zenzen ryōri o shimasen.	(I) don't cook at all.

Quantity

takusan	many, much
sukoshi	a few, a little
amari ... -masen	not many, not much
zenzen ... -masen	not at all

e.g. **Uchi no chikaku ni mise ga takusan arimasu.**	There are many stores near my house.
Uchi no chikaku ni mise ga sukoshi arimasu.	There are a few stores near my house.
Uchi no chikaku ni mise ga amari arimasen.	There aren't many stores near my house.
Uchi no chikau ni mise ga zenzen arimasen.	There are no stores near my house.

Target Dialogues (with kana)

LESSON 1
スミス：すみません。のぞみデパートの　たなかさんですか。
たなか：はい、そうです。
スミス：はじめまして。ABC フーズの　スミスです。よろしく　おねがいします。
たなか：はじめまして。たなかです。こちらこそ、よろしく　おねがいします。

LESSON 2
なかむら：これは　だれの　ペンですか。
すずき　：さあ、わかりません。スミスさんのですか。
スミス　：いいえ、わたしのじゃありません。
なかむら：たなかさん、これは　たなかさんの　ペンですか。
たなか　：はい、わたしのです。ありがとうございます。

LESSON 3
みせの　ひと：すしよしです。
スミス　　　：すみません。ランチタイムは　なんじからですか。
みせの　ひと：11 じはんからです。
スミス　　　：なんじまでですか。
みせの　ひと：2 じはんまでです。
スミス　　　：ラストオーダーは　なんじですか。
みせの　ひと：2 じです。
スミス　　　：ありがとうございます。
■ランチタイムは　11 じはんから　2 じはんまでです。

LESSON 4
みせの　ひと：いらっしゃいませ。
スミス　　　：それを　みせてください。
みせの　ひと：はい、どうぞ。
スミス　　　：ありがとう。これは　いくらですか。
みせの　ひと：3,000 えんです。
スミス　　　：あれは　いくらですか。
みせの　ひと：あれも　3,000 えんです。
スミス　　　：じゃ、これを　ください。
みせの　ひと：はい、ありがとうございます。

LESSON 5
スミス　　　　　　　　　　　：すみません。ワインショップは　どこですか。
インフォメーションの　ひと：ちか 1 かいです。
スミス　　　　　　　　　　　：どうも　ありがとう。
スミス　　　　　　　　　　　：すみません。その　ワインは　どこのですか。
みせの　ひと　　　　　　　　：フランスのです。
スミス　　　　　　　　　　　：いくらですか。
みせの　ひと　　　　　　　　：2,600 えんです。
スミス　　　　　　　　　　　：じゃ、それを　2ほん　ください。ふくろも　2まい　ください。

LESSON 6
チャン：はい、チャンです。
スミス：とうきょうししゃの　スミスです。おはようございます。
チャン：おはようございます。
スミス：あした　そちらに　いきます。かいぎは　1 じからですね。
チャン：はい、1 じからです。ひとりで　きますか。
スミス：いいえ、かとうさんと　いきます。
チャン：そうですか。では、あした。
スミス：しつれいします。
チャン：しつれいします。
■スミスさんは　あした　かとうさんと　おおさかししゃに　いきます。

LESSON 7

なかむら：あ、スミスさん、しゅっちょうですか。
スミス　：ええ、かとうさんと　おおさかししゃに　いきます。きんようびに　とうきょうに　かえります。
なかむら：ひこうきで　いきますか。
スミス　：いいえ、しんかんせんで　いきます。
なかむら：そうですか。いってらっしゃい。
■スミスさんは　かとうさんと　しんかんせんで　おおさかに　いきます。
　きんようびに　とうきょうに　かえります。

LESSON 8

ささき：しゅうまつに　なにを　しますか。
スミス：どようびに　ぎんざで　すずきさんと　てんぷらを　たべます。
ささき：そうですか。いいですね。
スミス：ささきさんは？
ささき：にちようびに　ともだちと　かぶきを　みます。
スミス：いいですね。
■スミスさんは　どようびに　ぎんざで　すずきさんと　てんぷらを　たべます。
　ささきさんは　にちようびに　ともだちと　かぶきを　みます。

LESSON 9

みせの　ひと　：いらっしゃいませ。
すずき　　　　：すずきです。
みせの　ひと　：すずきさまですね。どうぞ　こちらへ。
スミス　　　　：いい　みせですね。すずきさんは　よく　この　みせに　きますか。
すずき　　　　：ええ、ときどき　きます。せんしゅうは　ここで　グリーンさんに　あいました。
スミス　　　　：え、ほんとうですか。
スミス・すずき：あ、グリーンさん！
■スミスさんと　すずきさんは　ぎんざの　てんぷらやで　グリーンさんに　あいました。

LESSON 10

ささき：おちゃを　どうぞ。
エマ　：ありがとうございます。
ささき：おかしは　いかがですか。
エマ　：はい、いただきます。きれいな　おかしですね。にほんの　おかしですか。
ささき：ええ、そうです。きょうとの　おかしです。
エマ　：とても　おいしいです。
■エマさんは　ささきさんの　うちで　きれいな　にほんの　おかしを　たべました。

LESSON 11

エマ　：せんしゅう　ふじさんに　のぼりました。
ささき：どうでしたか。
エマ　：とても　きれいでした。
ささき：しゃしんを　とりましたか。
エマ　：ええ、これです。
ささき：ほんとうに　きれいですね。どのくらい　あるきましたか。
エマ　：8じかんぐらい　あるきました。たいへんでしたが、たのしかったです。
■エマさんは　ささきさんと　ささきさんの　ごしゅじんに　しゃしんを　みせました。

LESSON 12

なかむら：どようびに　エマさんと　にっこうに　いきます。
ラジャ　：そうですか。にっこうに　なにが　ありますか。
なかむら：おおきい　おてらや　じんじゃが　あります。おんせんも　あります。
ラジャ　：おんせんって　なんですか。
なかむら：これです。にほんの　スパですよ。
ラジャ　：いいですね。
■なかむらさんは　どようびに　エマさんと　にっこうに　いきます。にっこうに　おおきい　おてらや
じんじゃが　あります。

LESSON 13

なかむら　　　　：すみません。この　ちかくに　おいしい　おそばやさんが　ありますか。
みせの　ひと：ええ。そばいちが　おいしいですよ。
エマ　　　　　　：どこに　ありますか。
みせの　ひと：あそこに　おてらが　ありますね。そばいちは　あの　おてらの　まえです。
エマ　　　　　　：そうですか。それから、この　たきは　ここから　ちかいですか。
みせの　ひと：いいえ、ちょっと　とおいです。バスで　15ふんぐらいです。
エマ　　　　　　：そうですか。どうも　ありがとうございます。
▪そばいちは　おてらの　まえに　あります。

LESSON 14

エマ　　　　：ちょっと　さむいですね。
なかむら：あ、スカーフが　ありますよ。これ、どうぞ。
エマ　　　　：え、いいんですか。
なかむら：ええ、わたしは　さむくないですから。
エマ　　　　：ありがとうございます。すてきな　スカーフですね。
なかむら：ええ、たんじょうびに　ともだちに　もらいました。
▪なかむらさんは　エマさんに　スカーフを　かしました。

LESSON 15

スミス　　　　　　：いとこの　ポールです。
ポール　　　　　　：はじめまして。ポールです。よろしく　おねがいします。
　　　　　　　　　　わたしは　にほんの　アニメが　すきです。
すずき　　　　　　：どんな　アニメが　すきですか。
ポール　　　　　　：ロボットの　アニメが　すきです。
すずき　　　　　　：あ、わたしもです。かくのも　すきです。
スミス・ポール：わあ！　すごい！　じょうずですね！
▪ポールさんと　すずきさんは　ロボットの　アニメが　すきです。

LESSON 16

すずき：つぎの　にちようびに　あきはばらで　アニメの　イベントが　あります。
　　　　　おもしろい　イベントですから、いっしょに　いきませんか。
ポール：いいですね。ぜひ。イベントは　なんじからですか。
すずき：1じからです。ひるごはんも　いっしょに　たべましょう。スミスさんも　いっしょに　どうですか。
スミス：すみません。アニメは　ちょっと…。
すずき：そうですか。
▪すずきさんと　ポールさんは　つぎの　にちようびに　アニメの　イベントに　いきます。

LESSON 17

ポール：おとうとも　アニメが　すきですから、あきはばらで　おみやげを　かいたいです。
すずき：そうですか。じゃ、ひるごはんの　まえに、かいものを　しましょう。
ポール：ありがとうございます。
すずき：ポールさん、ホテルは　どこですか。
ポール：しんじゅくの　のぞみホテルです。
すずき：じゃ、10じに　ホテルの　ロビーで　あいましょう。
ポール：10じですね。わかりました。
▪すずきさんと　ポールさんは　ひるごはんを　たべる　まえに　かいものを　します。

LESSON 18

エマ　　：かとうさん、ちょっと　よろしいですか。
かとう：はい。
エマ　　：あした　おおさかに　いきます。
かとう：あ、パッケージフェアですね。
エマ　　：ええ。フェアの　あと、ししゃに　いって、チャンさんに　あいます。
　　　　　あさって　こうじょうを　みて、4じの　ひこうきで　とうきょうに　かえります。
かとう：わかりました。きを　つけて。
▪エマさんは　あした　おおさかに　いきます。あさって　こうじょうを　みて、とうきょうに　かえります。

LESSON 19

かとう：フェアは　どうでしたか。
エマ　：おもしろい　パッケージが　たくさん　ありました。
　　　　いろいろな　サンプルを　もらいましたから、たくはいびんで　おくりました。
かとう：そうですか。じゃ、げつようびの　かいぎで　ほうこくしてください。
エマ　：はい、わかりました。
かとう：いまから　おおさかししゃですか。
エマ　：はい、そうです。
かとう：チャンさんに　よろしく　つたえてください。
エマ　：はい、つたえます。
■エマさんは　げつようびの　かいぎで　パッケージフェアについて　ほうこくします。

LESSON 20

すずき：スミスさん、すみません。ねぼうしました。いま　うちを　でました。
スミス：ここまで　どのくらい　かかりますか。
すずき：30ぷんぐらい　かかります。
スミス：そうですか。じゃ、1かいの　カフェに　います。
すずき：すみません。
■すずきさんの　うちから　はくぶつかんまで　30ぷんぐらい　かかります。

LESSON 21

スミス　　　　　　　：これは　むかしの　おかねですか。
すずき　　　　　　　：ええ、そうです。あ、ここに　えいごの　パンフレットが　ありますよ。
スミス　　　　　　　：そうですね。
　　　　　　　　　　すみません。この　パンフレットを　もらっても　いいですか。
はくぶつかんの　ひと：はい、どうぞ。
すずき　　　　　　　：つかれましたね。
スミス　　　　　　　：そうですね。あしが　いたいです。すみません。ここに　すわっても　いいですか。
はくぶつかんの　ひと：はい、どうぞ。
■スミスさんは　はくぶつかんで　えいごの　パンフレットを　もらいました。

LESSON 22

スミス　　　　　　　：きれいな　きものですね。
すずき　　　　　　　：ほんとうに　きれいですね。これは　300ねんぐらいまえの　きものです。
スミス　　　　　　　：そうですか。いもうとに　みせたいです。
はくぶつかんの　ひと：すみません。ここで　しゃしんを　とらないでください。
スミス　　　　　　　：わかりました。すみません。
すずき　　　　　　　：スミスさん、あそこにも　きれいな　きものが　ありますよ。
スミス　　　　　　　：あ、そうですね。いきましょう。

LESSON 23

かとう：もう　かいぎの　じゅんびは　できましたか。
スミス：すみません。まだです。かいぎしつは　よやくしましたが、しりょうは　いま　つくっています。
かとう：そうですか。3じまでに　おわりますか。
スミス：はい、もうすぐ　できます。
スミス：かとうさん、しりょうが　できました。チェックを　おねがいします。
かとう：はい。

LESSON 24

すずき：スミスさん、いもうとさんは　にほんごが　わかりますか。
スミス：はい、すこし　わかりますよ。
すずき：リサさん、おしごとは？
リサ　：デザイナーです。ニューヨークの　アパレルメーカーに　つとめています。
すずき：おしごとは　たのしいですか。
リサ　：ええ、とても　たのしいです。わたしの　ゆめは　じぶんの　ブランドを　つくる　ことです。
すずき：そうですか。がんばってください。
リサ　：はい、ありがとうございます。
■リサさんは　ニューヨークの　アパレルメーカーに　つとめています。ゆめは　じぶんの　ブランドを
　つくる　ことです。

GLOSSARY

Japanese-English Glossary

A

a ah, oh 61
ABC Fūzu ABC Foods (fictitious company name) 2
abunai dangerous 212
achira over there 47
agemasu (R2) give 132
aimasu meet 84
aisu-kurīmu ice cream 76
Ajaruto Sukūru AJALT School (fictitious school name) 165
akai red 40
Akasaka Akasaka (district in Tokyo) 194
aka-wain red wine 45
akemasu (R2) open 201
Akihabara Akihabara (district in Tokyo) 151
amari . . . -masen not often, not very 85
Amerika United States 4
Amerika-jin American (person) 3
anata you 6
Andō Ando (surname) 232
ane (my) older sister 230
ani (my) older brother 230
anime anime, animation 142
ano that (over there) 39
antīku antiques 165
Antīku Tōkyō Antique Tokyo (fictitious shop name) 165
aoi blue 39
apareru apparel 228
apareru-mēkā apparel maker 228
appuru-pai apple pie 47
apuri application 101
araimasu wash 163
are that one over there 28
Aren Allen (surname) 57
Arigatō gozaimasu. Thank you. 9
arimasu be, exist 114
arimasu have 131
arimasu there is, take place 151
aruite on foot, walking 67
arukimasu walk 105
asa morning 26
asa-gohan breakfast 26
Asakusa Asakusa (district in Tokyo) 102
asatte day after tomorrow 54
ashi foot, leg 199
ashita tomorrow 21
asoko over there 123
atama head 200
atarashii new, fresh 97
atatakai warm 98
ato→. . . no ato after 172
ato de later 226
atsui hot 98
azukarimasu keep, take care of 187

B

bā bar 79
baggu bag 133
baiku motorbike 64
baikubin motorbike courier service 182
baiotekunorojī biotechnology 236
ban evening 26
-ban number. . . (suffix for number) 60
bangō number 11
ban-gohan evening meal, dinner, supper 26
-bansen platform. . . 198
Barentain-dē Valentine's Day 136
basho location 85
basu bus 60
basu-noriba bus terminal 125
basutei bus stop 129
beddo bed 116
bengoshi lawyer 233
benkyō o shimasu study 76
benkyōshimasu study 165
benri (na) convenient 97
bentō box lunch, bento 100
Berurin Berlin 6
Berurin Mōtāzu Berlin Motors (fictitious company name) 6
betsubetsu ni separately 93
bīchi beach 122
bijutsukan art museum 149
biru building 186
bīru beer 40
biyōin hair dresser 166
bōrupen ballpoint pen 36
bōto-noriba boat dock 129
burando brand 228
Buraun Brown (surname) 5
burausu blouse 133
byōin hospital, clinic 125

C

chekku check 218
chekkushimasu check 167
chichi (my) father 86
chiisai small 40
chika basement 38
chikai near, close 123
chika 1-kai (ikkai) first-floor basement 38
chikaku vicinity, near 117
chikatetsu subway 64
chiketto ticket 133
chīzu cheese 43
chīzu-bāgā cheese burger 215
chīzu-kēki cheese cake 47
chokorēto chocolate 135
chokorēto-kēki chocolate cake 35
chotto a little bit 104
chotto. . . 151
Chūgoku China 4
Chūgoku-go Chinese 234
chūsha-jō parking lot 116
chūsha-kinshi no parking 211

D

daibingu scuba diving 144
daibingu o shimasu scuba dive 197
daigaku university, college 4
Daijōbu desu ka. Are you all right? 139
dansu dance 146
dare who 9
dare mo . . . -masen no one 120
dare no whose 9
daunrōdo download 224
daunrōdoshimasu download 166
de by means of (particle) 37
de by means of (particle) 61
de at, in, on (particle) 74
. . . de gozaimasu (polite form of . . . desu) 83
deguchi exit 153
dekimasu (R2) be done 218
demasu (R2) leave 190
demo but 150
denki lights 202
denki-potto electric kettle 116
densha train 64
denshi-renji microwave oven 30
denwa telephone 11
denwa-bangō telephone number 11
denwa o shimasu telephone 86
denwashimasu telephone, call 226
depāto department store 2
. . . desu be 2
dēto date 108
dewa well then 50
dezainā designer 228
-do . . . degree 207
dō how (in question) 105
doa door 212
dochira where (polite word for **doko**) 8
Dō deshita ka. How was it? 105
dō desu ka how about you? 151
Dō itashimashite. You're welcome. 111
Doitsu Germany 4
Doitsu-go German 234
doko where 38
Dōmo. Thanks. 47
Dōmo arigatō. Thank you. 27
Dōmo arigatō gozaimashita. Thank you very much. 111
donata who (polite word for **dare**) 104
donna what kind of 102
dono which (of three or more things) 60
donokurai how long 105
doraibu o shimasu go for a drive 176
dore which one (of three or more things) 46
dōryō colleague, coworker 53
Dō shimashita ka. What seems to be the problem? 207
dōyatte how, in what way 195
do-yōbi Saturday 63
Dōzo. Please (have one). 18
Dōzo kochira e. Please come in. 84

E

e 72
e painting, picture 101
eakon air conditioner 30
Ebisu Ebisu (district in Tokyo) 186

Ebisu Eki Ebisu Station 186
ee yes (a softer way of saying hai) 61
eiga movie 78
Eigo English 199
eki station 53
ekiin station employee 198
-en . . . yen 28
enjinia engineer 233
enpitsu pencil 125

F

fairu file 11
fea fair 172
fōku fork 127
Fujisan Mt. Fuji 100
fukuro bag 38
-fun/pun . . . minute(s) 22
-fun/pun (kan) . . . minutes 192
Furansu France 38
Furansu-go French 220
furī-māketto flea market 83
furonto reception desk 26
furui old 98
futari two people 77
futatsu two 40
futatsu-me second 184
futsuka second (of the month) 63

G

ga (particle) 60
ga but (particle) 105
ga (particle) 114
gakkō school 88
gakusei student 53
ganbarimasu do one's best 228
Ganbatte kudasai. I hope it works out.
   228
-gatsu month 63
getsu-yōbi Monday 63
Gibuson Gibson (surname) 66
ginkō bank 4
Ginza Ginza (district in Tokyo) 55
Ginza Dōri Ginza Street 184
gitā guitar 220
go five 11
-go language 88
go- (honorific prefix) 86
Goa Goa (state in India) 122
5-bansen Platform 5 198
go-gatsu May 63
gogo P.M., in the afternoon 22
gohan meal, cooked rice 26
5-ji 5:00, five o'clock 21
gojū fifty 22
go-jūsho your address 185
5-kai fifth floor 39
go-kazoku (another person's) family
   86
gomi-bako trash basket 116
. . . goro about (time) 130
gorufu golf 146
gorufu o shimasu play golf 82
go-shujin (another person's) husband
   86
gozen A.M., in the morning 22
. . . gurai about (amount) 105
gurasu glass, wine glass 91
gyūniku beef 43

H

ha tooth 201
hachi eight 11
hachi-gatsu August 63
8-jikan 8 hours 105

hachijū eighty 22
haha (my) mother 86
hai yes 2
hairimasu enter 201
Hajimemashite. Nice to meet you. 2
hajimemasu (R2) start, begin 163
Hakone Hakone (popular travel
   destination southwest of Tokyo) 82
hakubutsukan museum 190
-han . . . thirty, half past (hour) 20
hana flower 100
hanabi fireworks 153
hanabi-taikai fireworks festival 153
hanami o shimasu view cherry
   blossoms 165
hanashimasu talk, speak 145
hana-ya florist 127
hanbāgā hamburger 215
Haneda Kūkō Haneda Airport 196
happī awā happy hour 25
Harisu Harris (surname) 6
hasami scissors 125
hashi bridge 184
hashirimasu run 145
hatsuka twentieth (of the month) 63
heya room 116
hidari left 182
higashi east 153
higashi-guchi east exit 153
hikidashi drawer 120
hikōki airplane 61
hima (na) free, not busy 107
Hiroshima Hiroshima (city in western
   Japan) 191
Hiroshima Eki Hiroshima Station 191
hiru noon 21
hiru-gohan lunch 76
hiru-yasumi lunch break 21
hito person, employee 20
hitori one person 77
hitori de alone 50
hito-tachi people 59
hitotsu one 40
Hofuman Hoffman (surname) 5
Hokkaidō Hokkaido (island in northern
   Japan) 56
hōkokushimasu report 180
hōkokushite kudasai please
   report 180
hōmu platform 153
hon book 11
-hon/bon/pon (counter for long,
   slender objects) 40
Honkon Hong Kong 54
Hontō desu ka. Really? 84
hontō ni really 103
hon-ya bookstore 125
hoteru hotel 69
Howaito White (surname) 231
hyaku one hundred 22
hyaku-man one million 31
hyaku-oku ten billion
   (=10,000,000,000) 31

I

ibento event 151
ichi one 11
ichi-do one time 18
ichi-gatsu January 63
ichi-man ten thousand 31
ichi-oku one hundred million 31
Igirisu United Kingdom 4

ii nice, good 84
Ii desu ne. That's good. 74
iie no 6
iimasu say 181
Ii n desu ka. Are you sure? 131
Ikaga desu ka. How about . . . ? 96
ikebana flower arrangement 163
ikimasen ka shall we go? 151
ikimashita went 51
ikimashō let's go 152
ikimasu go 50
ikitai n desu ga I'd like to go 198
1-kai (ikkai) first floor 38
ikura how much 28
ikutsu how many 126
ima now 21
imasu (R2) be, exist 115
imasu (R2) stay, be 191
imōto (my) younger sister 209
imōto-san (another person's) younger
   sister 228
Indo India 4
infomēshon information desk 38
intān intern 59
Irasshaimase. May I help you?,
   Welcome. 28
iremasu (R2) put in, add 210
irenaide kudasai please don't add/put
   in 210
iriguchi entrance 213
iroiro (na) various 180
isha medical doctor 207
isogashii busy 107
issho ni together 151
1-shūkan (isshūkan) one week 191
isu chair 116
itadakimasu 96
Itadakimasu. [said before eating] 168
itai hurt, sore, painful 199
Itai! Ouch! 139
Itaria Italy 43
Itaria-ryōri Italian cuisine 148
itchō one trillion 31
Itō Ito (surname) 233
itoko cousin 142
itsu when 25
itsuka fifth (of the month) 63
itsumo always 87
itsutsu five 40
itte go (te-form of ikimasu) 172
Itterasshai. Have a good trip., Have a
   good day. 61
iyaringu earrings 133

J

ja well then 28
. . . ja arimasen is/are not 9
jazu jazz 148
JBP Japan JBP Japan (fictitious
   company name) 231
-ji . . . o'clock 22
jibun no one's own 228
jikan time 133
-jikan (number of) hours 105
jimu gym 21
-jin -ese, -ian (person from) 4
jinja Shinto shrine 114
jitensha bicycle 64
jogingu o shimasu jog 227
jōshi boss, superior 53
jōzu (na) skilled, be good at 142
jū ten 22

jūdenshimasu recharge 203
jū-gatsu October 63
jūichi-gatsu November 63
11-ji han 11:30, eleven-thirty, half past eleven 20
jū-man one hundred thousand 31
junbi preparation 218
junbi o shimasu prepare 225
jūni-gatsu December 63
jū-oku one billion (=1,000,000,000) 31
jūsho address 11
jūsu juice 30
jūyokka the fourteenth (of the month) 63

K

ka (particle) 2
-ka (kan) . . . days 192
kaban bag 11
kabin vase 212
kabuki kabuki 74
kado corner 182
kādo credit card 37
kaerimasu return, come back 61
kafe café 190
-kagetsu (kan) . . . months 192
kagi key 11
kagu furniture 165
-kai/gai . . . floor 40
kaigi meeting 21
kaigi o shimasu have a meeting 178
kaigi-shitsu meeting room 116
kaikei bill, check 93
kaimasu buy 76
kaimono o shimasu shop 76
kaisha company 11
kaishain company employee 233
kaisha no namae company name 11
kaitai desu want to buy 161
kakarimasu take [time] 190
kakimasu draw 142
kakimasu write 163
kaku draw 142
Kamakura Kamakura (historic area south of Tokyo) 121
kamera camera 43
kanai (my) wife 86
kane money 133
kanji kanji 224
Kankoku South Korea, ROK 54
Kankoku-go Korean 234
kantan (na) simple, easy 107
kara from (particle) 20
kara from (particle) 51
kara because (particle) 131
kara because, so (particle) 151
karate karate 163
karē curry 29
karimasu (R2) borrow 133
kasa umbrella 11
kashi sweets 18
kashimasu lend, loan 131
kashū-nattsu cashew nuts 122
kata shoulder 201
katarogu catalog 183
kāten curtain 202
ka-yōbi Tuesday 63
kazoku family 53
kechappu ketchup 215
keitai mobile phone 234
kēki cake 101

kekkon wedding, marriage 138
kekkon-kinenbi wedding anniversary 138
keshigomu eraser 125
keshimasu turn off 201
kibun feeling 201
kibun ga warui feel sick, unwell 201
kikimasu listen to 76
kikimasu ask 86
kimashita came 51
kimasu come 50
kimono kimono 209
kin'en no smoking 211
kinenbi anniversary 138
ki ni shimasu worry about 216
Ki ni shinaide kudasai. Please don't worry about it. 216
kinō yesterday 51
kin-yōbi Friday 61
Ki o tsukete. Take care. 172
kirei (na) pretty, beautiful, clean 96
kirei deshita it was beautiful 105
kita north 153
kita-guchi north exit 153
kite kudasai please come 111
ko child 126
kōban police box 125
Kobayashi Kobayashi (surname) 233
Kōbe Kobe (city near Osaka) 178
Kōbe Bīfu Kobe Beef (famous, high-quality beef) 179
kōcha (black) tea 30
kochira this one (polite for "this person") 3
kochira this one (polite word for **kore**) 93
kochirakoso same here 2
kodomo child 230
kōen park 53
kōhī coffee 30
kōhī-kappu coffee cup 45
Kojima Kojima (surname) 233
kōjō factory 172
koko here 84
kokonoka ninth (of the month) 63
kokonotsu nine 40
konban this evening 137
konbini convenience store 79
kondo next, next time 92
kongetsu this month 53
kono this 39
kono chikaku vicinity, near here 123
konsāto concert 25
konshū this week 53
kopī o shimasu make a copy 221
kopīshimasu make a copy 203
koppu glass 40
kore this one 9
kōsaten intersection 182
koshi lower back 201
koto (nominalizer) 228
kotoshi this year 53
ku nine 11
kudamono fruit 147
kudasai please give me 28
ku-gatsu September 63
9-ji (ku-ji) 9:00, nine o'clock 21
kūkō airport 53
Kumano Jinja Kumano Shrine 129
kuni country 8
kurabu club 165

kurasu class 107
kuria-fairu clear file 125
kurippu paper clip 126
Kurisumasu Christmas 136
kuroi black 40
kuruma car 64
kutsu shoes 43
kyabinetto cabinet 125
kyō today 22
kyōkai church 122
kyonen last year 51
Kyōto Kyoto 54
kyū nine 11
kyūjū ninety 22

M

machi town 165
machimasu wait 104
mada desu not yet 218
made until (particle) 20
made to, as far as (particle) 186
made ni by [specified time] 185
mado window 202
mae in front 117
mae before 161
. . . mae . . . ago 209
mafurā muffler, scarf 133
magarimasu turn 181
magatte kudasai please turn 181
magu-kappu mug 42
-mai (counter for flat objects) 40
maiasa every morning 87
maiban every evening 87
mainichi every day 85
maishū every week 87
manshon condominium 186
massugu straight 182
mata again 111
Mata kite kudasai. Please come again. 111
Mata kondo. Next time., Another time. 155
matsuri festival 64
matte kudasai please wait 104
mayonēzu mayonnaise 215
me eye 201
-me (suffix that attaches to a number and turns it into ordinal number) 184
megane glasses 11
meishi business card 11
mēkā maker 228
menyū menu 183
mēru e-mail 88
mēru-adoresu mail address 11
michi road 182
migi right 181
mikan mikan orange 45
mikka third (of the month) 63
mimasen ka shall we see? 152
mimasu (R2) see 74
minami south 153
minami-guchi south exit 153
Minato Tenisu Kurabu Minato Tennis Club (fictitious club name) 165
miru (R2) see, watch 143
mise restaurant, shop 20
misemasu (R2) show 105
mise no hito restaurant employee 20
misete kudasai please show me 28
mite see (**te**-form of **mimasu**) 172
mittsu three 40

257

miyage souvenir 112
mizu water 76
mizuumi lake 117
mo also, too, either (particle) 28
mō more 18
mō already 218
mōfu blanket 187
mō ichi-do one more time 18
Mō ichi-do onegaishimasu. One more time, please. 18
moku-yōbi Thursday 63
moraimasu receive 131
moratte mo ii desu ka May I have . . . ? 199
Mori Mori (surname) 236
Mori-sensei Professor Mori 236
Moshimoshi. Hello. (greeting when making or answering a telephone call) 226
mō sugu soon 218
mō sukoshi a little longer 224
mottekimasu bring 181
muika sixth (of the month) 63
mukashi a long time ago 199
musuko (my) son 230
musuko-san (another person's) son 230
musume (my) daughter 230
musume-san (another person's) daughter 230
muttsu six 40
muzukashii difficult 107
myūjikaru musical 197

N

naka inside 117
nama-bīru draft beer 93
namae name 11
nan what 13
nana seven 11
nanajū seventy 22
nanatsu seven 40
nan-bon how many (long, thin objects) 127
nan de by what means 67
nan-gatsu what month 64
nani what 74
nani ka something 158
nani mo -masen nothing 75
nani mo tabemasendeshita didn't eat anything 75
nan-ji what time 20
nan-mai how many (flat objects) 127
Nan-mei sama desu ka. How many people? (polite expression of **Nan-nin desu ka**) 81
nan-nichi what day 64
nan-nin how many people 77
nanoka seventh (of the month) 63
nan-yōbi what day of the week 64
Nara Nara (old city in western Japan) 178
naraimasu learn, take lessons in 163
naratte imasu be taking lessons in 219
natsu summer 65
natsu-yasumi summer vacation 65
ne right?, isn't it? (particle) 50
ne (particle) 84
nebōshimasu oversleep 190
nekkuresu necklace 133
nekutai tie 133

nemasu (R2) sleep, go to bed 162
-nen the year. . . 63
-nen (kan) . . . years 192
neru mae ni before sleeping/going to bed 162
netsu fever 201
netsu ga arimasu have a fever 201
ni two 11
ni to (particle) 50
ni at, in, on (particle) 61
ni (particle) 84
ni from (particle) 131
ni on (particle) 199
ni in, on, at (particle) 114
niaimasu suit, look good on 138
-nichi day 63
-nichi (kan) . . . days 192
nichi-yōbi Sunday 63
ni-gatsu February 63
nigiyaka (na) lively 98
nigiyaka deshita it was lively 106
2-hon two (long objects) 38
Nihon Japan 4
Nihon-go Japanese 88
Nihon no o-kashi Japanese sweets 18
nihonshu sake (Japanese rice liquor) 76
2-ji 2:00, two o'clock 20
2-ji han 2:30, two-thirty, half past two 20
nijū twenty 22
nijūyokka twenty-fourth (of the month) 63
ni-kai (2-kai) second floor 40
Nikkō Nikko (scenic area north of Tokyo) 102
2-mai two (flat objects) 38
nimotsu package, luggage 183
-nin . . . people 77
nishi west 153
nishi-guchi west exit 153
. . . ni tsuite about . . . 180
niwa garden, yard 204
no (particle) 2
no (particle) 9
no (particle) 59
no (nominalizer) 142
. . . no ato after . . . 172
noborimasu climb 105
nodo throat 201
Nodo ga kawakimashita. I'm thirsty. 153
. . . no mae ni before . . . 161
nomimasu drink 76
nomimono beverage 93
norimasu get on, take [train, bus, etc.] 191
Nozomi Depāto Nozomi Department Store (fictitious company name) 2
Nozomi Hoteru Nozomi Hotel (fictitious hotel name) 161
nyūsu news 78
Nyūyōku New York 196

O

o (particle) 74
o (particle) 190
o- (honorific prefix) 8
o- (polite prefix) 18
o-bentō→bentō box lunch, bento 100
ocha green tea 76
Odaiba Odaiba (district in Tokyo) 102

o-denwa-bangō your phone number 83
o-hanami o shimasu→hanami o shimasu view cherry blossoms 165
Ohayō gozaimasu. Good morning. 50
oishii delicious, tasty 96
Ojamashimasu. May I come in? 104
ojōsan (another person's) daughter 230
o-kaikei→kaikei bill, check 93
Okake kudasai. Please have a seat. 71
o-kane→kane money 133
okāsan (another person's) mother 86
o-kashi→kashi sweets 18
ōkii big, large 40
okimasu put, place 201
Okinawa Okinawa (islands in southern Japan) 101
okosan (another person's) child 230
o-kuni your country 8
okurimasu send 86
okusan (another person's) wife 86
o-kyaku-san guest, customer 124
o-matsuri→matsuri festival 64
o-miyage→miyage souvenir 112
omoshiroi interesting 97
onaka stomach, belly 201
Onaka ga sukimashita. I'm hungry. 153
o-namae your name 83
Onegaidekimasu ka. May I ask [you to do this]? 187
onegaishimasu please (lit. "I request you") 18
onēsan (another person's) older sister 230
ongaku music 78
onīsan (another person's) older brother 230
onna female, woman 115
onna no hito woman 115
onna no ko girl 126
o-nomimono→nomimono beverage 93
onrain-kaigi o shimasu have an online meeting 221
onsen hot spring 114
. . . o onegaishimasu please (get me . . .) 8
. . . o oshiete kudasai please tell me 16
orenji-jūsu orange juice 35
orimasu (R2) get off 191
Ōsaka Osaka (city in western Japan) 50
Ōsaka-shisha Osaka branch 50
o-sake→sake alcoholic drink, sake 216
o-sara→sara dish, plate 40
oshiemasu (R2) tell, teach 85
oshiete kudasai→. . . o oshiete kudasai please tell me 16
o-shigoto your work 228
o-sobaya-san soba shop 123
o-sushi→sushi sushi 76
o-susume recommendation 93
Ōsutoraria Australia 4
otearai restroom 47
Ōtemachi Otemachi (district in Tokyo) 194
o-tera→tera temple 114
otoko male, man 118

otoko no hito man 118
otoko no ko boy 126
otōsan (another person's) father 86
otōto (my) younger brother 161
ototoi day before yesterday 54
otōto-san (another person's) younger
  brother 230
otto (my) husband 86
owarimasu finish 218
oyogimasu swim 145

P

pakkēji package 172
pakkēji-fea package fair 172
Paku Pak, Park (surname) 66
pan bread 125
panfuretto pamphlet 199
pan-ya bakery 125
pasokon (personal) computer 30
pātī party 21
pātī o shimasu have a party 158
pen pen 9
piano piano 163
piza pizza 148
poketto pocket 120
purezen presentation 25
purezen o shimasu give a presentation
  176
purojekuto project 221
pūru swimming pool 26

R

raigetsu next month 53
rainen next year 53
raishū next week 53
rajio radio 78
rāmen ramen (Chinese noodle) 76
rāmen-ya ramen shop 125
ranchi-taimu lunchtime 20
rasuto-ōdā last order 20
rei zero 11
reizōko refrigerator 30
repōto report 173
resutoran restaurant 21
Resutoran Rōma Restaurant Rome
  (fictitious restaurant name) 90
ringo apple 40
robī lobby 161
robotto robot 142
rokkai (6-kai) sixth floor 40
roku six 11
roku-gatsu June 63
rokujū sixty 22
Rōma Rome 90
rōmaji romaji, romanized Japanese
  208
Rondon London 6
Rondon Ginkō Bank of London
  (fictitious bank name) 6
Ropesu Lopez (surname) 66
Roppongi Roppongi (district in Tokyo)
  101
rūmu-sābisu room service 187
ryokan Japanese inn 119
ryokō trip 65
ryokō-gaisha travel agency 231
ryōri food, dish, cooking, cuisine 148
ryōri o shimasu cook 163

S

saifu wallet 11
sake alcoholic drink, sake 216
saki beyond 182
sakkā soccer, football 143

Sakura Kōen Sakura Park (fictitious
  park name) 165
-sama Mr., Mrs., Ms., Miss (more polite
  than -san) 84
samui cold 98
samukatta desu it was cold 106
san three 11
-san Mr., Mrs., Ms., Miss 2
sandoitchi sandwich 30
san-gai (3-gai) third floor 40
san-gatsu March 63
3-ji 3:00, three o'clock 21
sanjū thirty 22
38-do 38 degrees 207
sanpo o shimasu take a walk 90
sanpuru sample 180
3,000-en (sanzen-en) 3,000 yen 28
Sapporo Sapporo (city on the island of
  Hokkaido) 90
Sapporo-shisha Sapporo branch 90
sara dish, plate 40
sarada salad 29
Sā, wakarimasen. I don't know. 9
sawarimasu touch 211
sen one thousand 31
senaka back 201
sengetsu last month 53
senkō specialty, major 236
sen-man ten million 31
sen-oku one hundred billion 31
sensei (honorific used for teachers,
  doctors, etc.) 236
senshū last week 51
sēru sale 109
sētā sweater 101
setsumei o shimasu explain 220
shachō president (of a company) 88
shachō-shitsu president's office 128
shāpen mechanical pencil (colloquial
  shortening of shāpu-penshiru) 36
shashin photo 105
Shashin o totte mo ii desu ka. May I
  take photos? 200
shawā o abimasu (R2) take a shower
  163
shi four 11
shiai game, match 153
Shibuya Shibuya (district in Tokyo) 60
Shibuya Toshokan Shibuya Library
  (fictitious library name) 92
shichi seven 11
shichi-gatsu July 63
Shidonī Sydney 100
4-gatsu (shi-gatsu) April 62
shigoto work 21
shigoto o shimasu work 76
shimasu do 74
shimemasu (R2) close 201
Shinagawa Shinagawa (district in
  Tokyo) 232
shinbun newspaper 221
shingō traffic light 181
Shinjuku Shinjuku (district in
  Tokyo) 159
shinkansen superexpress train,
  Shinkansen 61
shiroi white 40
shiro-wain white wine 45
shiryō material, data, documents 162
shisha branch (office of a company)
  50

shita under 117
Shitsureishimasu. Good bye. 50
Shitsureishimasu. Excuse me. 71
shitte imasu know 229
shizuka (na) quiet 98
Shōchishimashita. Yes, certainly. 187
shodō calligraphy 220
shōhin product, goods 225
shokuji o shimasu have a meal 154
shōrai in the future 165
shorui documents 183
shujin (my) husband 86
-shūkan . . . weeks 192
shūmatsu weekend 74
shumi hobby, pastime 229
shutchō business trip 61
soba soba (buckwheat noodle) 119
Sobaichi Sobaichi (fictitious soba
  shop) 123
soba-ya soba shop 119
sochira there [where you are] 50
sō desu that's right 2
Sō desu ka. I see. 27
sofā sofa 116
sōjiki vacuum cleaner 41
sōji o shimasu clean 220
soko there 126
sono that 38
sore that one 28
sorekara also 123
sorosoro in a little while 111
Sorosoro shitsureishimasu. I need to
  be going in a little while. 111
Sō shimashō. Let's do that. 158
Souru Seoul 34
Sugoi! That's great! 142
sugu soko right [over] there 129
Suidōbashi Suidobashi (station in
  Tokyo) 198
Suisu Switzerland 43
sui-yōbi Wednesday 63
sukāfu scarf 131
sukī skiing 144
suki (na) like, favorite 142
sukī o shimasu ski 110
sukoshi a bit, a little 158
sumaho smart phone 11
Sumimasen. Excuse me. 2
Sumimasendeshita. I'm sorry (for what
  I did a while ago). 139
sumimasu live 165
Sumisu-san no Smith-san's 9
sumō sumo [wrestling] 176
sunde imasu live 229
sunōbōdo o shimasu snowboard 224
supa spa 114
sūpā supermarket 21
supōtsu sports 147
sūpu soup 76
sushi sushi 76
Sushiyoshi Sushiyoshi (fictitious
  restaurant name) 20
suteki (na) lovely, nice 131
sutēki steak 76
sutoretchi o shimasu do stretching
  exercises 162
suwarimasu sit down 199
suwatte mo ii desu ka May I sit [here]?
  199
Suzuki-sama Mr. Suzuki 84
suzushii cool 98

T

tabako o suimasu smoke a cigarette 211
tabemasendeshita did not eat 75
tabemasen ka shall we eat? 152
tabemashita ate 75
tabemashō let's eat 151
tabemasu (R2) eat 74
taberu mae ni before eating 161
tabetai desu want to eat 162
tabete imasu be eating 219
taburetto tablet 29
-tachi (plural for people) 59
tachiiri-kinshi no entry 211
tachimasu stand up 211
taihen (na) hard, tough 105
taihen deshita it was hard 105
taikai festival, event 153
taishikan embassy 4
takai expensive 98
taki waterfall 117
takuhaibin parcel delivery service 180
takusan many, much 126
takushī taxi 64
takushī-noriba taxi stand 124
tanjōbi birthday 65
tanoshii fun, pleasant, enjoyable 105
tanoshikatta desu it was fun, it was enjoyable 105
taoru towel 46
te hand 167
tēburu table 115
tegami letter 164
temae just before 182
tēma-pāku theme park 121
tenisu-kōto tennis court 82
tenisu o shimasu play tennis 75
tenki weather 103
Tenmasa Tenmasa (fictitious restaurant name) 83
tenpura tempura 74
tenpura-ya tempura restaurant 84
tera temple 114
terebi television 30
tesuto test 110
to and (particle) 29
to with, together with (particle) 50
tō ten 40
todokemasu (R2) deliver 181
tōi far 123
tōka tenth (of the month) 63
tokei watch, clock 10
tokidoki sometimes 84
tokoro place 102
Tōkyō Tokyo 6
Tōkyō Daigaku University of Tokyo 6
Tōkyō Dōmu Tokyo Dome 198
Tōkyō Eki Tokyo Station 55
Tōkyō Hoteru Tokyo Hotel (fictitious hotel name) 69
Tōkyō-shisha Tokyo branch 50
Tōkyō Tawā Tokyo Tower 186
tomato tomato 215
tomemasu (R2) stop 181
tomemasu (R2) park 205
tomenaide kudasai please don't park 210
tomodachi friend 51
tonari next to 117
toranaide kudasai please don't take [photos] 209

torimasu take (a photo) 105
toshokan library 80
tōsutā toaster 36
totemo very 96
totte mo ii desu ka→(shashin o) **totte mo ii desu ka** May I take [photos]? 200
T-shatsu T-shirt 39
tsugi next 151
tsuitachi first (of the month) 63
tsukaimasu use 201
Tsukaremashita. I'm tired. 153
tsukemasu (R2) turn on 201
Tsukiji Tsukiji (district in Tokyo) 194
tsukimasu arrive 192
tsukue desk 116
tsukurimasu make 218
tsukutte imasu be making 218
tsuma (my) wife 86
tsumaranai boring, uninteresting 107
tsutaemasu (R2) relay a message 180
tsutomete imasu work for, be employed 228
... tte nan desu ka. What is a/an ...? 114

U

uchi house, home 53
uchiawase o shimasu have a preparatory meeting 178
ue on, above 115
uisukī whiskey 146
uketsuke reception desk, receptionist 8
umi ocean 101
undō o shimasu do exercise 227
untenshu driver 60
ushiro behind 117
uta song 146
utaimasu sing 145

W

wa (particle) 3
Wā! Wow! (exclamation of surprise) 142
... wa dō desu ka how about ... 157
wain wine 38
wain-shoppu wine shop 38
wakarimasen I don't know 9
wakarimashita understood, I see, I understand 83
wakarimasu understand, see, get it 83
wakarimasu understand 228
Wan Wang (surname) 233
warui bad 98
wasabi wasabi 210
watashi I 3
watashi no my, mine 9
watashi-tachi we 111

Y

ya and, and so on (particle) 114
-ya (suffix for shop or restaurant) 84
yakusoku appointment, promise 133
yakyū baseball 144
Yamamoto Yamamoto (surname) 177
Yamashita Yamashita (surname) 233
yasai vegetable 90
yasai-jūsu vegetable juice 90
yasui inexpensive 98
yasumi break, time off 21
yasumi vacation 65
yasumimasu rest 158
yasumimasu take a day off 202

yattsu eight 40
yo (particle) 114
-yōbi day of the week 63
yōguruto yogurt 90
4-ji (yo-ji) 4:00, four o'clock 21
yōka eighth (of the month) 62
Yokatta desu. I'm glad to hear that. 112
yokka fourth (of the month) 62
Yokohama Yokohama (city near Tokyo) 58
yoku often 84
yoku well 138
Yoku niaimasu ne. It suits you well. 138
yomimasu read 76
yon four 11
yo ne ... right? (confirming expression) 236
yo-nin four people 77
yonjū forty 22
yon-kai (4-kai) fourth floor 40
yoroshii be all right (polite expression of ii) 172
Yoroshiku onegaishimasu. I look forward to working with you. 2
Yoroshiku tsutaete kudasasi. Please give him/her my regards. 180
yoru night 138
yotei schedule, plan 133
yottsu four 40
yoyaku reservation 83
yoyakushimasu make a reservation 218
yūbin mail 182
yūbinkyoku post office 116
yubiwa ring 133
yūgata evening 226
yuki snow 153
yuki-matsuri snow festival 153
yume dream 228
yūmei (na) famous 97

Z

zannen desu it is unfortunate 155
zehi I'd love to, by all means 151
zenzen ... -masen not at all 87
zero zero 11

English-Japanese Glossary

Note: Idiomatic expressions have been omitted, as have words that do not translate into English. Counters and particles are listed in the Appendixes of this book.

A

a bit **sukoshi** 158
a little **sukoshi** 158
a little bit **chotto** 104
a little longer **mō sukoshi** 224
a long time ago **mukashi** 199
A.M. **gozen** 22
ABC Foods (fictitious company name) **ABC Fūzu** 2
about (amount) . . . **gurai** 105
about (time) . . . **goro** 130
about . . . . . . **ni tsuite** 180
above **ue** 115
add **iremasu** (R2) 210
address **jūsho** 11
after **ato** →. . . **no ato** 172
after . . . . . . **no ato** 172
again **mata** 111
. . . ago . . . **mae** 209
ah **a** 61
air conditioner **eakon** 30
airplane **hikōki** 61
airport **kūkō** 53
AJALT School (fictitious school name) **Ajaruto Sukūru** 165
Akasaka (district in Tokyo) **Akasaka** 194
Akihabara (district in Tokyo) **Akihabara** 151
alcoholic drink **sake, o-sake** 216
Allen (surname) **Aren** 57
alone **hitori de** 50
already **mō** 218
also **sorekara** 123
also (particle) **mo** 28
always **itsumo** 87
American (person) **Amerika-jin** 3
and (particle) **to** 29
and (particle) **ya** 114
and so on (particle) **ya** 114
Ando (surname) **Andō** 232
animation **anime** 142
anime **anime** 142
anniversary **kinenbi** 138
Another time. **Mata kondo.** 155
Antique Tokyo (fictitious shop name) **Antīku Tōkyō** 165
antiques **antīku** 165
apparel **apareru** 228
apparel maker **apareru-mēkā** 228
apple **ringo** 40
apple pie **appuru-pai** 47
application **apuri** 101
appointment **yakusoku** 133
April **4-gatsu (shi-gatsu)** 62
Are you all right? **Daijōbu desu ka.** 139
Are you sure? **Ii n desu ka.** 131
arrive **tsukimasu** 192
art museum **bijutsukan** 149
as far as (particle) **made** 186
Asakusa (district in Tokyo) **Asakusa** 102
ask **kikimasu** 86
at (particle) **ni** 61, 114

at (particle) **de** 74
ate **tabemashita** 75
August **hachi-gatsu** 63
Australia **Ōsutoraria** 4

B

back **senaka** 201
bad **warui** 98
bag **kaban** 11
bag **fukuro** 38
bag **baggu** 133
bakery **pan-ya** 125
ballpoint pen **bōrupen** 36
bank **ginkō** 4
Bank of London (fictitious bank name) **Rondon Ginkō** 6
bar **bā** 79
baseball **yakyū** 144
basement **chika** 38
be . . . **desu** 2
be **arimasu** 114
be **imasu** (R2) 115, 191
be all right (polite expression of **ii**) **yoroshii** 172
be done **dekimasu** (R2) 218
be eating **tabete imasu** 219
be employed **tsutomete imasu** 228
be good at **jōzu (na)** 142
be making **tsukutte imasu** 218
be taking lessons in **naratte imasu** 219
beach **bīchi** 122
beautiful **kirei (na)** 96
because (particle) **kara** 131, 151
bed **beddo** 116
beef **gyūniku** 43
beer **bīru** 40
before **mae** 161
before . . . . . . **no mae ni** 161
before eating **taberu mae ni** 161
before sleeping/going to bed **neru mae ni** 162
begin **hajimemasu** (R2) 163
behind **ushiro** 117
belly **onaka** 201
bento **bentō, o-bentō** 100
Berlin **Berurin** 6
Berlin Motors (fictitious company name) **Berurin Mōtāzu** 6
beverage **nomimono, o-nomimono** 93
beyond **saki** 182
bicycle **jitensha** 64
big **ōkii** 40
bill **kaikei, o-kaikei** 93
biotechnology **baiotekunorojī** 236
birthday **tanjōbi** 65
black **kuroi** 40
black tea **kōcha** 30
blanket **mōfu** 187
blouse **burausu** 133
blue **aoi** 39
boat dock **bōto-noriba** 129
book **hon** 11
bookstore **hon-ya** 125
boring **tsumaranai** 107
borrow **karimasu** (R2) 133

boss **jōshi** 53
box lunch **bentō, o-bentō** 100
boy **otoko no ko** 126
branch (office of a company) **shisha** 50
brand **burando** 228
bread **pan** 125
break **yasumi** 21
breakfast **asa-gohan** 26
bridge **hashi** 184
bring **mottekimasu** 181
Brown (surname) **Buraun** 5
building **biru** 186
bus **basu** 60
bus stop **basutei** 129
bus terminal **basu-noriba** 125
business card **meishi** 11
business trip **shutchō** 61
busy **isogashii** 107
but (particle) **ga** 105
but **demo** 150
buy **kaimasu** 76
by [specified time] **made ni** 185
by means of (particle) **de** 37, 61
by what means **nan de** 67

C

cabinet **kyabinetto** 125
café **kafe** 190
cake **kēki** 101
call **denwashimasu** 226
calligraphy **shodō** 220
came **kimashita** 51
camera **kamera** 43
car **kuruma** 64
cashew nuts **kashū-nattsu** 122
catalog **katarogu** 183
chair **isu** 116
check **kaikei, o-kaikei** 93
check **chekkushimasu** 167
check **chekku** 218
cheese **chīzu** 43
cheese burger **chīzu-bāgā** 215
cheese cake **chīzu-kēki** 47
child (another person's) **okosan** 230
child **ko** 126
child **kodomo** 230
China **Chūgoku** 4
Chinese **Chūgoku-go** 234
chocolate **chokorēto** 135
chocolate cake **chokorēto-kēki** 35
Christmas **Kurisumasu** 136
church **kyōkai** 122
class **kurasu** 107
clean **kirei (na)** 96
clean **sōji o shimasu** 220
clear file **kuria-fairu** 125
climb **noborimasu** 105
clinic **byōin** 125
clock **tokei** 10
close **chikai** 123
close **shimemasu** (R2) 201
club **kurabu** 165
coffee **kōhī** 30
coffee cup **kōhī-kappu** 45
cold **samui** 98

colleague **dōryō** 53
college **daigaku** 4
come **kimasu** 50
come back **kaerimasu** 61
company **kaisha** 11
company employee **kaishain** 233
company name **kaisha no namae** 11
computer **pasokon** 30
concert **konsāto** 25
condominium **manshon** 186
convenience store **konbini** 79
convenient **benri (na)** 97
cook **ryōri o shimasu** 163
cooked rice **gohan** 26
cooking **ryōri** 148
cool **suzushii** 98
corner **kado** 182
country **kuni** 8
cousin **itoko** 142
coworker **dōryō** 53
credit card **kādo** 37
cuisine **ryōri** 148
curry **karē** 29
curtain **kāten** 202
customer **o-kyaku-san** 124

D

dance **dansu** 146
dangerous **abunai** 212
data **shiryō** 162
date **dēto** 108
daughter (another person's)
  musume-san, ojōsan 230
daughter (my) **musume** 230
day **-nichi** 63
day after tomorrow **asatte** 54
day before yesterday **ototoi** 54
day of the week **-yōbi** 63
. . . days **-ka/nichi (kan)** 192
December **jūni-gatsu** 63
. . . degree **-do** 207
delicious **oishii** 96
deliver **todokemasu (R2)** 181
department store **depāto** 2
designer **dezainā** 228
desk **tsukue** 116
did not eat **tabemasendeshita** 75
didn't eat anything **nani mo
  tabemasendeshita** 75
difficult **muzukashii** 107
dinner **ban-gohan** 26
dish **sara, o-sara** 40
dish **ryōri** 148
do **shimasu** 74
do exercise **undō o shimasu** 227
do one's best **ganbarimasu** 228
do stretching exercises **sutoretchi o
  shimasu** 162
documents **shiryō** 162
documents **shorui** 183
door **doa** 212
download **daunrōdo** 224
download **daunrōdo shimasu** 166
draft beer **nama-bīru** 93
draw **kaku, kakimasu** 142
drawer **hikidashi** 120
dream **yume** 228
drink **nomimasu** 76
driver **untenshu** 60

E

earrings **iyaringu** 133
east **higashi** 153

east exit **higashi-guchi** 153
easy **kantan (na)** 107
eat **tabemasu (R2)** 74
Ebisu (district in Tokyo) **Ebisu** 186
Ebisu Station **Ebisu Eki** 186
eight **hachi** 11
eight **yattsu** 40
eighth (of the month) **yōka** 62
eighty **hachijū** 22
either (particle) **mo** 28
electric kettle **denki-potto** 116
eleven-thirty **11-ji han** 20
e-mail **mēru** 88
embassy **taishikan** 4
employee **hito** 20
engineer **enjinia** 233
English **Eigo** 199
enjoyable **tanoshii** 105
enter **hairimasu** 201
entrance **iriguchi** 213
eraser **keshigomu** 125
-ese (person from) **-jin** 4
evening **ban** 26
evening **yūgata** 226
evening meal **ban-gohan** 26
event **ibento** 151
event **taikai** 153
every day **mainichi** 85
every evening **maiban** 87
every morning **maiasa** 87
every week **maishū** 87
Excuse me. **Sumimasen.** 2
Excuse me. **Shitsureishimasu.** 71
exist **arimasu** 114
exist **imasu (R2)** 115
exit **deguchi** 153
expensive **takai** 98
explain **setsumei o shimasu** 220
eye **me** 201

F

factory **kōjō** 172
fair **fea** 172
family (another person's) **go-kazoku**
  86
family **kazoku** 53
famous **yūmei (na)** 97
far **tōi** 123
father (another person's) **otōsan** 86
father (my) **chichi** 86
favorite **suki (na)** 142
February **ni-gatsu** 63
feel sick **kibun ga warui** 201
female **onna** 115
festival **matsuri, o-matsuri** 64
festival **taikai** 153
fever **netsu** 201
fifth floor **5-kai** 39
fifth (of the month) **itsuka** 63
fifty **gojū** 22
file **fairu** 11
finish **owarimasu** 218
fireworks **hanabi** 153
fireworks festival **hanabi-taikai** 153
first (of the month) **tsuitachi** 63
first floor **1-kai (ikkai)** 38
first-floor basement **chika 1-kai (ikkai)**
  38
five **go** 11
five **itsutsu** 40
five o'clock **5-ji** 21
flea market **furī-māketto** 83

. . . floor **-kai/gai** 40
florist **hana-ya** 127
flower **hana** 100
flower arrangement **ikebana** 163
food **ryōri** 148
foot **ashi** 199
football **sakkā** 143
fork **fōku** 127
forty **yonjū** 22
four **yon, shi** 11
four **yottsu** 40
four o'clock **4-ji (yo-ji)** 21
four people **yo-nin** 77
fourteenth (of the month) **jūyokka** 63
fourth (of the month) **yokka** 62
fourth floor **yonkai (4-kai)** 40
France **Furansu** 38
free **hima (na)** 107
French **Furansu-go** 220
fresh **atarashii** 97
Friday **kin-yōbi** 61
friend **tomodachi** 51
from (particle) **kara** 20, 51
from (particle) **ni** 131
fruit **kudamono** 147
fun **tanoshii** 105
furniture **kagu** 165

G

game **shiai** 153
garden **niwa** 204
German **Doitsu-go** 234
Germany **Doitsu** 4
get it **wakarimasu** 83
get off **orimasu (R2)** 191
get on [train, bus, etc.] **norimasu** 191
Gibson (surname) **Gibuson** 66
Ginza (district in Tokyo) **Ginza** 55
Ginza Street **Ginza Dōri** 184
girl **onna no ko** 126
give **agemasu (R2)** 132
give a presentation **purezen o shimasu**
  176
glass **koppu** 40
glass **gurasu** 91
glasses **megane** 11
go **ikimasu** 50
go (te-form of ikimasu) **itte** 172
go for a drive **doraibu o shimasu** 176
go to bed **nemasu (R2)** 162
Goa (state in India) **Goa** 122
golf **gorufu** 146
good **ii** 84
Good bye. **Shitsureishimasu.** 50
Good morning. **Ohayō gozaimasu.** 50
goods **shōhin** 225
green tea **o-cha** 76
guest **o-kyaku-san** 124
guitar **gitā** 220
gym **jimu** 21

H

hair dresser **biyōin** 166
Hakone (popular travel destination
  southwest of Tokyo) **Hakone** 82
half past (hour) . . . **han** 20
half past eleven **11-ji han** 20
half past two **2-ji han** 20
hamburger **hanbāgā** 215
hand **te** 167
Haneda Airport **Haneda Kūkō** 196
happy hour **happī awā** 25
hard **taihen (na)** 105

Harris (surname) **Harisu** 6
have **arimasu** 131
have a fever **netsu ga arimasu** 201
Have a good day. **Itterasshai.** 61
Have a good trip. **Itterasshai.** 61
have a meal **shokuji o shimasu** 154
have a meeting **kaigi o shimasu** 178
have a party **pātī o shimasu** 158
have a preparatory meeting
uchiawase o shimasu 178
have an online meeting **onrain-kaigi o
shimasu** 221
head **atama** 200
Hello. (greeting when making or
answering a telephone call)
Moshimoshi. 226
here **koko** 84
Hiroshima (city in western Japan)
Hiroshima 191
Hiroshima Station **Hiroshima Eki** 191
hobby **shumi** 229
Hoffman (surname) **Hofuman** 5
Hokkaido (island in northern Japan)
Hokkaidō 56
home **uchi** 53
Hong Kong **Honkon** 54
hospital **byōin** 125
hot **atsui** 98
hot spring **onsen** 114
hotel **hoteru** 69
hours (number of) **-jikan** 105
house **uchi** 53
how **dōyatte** 195
how (in question) **dō** 105
how about . . . . . . **wa dō desu ka** 157
How about . . . ? **Ikaga desu ka.** 96
how about you? **dō desu ka** 151
How are you feeling? **Dō shimashita
ka.** 207
how long **donokurai** 105
how many **ikutsu** 126
how many (flat objects) **nan-mai** 127
how many (long, thin objects) **nan-bon**
127
how many people **nan-nin** 77
How many people? (polite expression
of **Nan-nin desu ka**) **Nan-mei sama
desu ka.** 81
how much **ikura** 28
How was it? **Dō deshita ka.** 105
husband (another person's) **go-shujin**
86
husband (my) **otto** 86
husband (my) **shujin** 86

I
I **watashi** 3
I don't know **wakarimasen** 9
I don't know. **Sā, wakarimasen.** 9
I hope it works out. **Ganbatte kudasai.**
228
I look forward to working with you.
Yoroshiku onegaishimasu. 2
I need to be going in a little while.
Sorosoro shitsureishimasu. 111
I see **wakarimashita** 83
I see. **Sō desu ka.** 27
I understand **wakarimashita** 83
-ian (person from) **-jin** 4
ice cream **aisu-kurīmu** 76
I'd like to go **ikitai n desu ga** 198
I'd love to **zehi** 151

I'm glad to hear that. **Yokatta desu.**
112
I'm hungry. **Onaka ga sukimashita.**
153
I'm sorry (for what I did a while ago).
Sumimasendeshita. 139
I'm thirsty. **Nodo ga kawakimashita.**
153
I'm tired. **Tsukaremashita.** 153
in (particle) **ni** 61
in (particle) **de** 74, 114
in a little while **sorosoro** 111
in front **mae** 117
in the afternoon **gogo** 22
in the future **shōrai** 165
in the morning **gozen** 22
in what way **dōyatte** 195
India **Indo** 4
inexpensive **yasui** 98
information desk **infomēshon** 38
inside **naka** 117
interesting **omoshiroi** 97
intern **intān** 59
intersection **kōsaten** 182
is/are not **. . . ja arimasen** 9
isn't it? (particle) **ne** 50
it is unfortunate **zannen desu** 155
It suits you well. **Yoku niaimasu ne.**
138
it was beautiful **kirei deshita** 105
it was cold **samukatta desu** 106
it was enjoyable **tanoshikatta desu**
105
it was fun **tanoshikatta desu** 105
it was hard **taihen deshita** 105
it was lively **nigiyaka deshita** 106
Italian cuisine **Itaria-ryōri** 148
Italy **Itaria** 43
Ito (surname) **Itō** 233

J
January **ichi-gatsu** 63
Japan **Nihon** 4
Japanese **Nihon-go** 88
Japanese inn **ryokan** 119
Japanese sweets **Nihon no o-kashi** 18
jazz **jazu** 148
JBP Japan (fictitious company name)
JBPJapan 231
jog **jogingu o shimasu** 227
juice **jūsu** 30
July **shichi-gatsu** 63
June **roku-gatsu** 63
just before **temae** 182

K
kabuki **kabuki** 74
Kamakura (historic area south of Tokyo)
Kamakura 121
kanji **kanji** 224
karate **karate** 163
keep **azukarimasu** 187
ketchup **kechappu** 215
key **kagi** 11
kimono **kimono** 209
know **shitte imasu** 229
Kobayashi (surname) **Kobayashi** 233
Kobe (city near Osaka) **Kōbe** 178
Kobe Beef (famous, high-quality beef)
Kōbe Bīfu 179
Kojima (surname) **Kojima** 233
Korean **Kankoku-go** 234
Kumano Shrine **Kumano Jinja** 129

Kyoto **Kyōto** 54
L
lake **mizuumi** 117
language **-go** 88
large **ōkii** 40
last month **sengetsu** 53
last order **rasuto-ōdā** 20
last week **senshū** 51
last year **kyonen** 51
later **ato de** 226
lawyer **bengoshi** 233
learn **naraimasu** 163
leave **demasu** (R2) 190
left **hidari** 182
leg **ashi** 199
lend **kashimasu** 131
Let's do that. **Sō shimashō.** 158
let's eat **tabemashō** 151
let's go **ikimashō** 152
letter **tegami** 164
library **toshokan** 80
lights **denki** 202
like **suki (na)** 142
listen to **kikimasu** 76
live **sumimasu** 165
live **sunde imasu** 229
lively **nigiyaka (na)** 98
loan **kashimasu** 131
lobby **robī** 161
location **basho** 85
London **Rondon** 6
look good on **niaimasu** 138
Lopez (surname) **Ropesu** 66
lovely **suteki (na)** 131
lower back **koshi** 201
luggage **nimotsu** 183
lunch **hiru-gohan** 76
lunch break **hiru-yasumi** 21
lunchtime **ranchi-taimu** 20

M
mail **yūbin** 182
mail address **mēru-adoresu** 11
major **senkō** 236
make **tsukurimasu** 218
make a copy **kopīshimasu** 203
make a copy **kopī o shimasu** 221
make a reservation **yoyakushimasu**
218
maker **mēkā** 228
male **otoko** 118
man **otoko, otoko no hito** 118
many **takusan** 126
March **san-gatsu** 63
marriage **kekkon** 138
match **shiai** 153
material **shiryō** 162
May **go-gatsu** 63
May I ask [you to do this]?
Onegaidekimasu ka. 187
May I come in? **Ojamashimasu.** 104
May I have . . . ? **moratte mo ii desu ka**
199
May I help you? **Irasshaimase.** 28
May I sit [here]? **suwatte mo ii desu ka**
199
May I take [photos]? **(shashin o) totte
mo ii desu ka** 200
mayonnaise **mayonēzu** 215
meal **gohan** 26
mechanical pencil (colloquial
shortening of **shāpu-penshiru**)

shāpen 36
medical doctor isha 207
meet aimasu 84
meeting kaigi 21
meeting room kaigi-shitsu 116
menu menyū 183
microwave oven denshi-renji 30
mikan orange mikan 45
Minato Tennis Club (fictitious club
  name) Minato Tenisu Kurabu 165
mine watashi no 9
...minute(s) -fun/pun 22
...minutes -fun/pun (kan) 192
Miss -san 2, 84
mobile phone keitai 234
Monday getsu-yōbi 63
money kane, o-kane 133
month -gatsu 63
...months -kagetsu (kan) 192
more mō 18
Mori (surname) Mori 236
morning asa 26
mother (another person's) okāsan 86
mother (my) haha 86
motorbike baiku 64
motorbike courier service baikubin
  182
movie eiga 78
Mr. -san 2
Mr. (more polite than -san) -sama 84
Mr. Suzuki Suzuki-sama 84
Mrs. -san 2
Mrs. (more polite than -san) -sama
  84
Ms. -san 2
Ms. (more polite than -san) -sama 84
Mt. Fuji Fujisan 100
much takusan 126
muffler mafurā 133
mug magu-kappu 42
museum hakubutsukan 190
music ongaku 78
musical myūjikaru 197
my watashi no 9

N
name namae 11
Nara (old city in western Japan) Nara
  178
near chikaku 117
near chikai 123
necklace nekkuresu 133
new atarashii 97
New York Nyūyōku 196
news nyūsu 78
newspaper shinbun 221
next kondo 92
next tsugi 151
next month raigetsu 53
next time kondo 92
Next time. Mata kondo. 155
next to tonari 117
next week raishū 53
next year rainen 53
nice ii 84
nice suteki (na) 131
Nice to meet you. Hajimemashite. 2
night yoru 138
Nikko (scenic area north of Tokyo)
  Nikkō 102
nine kyū, ku 11
nine kokonotsu 40

nine o'clock 9-ji (ku-ji) 21
ninth (of the month) kokonoka 63
ninety kyūjū 22
no iie 6
no entry tachiiri-kinshi 211
no one dare mo ... -masen 120
no parking chūsha-kinshi 211
no smoking kin'en 211
noon hiru 21
north kita 153
north exit kita-guchi 153
not at all zenzen ... -masen 87
not busy hima (na) 107
not often amari ... -masen 85
not very amari ... -masen 85
not yet mada desu 218
nothing nani mo -masen 75
November jūichi-gatsu 63
now ima 21
Nozomi Department Store (fictitious
  company name) Nozomi Depāto 2
Nozomi Hotel (fictitious hotel name)
  Nozomi Hoteru 161
number bangō 11
number... (suffix for number) -ban 60

O
ocean umi 101
...o'clock -ji 22
October jū-gatsu 63
Odaiba (district in Tokyo) Odaiba 102
often yoku 84
oh a 61
Okinawa (islands in southern Japan)
  Okinawa 101
old furui 98
older brother (another person's)
  onīsan 230
older brother (my) ani 230
older sister (another person's)
  onēsan 230
older sister (my) ane 230
on (particle) ni 61, 114, 199
on (particle) de 74
on ue 115
on foot aruite 67
one ichi 11
one hitotsu 40
one billion (=1,000,000,000) jū-
  oku 31
one hundred hyaku 22
one hundred billion sen-oku 31
one hundred million ichi-oku 31
one hundred thousand jū-man 31
one million hyaku-man 31
one more time mō ichi-do 18
One more time, please. Mō ichi-do
  onegaishimasu. 18
one person hitori 77
one thousand sen 31
one time ichi-do 18
one trillion itchō 31
one week 1-shūkan (isshūkan) 191
one's own jibun no 228
open akemasu (R2) 201
orange juice orenji-jūsu 35
Osaka (city in western Japan) Ōsaka
  50
Osaka branch Ōsaka-shisha 50
Otemachi (district in Tokyo) Ōtemachi
  194
Ouch! Itai! 139

over there achira 47
over there asoko 123
oversleep nebōshimasu 190

P
P.M. gogo 22
package pakkēji 172
package nimotsu 183
package fair pakkēji-fea 172
painful itai 199
painting e 101
Pak (surname) Paku 66
pamphlet panfuretto 199
paper clip kurippu 126
parcel delivery service takuhaibin 180
park kōen 53
park tomemasu (R2) 205
Park (surname) Paku 66
parking lot chūsha-jō 116
party pātī 21
pastime shumi 229
pen pen 9
pencil enpitsu 125
people hito-tachi 59
...people -nin 77
person hito 20
personal computer pasokon 30
photo shashin 105
piano piano 163
picture e 101
pizza piza 148
place tokoro 102
place okimasu 201
plan yotei 133
plate sara, o-sara 40
platform hōmu 153
platform... -bansen 198
Platform 5 5-bansen 198
play golf gorufu o shimasu 82
play tennis tenisu o shimasu 75
pleasant tanoshii 105
please (get me ...) ...o onegai
  shimasu 8
Please (have one). Dōzo. 18
please (lit. "I request you")
  onegaishimasu 18
please come kite kudasai 111
Please come again. Mata kite kudasai.
  111
Please come in. Dōzo kochira e. 84
please don't add/put in irenaide
  kudasai 210
please don't park tomenaide kudasai
  210
please don't take [photos] toranaide
  kudasai 209
Please don't worry about it. Ki ni
  shinaide kudasai. 216
Please give him/her my
  regards. Yoroshiku tsutaete
  kudasai. 180
please give me kudasai 28
Please have a seat. Okake kudasai. 71
please report hōkokushite kudasai
  180
please show me misete kudasai 28
please tell me ...o oshiete kudasai
  16
please turn magatte kudasai 181
please wait matte kudasai 104
(plural for people) -tachi 59
pocket poketto 120

police box **kōban** 125
post office **yūbinkyoku** 116
preparation **junbi** 218
prepare **junbi o shimasu** 225
presentation **purezen** 25
president (of a company) **shachō** 88
president's office **shachō-shitsu** 128
pretty **kirei (na)** 96
product **shōhin** 225
Professor Mori **Mori-sensei** 236
project **purojekuto** 221
promise **yakusoku** 133
put **okimasu** 201
put in **iremasu (R2)** 210

Q

quiet **shizuka (na)** 98

R

radio **rajio** 78
ramen (Chinese noodle) **rāmen** 76
ramen shop **rāmen-ya** 125
read **yomimasu** 76
really **hontō ni** 103
Really? **Hontō desu ka.** 84
receive **moraimasu** 131
reception desk **uketsuke** 8
reception desk **furonto** 26
receptionist **uketsuke** 8
recharge **jūdenshimasu** 203
recommendation **o-susume** 93
red **akai** 40
red wine **aka-wain** 45
refrigerator **reizōko** 30
relay a message **tsutaemasu (R2)** 180
report **repōto** 173
report **hōkokushimasu** 180
reservation **yoyaku** 83
rest **yasumimasu** 158
restaurant **mise** 20
restaurant **resutoran** 21
restaurant employee **mise no hito** 20
Restaurant Rome (fictitious restaurant
    name) **Resutoran Rōma** 90
restroom **otearai** 47
return **kaerimasu** 61
right **migi** 181
. . . right? (confirming expression) **yo
ne** 236
right [over] there **sugu soko** 129
right? (particle) **ne** 50
ring **yubiwa** 133
road **michi** 182
robot **robotto** 142
ROK **Kankoku** 54
romaji **rōmaji** 208
romanized Japanese **rōmaji** 208
Rome **Rōma** 90
room **heya** 116
room service **rūmu-sābisu** 187
Roppongi (district in Tokyo) **Roppongi**
    101
run **hashirimasu** 145

S

(said before eating) **itadakimasu** 168
sake (Japanese rice liquor) **nihonshu**
    76, 216
Sakura Park (fictitious park name)
    Sakura Kōen 165
salad **sarada** 29
sale **sēru** 109
same here **kochirakoso** 2
sample **sanpuru** 180

sandwich **sandoitchi** 30
Sapporo (city on the island of
    Hokkaido) **Sapporo** 90
Sapporo branch **Sapporo-shisha** 90
Saturday **do-yōbi** 63
say **iimasu** 181
scarf **sukāfu** 131
scarf **mafurā** 133
schedule **yotei** 133
school **gakkō** 88
scissors **hasami** 125
scuba dive **daibingu o shimasu** 197
scuba diving **daibingu** 144
second **futatsu-me** 184
second (of the month) **futsuka** 63
second floor **ni-kai (2-kai)** 40
see **mimasu (R2)** 74
see **miru (R2)** 143
see **wakarimasu** 83
see (**te**-form of **mimasu**) **mite** 172
send **okurimasu** 86
Seoul **Souru** 34
separately **betsubetsu ni** 93
September **ku-gatsu** 63
seven **nana, shichi** 11
seven **nanatsu** 40
seventh (of the month) **nanoka** 63
seventy **nanajū** 22
shall we eat? **tabemasen ka** 152
shall we go? **ikimasen ka** 151
shall we see? **mimasen ka** 152
Shibuya (district in Tokyo) **Shibuya** 60
Shibuya Library (fictitious library name)
    Shibuya Toshokan 92
Shinagawa (district in Tokyo)
    Shinagawa 232
Shinjuku (district in Tokyo) **Shinjuku**
    159
Shinkansen **shinkansen** 61
Shinto shrine **jinja** 114
shoes **kutsu** 43
shop **mise** 20
shop **kaimono o shimasu** 76
shoulder **kata** 201
show **misemasu (R2)** 105
simple **kantan (na)** 107
sing **utaimasu** 145
sit down **suwarimasu** 199
six **roku** 11
six **muttsu** 40
sixth (of the month) **muika** 63
sixth floor **rokkai (6-kai)** 40
sixty **rokujū** 22
ski **sukī o shimasu** 110
skiing **sukī** 144
skilled **jōzu (na)** 142
sleep **nemasu (R2)** 162
small **chiisai** 40
smart phone **sumaho** 11
Smith-san's **Sumisu-san no** 9
smoke a cigarette **tabako o suimasu**
    211
snow **yuki** 153
snow festival **yuki-matsuri** 153
snowboard **sunōbōdo o shimasu** 224
so (particle) **kara** 151
soba (buckwheat noodle) **soba** 119
soba shop **soba-ya** 119
soba shop **o-sobaya-san** 123
Sobaichi (fictitious soba shop)
    Sobaichi 123

soccer **sakkā** 143
sofa **sofā** 116
something **nani ka** 158
sometimes **tokidoki** 84
son (another person's) **musuko-san**
    230
son (my) **musuko** 230
song **uta** 146
soon **mō sugu** 218
sore **itai** 199
soup **sūpu** 76
south **minami** 153
south exit **minami-guchi** 153
South Korea **Kankoku** 54
souvenir **miyage, o-miyage** 112
spa **supa** 114
speak **hanashimasu** 145
specialty **senkō** 236
sports **supōtsu** 147
stand up **tachimasu** 211
start **hajimemasu (R2)** 163
station **eki** 53
station employee **ekiin** 198
stay **imasu (R2)** 191
steak **sutēki** 76
stomach **onaka** 201
stop **tomemasu (R2)** 181
straight **massugu** 182
student **gakusei** 53
study **benkyō o shimasu** 76
study **benkyōshimasu** 165
subway **chikatetsu** 64
suffix for number **-ban** 60
Suidobashi (station in Tokyo)
    Suidōbashi 198
suit **niaimasu** 138
summer **natsu** 65
summer vacation **natsu-yasumi** 65
sumo [wrestling] **sumō** 176
Sunday **nichi-yōbi** 63
superexpress train **shinkansen** 61
superior **jōshi** 53
supermarket **sūpā** 21
supper **ban-gohan** 26
sushi **sushi, o-sushi** 76
Sushiyoshi (fictitious restaurant name)
    Sushiyoshi 20
sweater **sētā** 101
sweets **o-kashi, kashi** 18
swim **oyogimasu** 145
swimming pool **pūru** 26
Switzerland **Suisu** 43
Sydney **Shidonī** 100

T

table **tēburu** 115
tablet **taburetto** 29
take [train, bus, etc.] **norimasu** 191
take (a photo) **torimasu** 105
take [time] **kakarimasu** 190
take a day off **yasumimasu** 202
take a shower **shawā o abimasu (R2)**
    163
take a walk **sanpo o shimasu** 90
Take care. **Ki o tsukete.** 172
take care of **azukarimasu** 187
take lessons in **naraimasu** 163
take place **arimasu** 151
talk **hanashimasu** 145
tasty **oishii** 96
taxi **takushī** 64
taxi stand **takushī-noriba** 124

tea **kōcha** 30
teach **oshiemasu** (R2) 85
telephone **denwa** 11
telephone **denwa o shimasu** 86
telephone **denwashimasu** 226
telephone number **denwa-bangō** 11
television **terebi** 30
tell **oshiemasu** (R2) 85
temple **tera, o-tera** 114
tempura **tenpura** 74
tempura restaurant **tenpura-ya** 84
ten **jū** 22
ten **tō** 40
ten billion (=10,000,000,000)
    hyaku-oku 31
ten million **sen-man** 31
tenth (of the month) **tōka** 63
ten thousand **ichi-man** 31
Tenmasa (fictitious restaurant name)
    Tenmasa 83
tennis court **tenisu-kōto** 82
test **tesuto** 110
Thank you very much. **Dōmo arigatō
    gozaimashita.** 111
Thank you. **Dōmo arigatō.** 27
Thank you. **Arigatō gozaimasu.** 9
Thanks. **Dōmo.** 47
that **sono** 38
that (over there) **ano** 39
that one **sore** 28
that one over there **are** 28
That's good. **Ii desu ne.** 74
That's great! **Sugoi!** 142
that's right **sō desu** 2
the year... **-nen** 63
theme park **tēma-pāku** 121
there **soko** 126
there [where you are] **sochira** 50
there is **arimasu** 151
third (of the month) **mikka** 63
third floor **san-gai** (3-gai) 40
thirty **sanjū** 22
...thirty **...han** 20
this **kono** 39
this evening **konban** 137
this is... (polite form of ... **desu**)
    ...de gozaimasu 83
this month **kongetsu** 53
this one **kore** 9
this one (polite for "this person")
    kochira 3
this one (polite word for **kore**)
    kochira 93
this week **konshū** 53
this year **kotoshi** 53
three **san** 11
three **mittsu** 40
three o'clock **3-ji** 21
throat **nodo** 201
Thursday **moku-yōbi** 63
ticket **chiketto** 133
tie **nekutai** 133
time **jikan** 133
time off **yasumi** 21
to (particle) **ni** 50
to (particle) **made** 186
toaster **tōsutā** 36
today **kyō** 22
together **issho ni** 151
together with (particle) **to** 50
Tokyo **Tōkyō** 6

Tokyo branch **Tōkyō-shisha** 50
Tokyo Dome **Tōkyō Dōmu** 198
Tokyo Hotel (fictitious hotel name)
    Tōkyō Hoteru 69
Tokyo Station **Tōkyō Eki** 55
Tokyo Tower **Tōkyō Tawā** 186
tomato **tomato** 215
tomorrow **ashita** 21
too (particle) **mo** 28
tooth **ha** 201
touch **sawarimasu** 211
tough **taihen (na)** 105
towel **taoru** 46
town **machi** 165
traffic light **shingō** 181
train **densha** 64
trash basket **gomi-bako** 116
travel agency **ryokō-gaisha** 231
trip **ryokō** 65
T-shirt **T-shatsu** 39
Tsukiji (district in Tokyo) **Tsukiji** 194
Tuesday **ka-yōbi** 63
turn **magarimasu** 181
turn off **keshimasu** 201
turn on **tsukemasu** (R2) 201
twentieth (of the month) **hatsuka** 63
twenty **nijū** 22
twenty-fourth (of the month) **nijūyokka**
    63
two **ni** 11
two **futatsu** 40
two (flat objects) **2-mai** 38
two (long objects) **2-hon** 38
two o'clock **2-ji** 20
two people **futari** 77
two-thirty **2-ji han** 20

U
umbrella **kasa** 11
under **shita** 117
understand **wakarimasu** 83, 228
understood **wakarimashita** 83
uninteresting **tsumaranai** 107
United Kingdom **Igirisu** 4
United States **Amerika** 4
university **daigaku** 4
University of Tokyo **Tōkyō Daigaku** 6
until (particle) **made** 20
unwell **kibun ga warui** 201
use **tsukaimasu** 201

V
vacation **yasumi** 65
vacuum cleaner **sōjiki** 41
Valentine's Day **Barentain-dē** 136
various **iroiro (na)** 180
vase **kabin** 212
vegetable **yasai** 90
vegetable juice **yasai-jūsu** 90
very **totemo** 96
vicinity **chikaku** 117
vicinity **kono chikaku** 123
view cherry blossoms **hanami o
    shimasu, o-hanami o shimasu** 165

W
wait **machimasu** 104
walk **arukimasu** 105
walking **aruite** 67
wallet **saifu** 11
Wang (surname) **Wan** 233
want to buy **kaitai desu** 161
want to eat **tabetai desu** 162
warm **atatakai** 98

wasabi **wasabi** 210
wash **araimasu** 163
watch **tokei** 10
watch **miru** (R2) 143
water **mizu** 76
waterfall **taki** 117
we **watashi-tachi** 111
weather **tenki** 103
wedding **kekkon** 138
wedding anniversary **kekkon-kinenbi**
    138
Wednesday **sui-yōbi** 63
weekend **shūmatsu** 74
...weeks **-shūkan** 192
Welcome. **Irasshaimase.** 28
well **yoku** 138
well then **ja** 28
well then **dewa** 50
went **ikimashita** 51
west **nishi** 153
west exit **nishi-guchi** 153
what **nan** 13
what **nani** 74
what day **nan-nichi** 64
what day of the week **nan-yōbi** 64
What is a/an...? **...tte nan desu ka.**
    114
what kind of **donna** 102
what month **nan-gatsu** 64
What seems to be the problem? **Dō
    shimashita ka.** 207
what time **nan-ji** 20
when **itsu** 25
where **doko** 38
where (polite word for **doko**) **dochira**
    8
which one (of three or more things)
    dore 46
which (of three or more things) **dono**
    60
whiskey **uisukī** 146
white **shiroi** 40
White (surname) **Howaito** 231
white wine **shiro-wain** 45
who **dare** 9
who (polite word for **dare**) **donata** 104
whose **dare no** 9
wife (another person's) **okusan** 86
wife (my) **tsuma** 86
wife (my) **kanai** 86
window **mado** 202
wine **wain** 38
wine glass **gurasu** 91
wine shop **wain-shoppu** 38
with (particle) **to** 50
woman **onna, onna no hito** 115
work **shigoto** 21
work **shigoto o shimasu** 76
work for **tsutomete imasu** 228
worry about **ki ni shimasu** 216
Wow! (exclamation of surprise) **Wā!**
    142
write **kakimasu** 163

Y
Yamamoto (surname) **Yamamoto** 177
Yamashita (surname) **Yamashita** 233
yard **niwa** 204
...years **-nen (kan)** 192
...yen **-en** 28
yes **hai** 2
yes (a softer way of saying **hai**) **ee** 61

Yes, certainly. **Shōchishimashita.** 187
yesterday **kinō** 51
yogurt **yōguruto** 90
Yokohama (city near Tokyo)
    Yokohama 58
you **anata** 6
You're welcome.
    Dō itashimashite. 111
younger brother (another person's)
    otōto-san 230
younger brother (my) **otōto** 161
younger sister (another person's)
    imōto-san 228
younger sister (my) **imōto** 209
your address **go-jūsho** 185
your country **o-kuni** 8
your name **o-namae** 83
your phone number **o-denwa-bangō**
    83
your work **o-shigoto** 228

Z

zero **zero, rei** 11

2:00 **2-ji** 20
2:30 **2-ji han** 20
3:00 **3-ji** 21
4:00 **4-ji (yo-ji)** 21
5:00 **5-ji** 21
9:00 **9-ji (ku-ji)** 21
11:30 **11-ji han** 20
3,000 yen **3,000-en (sanzen-en)** 28
38 degrees **38-do** 207
4th (of the month) **yokka** 62
8 hours **8-jikan** 105
8th (of the month) **yōka** 62

Basic Hiragana

あ a	い i	う u	え e	お o
か ka	き ki	く ku	け ke	こ ko
さ sa	し shi	す su	せ se	そ so
た ta	ち chi	つ tsu	て te	と to
な na	に ni	ぬ nu	ね ne	の no
は ha	ひ hi	ふ fu	へ he	ほ ho
ま ma	み mi	む mu	め me	も mo
や ya		ゆ yu		よ yo
ら ra	り ri	る ru	れ re	ろ ro
わ wa				を o
ん n				

Combination Hiragana

きゃ kya	きゅ kyu	きょ kyo
しゃ sha	しゅ shu	しょ sho
ちゃ cha	ちゅ chu	ちょ cho
にゃ nya	にゅ nyu	にょ nyo
ひゃ hya	ひゅ hyu	ひょ hyo
みゃ mya	みゅ myu	みょ myo

りゃ rya	りゅ ryu	りょ ryo

Voiced Hiragana

が ga	ぎ gi	ぐ gu	げ ge	ご go
ざ za	じ ji	ず zu	ぜ ze	ぞ zo
だ da	ぢ ji	づ zu	で de	ど do
ば ba	び bi	ぶ bu	べ be	ぼ bo
ぱ pa	ぴ pi	ぷ pu	ぺ pe	ぽ po

ぎゃ gya	ぎゅ gyu	ぎょ gyo
じゃ ja	じゅ ju	じょ jo

びゃ bya	びゅ byu	びょ byo
ぴゃ pya	ぴゅ pyu	ぴょ pyo

Basic Katakana

ア a	イ i	ウ u	エ e	オ o
カ ka	キ ki	ク ku	ケ ke	コ ko
サ sa	シ shi	ス su	セ se	ソ so
タ ta	チ chi	ツ tsu	テ te	ト to
ナ na	ニ ni	ヌ nu	ネ ne	ノ no
ハ ha	ヒ hi	フ fu	ヘ he	ホ ho
マ ma	ミ mi	ム mu	メ me	モ mo
ヤ ya		ユ yu		ヨ yo
ラ ra	リ ri	ル ru	レ re	ロ ro
ワ wa				ヲ o
ン n				

Combination Katakana

キャ kya	キュ kyu	キョ kyo
シャ sha	シュ shu	ショ sho
チャ cha	チュ chu	チョ cho
ニャ nya	ニュ nyu	ニョ nyo
ヒャ hya	ヒュ hyu	ヒョ hyo
ミャ mya	ミュ myu	ミョ myo
リャ rya	リュ ryu	リョ ryo

Voiced Katakana

ガ ga	ギ gi	グ gu	ゲ ge	ゴ go
ザ za	ジ ji	ズ zu	ゼ ze	ゾ zo
ダ da	ヂ ji	ヅ zu	デ de	ド do
バ ba	ビ bi	ブ bu	ベ be	ボ bo
パ pa	ピ pi	プ pu	ペ pe	ポ po

ギャ gya	ギュ gyu	ギョ gyo
ジャ ja	ジュ ju	ジョ jo

ビャ bya	ビュ byu	ビョ byo
ピャ pya	ピュ pyu	ピョ pyo

Newly revised edition of the all-time best-selling textbook

JAPANESE FOR BUSY PEOPLE:
Revised 4th Edition

Association for Japanese-Language Teaching (AJALT)

The leading textbook series for conversational Japanese has been redesigned, updated, and consolidated to meet the needs of today's students and businesspeople.

- Free downloadable audio with each text and workbook
- Edited for smoother transition between levels
- Hundreds of charming illustrations make learning Japanese easy
- Clear explanations of fundamental grammar

VOLUME 1 Teaches survival Japanese, providing a comprehensive introduction to the three-volume series of *Japanese for Busy People*.

- **Japanese for Busy People I: Revised 4th Edition, Romanized Version**
  Paperback, ISBN: 978-1-56836-619-7, Spring 2022

- **Japanese for Busy People I: Revised 4th Edition, Kana Version**
  Paperback, ISBN: 978-1-56836-620-3, Spring 2022

- **Japanese for Busy People I: The Workbook for the Revised 4th Edition**
  Paperback, ISBN: 978-1-56836-621-0, Spring 2022

- **Japanese for Busy People: Kana Workbook for the Revised 4th Edition**
  Paperback, ISBN: 978-1-56836-622-7, Spring 2022

- **Japanese for Busy People I—App**
  Skill Practice on the Go app based on Volume I for iPhone, iPad, iPod and Android

VOLUME 2 Brings learners to the intermediate* level, enabling them to carry on basic conversations in everyday situations. (*upper beginners in Japan)

- **Japanese for Busy People II: Revised 4th Edition**
  Paperback, ISBN: 978-1-56836-627-2, Fall 2022

- **Japanese for Busy People II: The Workbook for the Revised 4th Edition**
  Paperback, ISBN: 978-1-56836-628-9, Fall 2022

VOLUME 3 Covers intermediate-level** Japanese. (**pre-intermediate in Japan)

- **Japanese for Busy People III: Revised 4th Edition**
  Paperback, ISBN: 978-1-56836-630-2, Spring 2023

- **Japanese for Busy People III: The Workbook for the Revised 4th Edition**
  Paperback, ISBN: 978-1-56836-631-9, Spring 2023

TEACHER'S MANUAL

Now available in eBook format (all in Japanese):

- **Japanese for Busy People I:**   ISBN: 978-1-56836-623-4, Spring 2022
- **Japanese for Busy People II:**   ISBN: 978-1-56836-629-6, Fall 2022
- **Japanese for Busy People III:**   ISBN: 978-1-56836-632-6, Spring 2023

JAPANESE LANGUAGE GUIDES

Easy-to-use Guides to Essential Language Skills

JAPANESE FOR PROFESSIONALS   *AJALT*
Revised Edition

A comprehensive course for students who need to use Japanese in a real-life business environment. Eight lessons introduce common business situations—first-time meetings, directing subordinates, client negotiations—with key sentences and a dialogue to illustrate how Japanese is used in a business context. Free audio recordings are available for download.

Paperback, 216 pages, ISBN 978-1-56836-599-2

JAPANESE SENTENCE PATTERNS FOR EFFECTIVE COMMUNICATION
A Self-Study Course and Reference   *Taeko Kamiya*

Presents 142 essential sentence patterns for daily conversation—all the ones an intermediate student should know, and all the ones a beginner should study to become minimally proficient in speaking. All in a handy, step-by-step format with pattern practice every few pages.

Paperback, 368 pages, ISBN 978-1-56836-420-9

THE HANDBOOK OF JAPANESE VERBS   *Taeko Kamiya*

An indispensable reference and guide to Japanese verbs, aimed at beginning and intermediate students. Precisely the book that verb-challenged students have been looking for.
- Verbs are grouped, conjugated, and combined with auxiliaries
- Different forms are used in sentences
- Each form is followed by reinforcing examples and exercises

Paperback, 256 pages, ISBN 978-1-56836-484-1

THE HANDBOOK OF JAPANESE ADJECTIVES AND ADVERBS   *Taeko Kamiya*

The ultimate reference manual for those seeking a deeper understanding of Japanese adjectives and adverbs and how they are used in sentences. Ideal, too, for those simply wishing to expand their vocabulary or speak livelier Japanese.

Paperback, 336 pages, ISBN 978-1-56836-416-2

MAKING SENSE OF JAPANESE   *Jay Rubin*
What the Textbooks Don't Tell You

"Brief, wittily written essays that gamely attempt to explain some of the more frustrating hurdles [of Japanese]… They can be read and enjoyed by students at any level."
—*Asahi Evening News*

Paperback, 144 pages, ISBN 978-1-56836-492-6

JAPANESE LANGUAGE GUIDES

Easy-to-use Guides to Essential Language Skills

BREAKING INTO JAPANESE LITERATURE   *Giles Murray*
Seven Modern Classics in Parallel Text
Read classics of modern Japanese fiction in the original with the aid of a built-in, customized dictionary, free MP3 sound files of professional Japanese narrators reading the stories, and literal English translations. Features Ryunosuke Akutagawa's "Rashomon" and other stories.
Paperback, 240 pages, ISBN 978-1-56836-589-3

EXPLORING JAPANESE LITERATURE   *Giles Murray*
Read Mishima, Tanizaki and Kawabata in the Original
Provides all the backup you need to enjoy three works of modern Japanese fiction in the original language: Yukio Mishima's "Patriotism," Jun'ichiro Tanizaki's "The Secret," and Yasunari Kawabata's "Snow Country Miniature."
Paperback, 352 pages, ISBN 978-1-56836-541-1

READ REAL JAPANESE FICTION   *Edited by Michael Emmerich*
Short Stories by Contemporary Writers
Short stories by cutting-edge writers, from Otsuichi to Tawada Yoko. Set in vertical text with translations, notes, and free downloadable audio containing narrations of the works.
Paperback, 256 pages, ISBN 978-1-56836-617-3

READ REAL JAPANESE ESSAYS   *Edited by Janet Ashby*
Contemporary Writings by Popular Authors
Essays by Japan's leading writers. Set in vertical text with translations, notes, and free downloadable audio containing narrations of the works.
Paperback, 240 pages, ISBN 978-1-56836-618-0

BASIC CONNECTIONS   *Kakuko Shoji*
Making Your Japanese Flow
Explains how words and phrases dovetail, how clauses pair up with other clauses, how sentences come together to create harmonious paragraphs. The goal is to enable the student to speak both coherently and smoothly.
Paperback, 160 pages, ISBN 978-1-56836-421-6

ALL ABOUT PARTICLES   *Naoko Chino*
The most common and less common particles brought together and broken down into some 200 usages, with abundant sample sentences.
Paperback, 160 pages, ISBN 978-1-56836-419-3

KODANSHA DICTIONARIES

Easy-to-use Dictionaries Designed for Learners of Japanese

KODANSHA'S FURIGANA JAPANESE DICTIONARY
JAPANESE-ENGLISH / ENGLISH-JAPANESE

Both of Kodansha's popular furigana dictionaries in one portable, affordable volume. A truly comprehensive and practical dictionary for English-speaking learners, and an invaluable guide to using the Japanese language.

- 30,000-word basic vocabulary
- Hundreds of special words, names, and phrases
- Clear explanations of semantic and usage differences
- Special information on grammar and usage

Hardcover, 1318 pages, ISBN 978-1-56836-457-5

KODANSHA'S FURIGANA JAPANESE-ENGLISH DICTIONARY

The essential dictionary for all students of Japanese.

- Furigana readings added to all kanji
- 16,000-word basic vocabulary

Paperback, 592 pages, ISBN 978-1-56836-422-3

KODANSHA'S FURIGANA ENGLISH-JAPANESE DICTIONARY

The companion to the essential dictionary for all students of Japanese.

- Furigana readings added to all kanji
- 14,000-word basic vocabulary

Paperback, 728 pages, ISBN 978-4-7700-2751-1

A DICTIONARY OF JAPANESE PARTICLES   *Sue A. Kawashima*

Treats over 100 particles in alphabetical order, providing sample sentences for each meaning.

- Meets students' needs from beginning to advanced levels
- Treats principal particle meanings as well as variants

Paperback, 368 pages, ISBN 978-4-7700-2352-0

THE KODANSHA KANJI LEARNER'S COURSE   *Andrew Scott Conning*
A Step-by-Step Guide to Mastering 2300 Characters

A complete, logical system for acquiring all the kanji characters needed for genuine literacy

- Includes all 2,136 official Jōyō Kanji plus 164 most useful non-Jōyō characters
- Summarizes kanji meanings in concise, easy-to-memorize keywords
- Mnemonic annotations for each kanji help in remembering its meaning(s)
- Cross-references, character meanings, readings, and sample vocabulary drawn from *The Kodansha Kanji Learner's Dictionary*

Paperback, 720 pages, ISBN 978-1-56836-526-8

www.kodansha.us

KODANSHA DICTIONARIES

Easy-to-use Dictionaries Designed for Learners of Japanese

THE KODANSHA KANJI LEARNER'S DICTIONARY   *Jack Halpern*
Revised and Expanded: 2nd Edition

The perfect kanji tool for beginners to advanced learners.

- Revolutionary SKIP lookup method
- Five lookup methods and three indices
- 3,002 kanji entries and approximately 46,000 senses for 35,000 words, word elements, and illustrative examples
- Includes latest 2020 revision of Education Kanji

"Up-to-date, and easy to use...this beautifully designed dictionary meets the needs of a wide range of Japanese language learners."
—*Y.-H. Tohsaku, former President, American Association of Teachers of Japanese*

Paperback, 1060 pages (2-color), ISBN 978-1-56836-625-8

THE KODANSHA'S KANJI DICTIONARY   *Jack Halpern*

The most sophisticated kanji dictionary ever developed

- Includes all the current Jōyō and Jinmei Kanji
- 5,458 character entries – all the kanji that advanced learners are likely to encounter
- 6 lookup methods, including the SKIP method; 3 indexes; 13 appendixes
- Features core meanings or concise keywords that convey the dominant sense of each character

Hardcover, 2,112 pages (53 in 2 color), ISBN 978-1-56836-408-7

THE KODANSHA'S KANJI SYNONYMS GUIDE   *Jack Halpern*

A groundbreaking bilingual kanji thesaurus that provides complete, precise guidance on the distinctions between characters of similar meanings

- 1,245 synonym groups, arranged alphabetically by shared concept
- Covers 5,630 synonym members from the Jōyō Kanji, Jinmei Kanji, and non-Jōyō Kanji character sets
- Over 22,000 compounds illustrate the function of kanji as word elements
- Compound words and readings in hiragana
- Two indexes to help locate synonym groups quickly

Paperback, 680 pages, ISBN 978-1-56836-585-5

THE KODANSHA'S KANJI USAGE GUIDE   *Jack Halpern*

An A to Z of Kun Homophones

- The first Japanese-English resource devoted exclusively to kun homophones
- Presents detailed usage articles that show the differences and similarities for 675 homophone groups
- Includes thousands of illustrative samples of kanji in context

Paperback, 352 pages, ISBN 978-1-56836-559-6

www.kodansha.us